*f*P

A COUNTRY CALLED
AMREEKA

Arab Roots, American Stories

Alia Malek

Free Press
NEW YORK · LONDON · TORONTO · SYDNEY

FREE PRESS

A Division of Simon & Schuster, Inc.

1230 Avenue of the Americas

New York, NY 10020

First Free Press hardcover edition October 2009

FREE PRESS and colophon are
trademarks of Simon & Schuster, Inc.

For information about special discounts for bulk purchases,
please contact Simon & Schuster Special Sales at
1-866-506-1949 or business@simonandschuster.com

The Simon & Schuster Speakers Bureau can bring authors to your live event.
For more information or to book an event
contact the Simon & Schuster Speakers Bureau at 1-866-248-3049
or visit our website at www.simonspeakers.com

Designed by Paul Dippolito

Manufactured in the United States of America

1 3 5 7 9 10 8 6 4 2

Library of Congress Cataloging-in-Publication Data
Malek, Alia.
A country called Amreeka: Arab roots, American stories / Alia Malek.
p. cm.
1. Arab Americans—Case studies. 2. Arab Americans—Social conditions—Case studies.
3. Immigrants—United States—Case studies. I. Title.
E184.A65M35 2009
973'.04927–dc22   2008055091

ISBN 978-1-4165-8972-3
ISBN 978-1-4165-9268-6 (ebook)

To
Leyla, for believing
Rana, for reading
Hussam, for faith
Samar, for common sense

CONTENTS

FOREWORD

Amreeka is the formal Arabic word for America, the country that approximately a million immigrants from the Arabic-speaking world have come to in search of a home for over a century. The word also represents a place and a myriad of experiences about which Americans—including many Arab Americans themselves—know very little. This book is an attempt to populate *Amreeka* with human faces, emotions, thoughts, and stories, adding another chapter to the story of the country that we all share.

This book traverses American history as it unfolded during and after the 1960s, stopping in moments of time that are important from an Arab-American perspective. Some of these dates are significant to all Americans, others barely familiar, and yet others virtually unknown. Each chapter introduces a different person, whose eyes and skin serve as our vicarious guides. I have chosen an ensemble cast to account for the diversity within Arab America itself. There are Christians and Muslims of different sects; naturalized and native-born citizens; newcomers and old-timers; Midwesterners, East Coasters, Southerners, Californians, and Texans; urban, suburban, and rural residents; Lebanese, Syrians, Jordanians, Palestinians, Egyptians, and Yemenis; women and men; rich and poor; adults and children; lovers and fighters.

Today there are at least an estimated 3.5 million Americans of Arabic-speaking descent, and they live in all fifty states. They are neighbors, classmates, coworkers, voters, consumers, producers, heroes, relatives, and friends. The purpose of this book isn't to separate them out but to fold their experience into the mosaic of American history and deepen our understanding of who we Americans are.

While there are reports that Arabs came to the Americas with the Spanish explorers in the fifteenth century as slaves, the appearance of Arabic-speaking peoples in significant numbers in the United States may be divided into three eras: the years of the Great Migration from 1880 to 1924, during which mostly Lebanese, Syrian, and Palestinian Christians arrived; the Nativist period from 1924 to 1965, in which Arab and other immigration was discouraged; and the period from 1965 to the present, in which immigrants from all over the world arrived.

The 1960s serve as the starting point of this book because Congress passed the Immigration and Naturalization Act in 1965. Like the Civil Rights and Voting Rights Acts of 1964 and 1965, this act was meant to redress past wrongs and move the United States toward a more equitable society.

Since its passage and until 2008, another 30,934,631 people have again arrived on American shores, 841,501 of whom have come from Arabic-speaking countries. These newer Arab immigrants have been different in many ways from their predecessors. Most significantly, many of them have been skilled professionals who were born or came of age after the end of colonialism and the rise of Arab nationalism, and many—nearly 60 percent—have been Muslims. Two important clarifications are important to note here: Arabs account for only about 25 percent of Muslims in America, and Arab-American Muslims still account for only about 24 percent of all Americans believed to be of Arab descent. In addition, technological advances like the airplane, phone, fax, Internet, and satellite television have increasingly shrunk the chasm between the Old and the New World. The post-1965 Arab immigrants also arrived at a time when assimilation pressures were relatively less than before 1924. Together with the other post-1965 immigrants, this wave has dramatically changed the racial, ethnic, and religious makeup of the United States.

For many of us living today in our post–civil rights, hyperconnected, and globalized world, it is impossible to imagine what America, let alone *Amreeka*, was like before 1965. To make this earlier time tangible, I've chosen to open the book with a prologue set in Birmingham, Alabama, where tragedy in 1963 sparked the legislative reforms that followed in 1964 and 1965.

Similarly, each chapter will move us through American history as the country contends with changes in its laws, society, and place in this world. The effects of these dynamics on Arab Americans have been mainly, though not exclusively, explored in academic contexts. This book invites readers to experience these elements vicariously by living the lives of the Arab Americans who have generously shared themselves in these pages.

In this book, readers will spend the 1960s with a football player in Birmingham and a feisty teacher and mother in Baltimore; the 1970s will take them to the auto factories of Detroit for the energy crisis and the streets of Chicago for the hostage crisis; the 1980s will introduce Americans to one of *Amreeka*'s biggest tragedies in California and let them experience adolescence, Arab-American style, in Texas; the 1990s will reveal how racism can lie just beneath the surface in a small town and how freedom to be yourself can change depending on where you are. At the same time we'll explore the first Gulf War and the Oklahoma City bombing; in the final three chapters of the 2000s, we'll encounter the sharp smarts of two political women whose stories illustrate both sides of election 2000, the loss of a community in Brooklyn in 2001, and the journey of a soldier in Baghdad in 2003.

All these stories are meant to answer collectively this question: What does American history look and feel like in the eyes and skin of Arab Americans?

A COUNTRY CALLED

AMREEKA

In the Great Migration of 1880–1924, during which 20 million immigrants entered the United States, approximately 95,000 of them came from Arabic-speaking countries. By 1924, they and their progeny were 200,000 strong.

Before 1924, 90 percent of the Arabic-speaking peoples who came to the States were Christian and mostly Lebanese, Syrians, and Palestinians. Many of their Jewish compatriots also emigrated at the same time. Their homelands had been brought under the yoke of the Ottoman Empire, which both tolerated and persecuted its religious minorities. When the ban on Christian and Jewish conscription into the Ottoman army was lifted early in the twentieth century, their emigration hastened.

For the most part, these Christian "Syrians," as they were called, were not skilled laborers. Once they came to the United States, they rarely returned to their homelands. They identified primarily along village lines and only after independence did they develop Syrian and Lebanese identities. While Arabic food, religious rites, and language peppered their lives, it was not and is not a given that they would identify themselves as Arabs.

Many of the Arabic-speaking immigrants settled in major cities and worked as peddlers, selling household goods door to door. Because of the nature of peddling, they also worked in areas not well served by stores, and so unlike other immigrant groups, Syrians could also be found in every state in the Union, in places where no other Syrian or immigrant families lived.

But there were many in America—in both its cities and rural areas—who disdained the newly arrived immigrants and who campaigned to end immigration of peoples they said were inherently un-American.

Seeking to replenish America with the same racial stock of the founding fathers, Congress in response passed a series of laws in 1917, 1921, and 1924 that slowed immigration from southern and eastern Europe while allowing for immigration from northern and western Europe. These laws also greatly reduced the immigration of Arabic-speaking peoples and outright excluded Asians, though Chinese and Japanese immigrants had also already arrived.

The Great Migration was over. Immigration to the United States from anywhere but the desirable areas of Europe would not resume until America—through a series of legislative revolutions in the 1960s—was forced to decide whether equality would remain merely a notion in its founding documents or whether it had a greater role to play as the nation emerged as a world superpower. The one exception worth noting here is the Refugee Relief Act of 1953, which allotted 2,000 visas during 1954–1958 for Palestinians displaced by the creation of the state of Israel.

The crusade for civil rights and the changes to American society that it ushered in had been escalating, ever since African Americans who had died for European equality had returned home to find their own country still hostile to them. They and their supporters began to experience victories in their struggle, particularly in the courts; in 1954, they achieved their greatest judicial win. The highest court in the land decided Brown v. Board of Education, *declaring that separate—segregation—could never be equal. But the lived reality of many African Americans in the country hardly changed immediately. Lawmakers and those who had put them in power needed a push to convince them that the South—where segregation was a way of life—would not come around on its own.*

That catalyst would finally come in the spring and summer of 1963, in Birmingham, Alabama.

PHOTO COURTESY PAUL W. BRYANT MUSEUM, THE UNIVERSITY OF ALABAMA

Prologue

On December 4, 1948, in Birmingham, Alabama, Ed Salem, native son and sophomore left halfback for the University of Alabama, was not going to get dressed and get on the field unless Coach Red Drew let in Ed's Lebanese friends from the city's Southside free of charge.

Some of the guys from the neighborhood had already managed to get into Legion Field by selling Cokes and programs in the stands, though they were really there to watch one of their own play in the big game against Auburn University.

"Salem!" Coach yelled. "Get your clothes on!"

"No sir, not till you open that gate and let our friends come in and see our ball game," Ed responded, referring to himself and the other Lebanese Southside kid on the team, Mike Mizerany.

"Let 'em buy a ticket," Coach said.

"They don't have the money to buy a ticket," Ed explained.

The 46,000 people who did have tickets, however, were already packed into the bleachers. It was the biggest crowd ever to attend a sports event in Alabama, and they were hungry for the action to start between the state's two football giants, who had not played against each other in forty-one famine-like years.

In a series that had started in 1893, Alabama's Crimson Tide and Auburn's Tigers had last met in 1907 in a draw. After that tie game, a disagreement about the amount of expenses to be paid to players, as well as about who was sufficiently neutral to officiate the games, had been enough to destroy all athletic relations between the two schools. The Alabama legislature had tried to force the universities to play again by threatening to cut off their funding, but to no avail, and so generations of Tigers and Tide had remained deprived of the kind of purpose an annual contest could bestow on their football-watching lives.

Only months before did both schools' presidents finally decide there was no *actual* reason not to play each other. The heads of the respective student governments met in a field in Birmingham, broke ground, threw in a hatchet, and buried it deep. Their teams would meet and unleash the pent-up rivalry not in Tuscaloosa or Auburn, but on Legion Field in Birmingham. At last, the day had come.

Eleven thousand of the schools' 17,000 students had tickets to be inside the stadium, while the other 35,000 seats had been saved for Alabama dignitaries—Governor Folsom and his wife were there—and alumni, though not even all of the old grads could be accommodated. The Lebanese guys with whom Ed had grown up certainly weren't Alabama dignitaries, and they were hardly alumni; most of them weren't able to afford college. Ed and Mike were both at the university on athletic scholarships. The team's families, of course, had tickets. Ed's mother, Zaki Zarzour Salem, was there with his siblings Helen and George, as was his high-school sweetheart Ann Dugger.

The fervor had spread far beyond Alabama's borders. All of Dixie's eyes were in fact watching. The game was the hottest show in town, and a week earlier scalpers were already getting ten dollars a ticket, twice face value. Alumni, journalists, and sports fanatics from across Alabama and the South had poured into Birmingham, filling its hotels to the roofs, crowding its cabs, and jamming its streets. The city was awash with the schools' colors—crimson and white, orange and blue.

The old-timers who had played in the '07 game met up in friendly reunions around town. Alumni of other years' teams had come as well, including Johnny Mack Brown, the Western actor who traveled all the way from Hollywood, Congressman Sam Hobbs, and Kentucky coach Paul "Bear" Bryant—none having forgotten his Crimson blood.

The real zeal had of course been on campus. The night before in Tuscaloosa, students danced hand-in-hand around a leaping bonfire. At the rally, brave talk and stories from the coaches, pep squads, and campus beauties had been heard while the band struck up old tunes that sent Tide spirits riding high, wide, and handsome.

Saturday finally arrived with weather that was crisp and cool. Fans took over the streets, waving colorful banners at a parade thrown in both schools' honor in Birmingham. Both Auburn and Alabama brought their bands, pep squads, and noisemaking power that morning for the 10:30 A.M. spectacle, whooping it up in advance of the 2 P.M. game. Regardless of the outcome, the *Birmingham News* predicted it would be a game they'd all be telling their grand- and great-grandchildren about.

Ed and the rest of the team had stayed away from the hullabaloo on Coach's orders, spending Friday evening in after a light limbering workout that afternoon. They had taken the bus from Tuscaloosa that morning and as they rode into Birmingham, they caught a glimpse of some of 'Bama's TNT signs—Tide Nip Tigers—plastered all over downtown store windows and lining the streets approaching Legion Field.

Alabama's record that season so far was 5–4–1—having just beaten Florida 34–28 the weekend before, in a game where the newspapers credited Ed with shouldering much of the attack. Auburn had been having a tougher year with a 1–7–1 record.

Though the Crimson Tide was a two-touchdown favorite to win, their punter, tackle, and sub fullback were all unable to play that day because of injuries. Those setbacks didn't worry some of Ed's teammates, who argued Auburn's team was just a bunch of country boys, but Ed took nothing for granted and stayed focused. He was there to do a job, and he was going to do it right. All Coach had to do was let the Southside guys in for free.

With the crowd near frenzy and a chance at legend on the line, Coach

Drew had to relent and let the Lebanese boys into the field. Ed recipro-
cated and pulled on his jersey and gear. The team was ready to play.

The boys entered a soggy Legion Field under a bright sky; the crowd's
hearts and throats screamed for their teams, but they stayed orderly. On
hand was Public Safety Commissioner Bull Connor, who had already
declared he would not tolerate drunkenness or drinking at this game,
which the papers had warned would earn a man a night in his Bastille.

That day, Ed was wearing number 14. The players changed numbers
with each game so spectators would have to buy a new program; times
were tough even for football both during the war and after, and a lot of
boys who might have played were away in the service. The university had
recruited players from the North, luring them down with lucrative scholarships. 'Bama even had a one-handed Polish kid from Ohio playing right
end. Ed had been spared the war because of his flat feet, which were terrible for marching but never slowed him down running a football field.

The first quarter started with Ed on the bench. In the game's opening
minutes, Auburn fumbled deep in its territory. Alabama recovered the
ball and within three plays and before the game could reach its fifth minute, the Tide took its first touchdown. Ed came in to kick the extra point,
and he scored. The board now said 7–0, Alabama.

In the second quarter, Coach put Ed in. Auburn's Tiger line was holding well defensively. Playing to the hometown crowd, Ed took to the air,
completing two passes before sending one twenty yards into the arms of
his right halfback for the game's second touchdown. Ed again kicked the
extra point, and the score stood 14–0 for the Crimson and White. With
the first half nearly over, Alabama drove deep into Auburn's territory on
several more of Ed's sailing passes and delivered yet another touchdown.
Ed again sealed it with the extra point. Going into halftime, Alabama led
Auburn 21–0.

When the players returned, the skies had clouded and fans settled in
to see if the break in play would change either team's fate. They did not
have to wait long.

Auburn fumbled the kickoff to start the second half, and Alabama
recovered again. When the ball got to Ed, he showed Legion Field what
made him so good—he could run with a ball as well as he could toss it,
and he charged off for another touchdown. The score had swollen to 28–0

with Ed's extra kick. Shortly after, on a bullet thrown by Ed, Alabama had its fifth touchdown, to which Ed added the extra point. The score was 35–0, and the game became a rout.

The fourth period brought only more humiliation and pain to the Plainsmen. Alabama started playing its third and fourth stringers and scored another three touchdowns, with Ed passing for one of them. He kicked extra points for two of them, with only his eighth finally being blocked. At the end of the day, the Crimson Tide drowned their Tiger rivals in a 55–0 trouncing and provided Alabama fans bragging rights forty-one years in the making.

The Lebanese boys who had known Ed all their lives were beaming. Not only did they now have a hero who was one of their own, but all of Alabama could see what their guys could do! Though Ed's father had not lived to see the day, his mother had been there to see it all. So had Ann— beautiful Ann with her fair skin and feisty green eyes.

The headlines were unequivocal:

SALEM SOCKS TIGERS WITH AERIAL BOMBS

ED SALEM STARS

SALEM SHINES AS TIDE PASSES ROUT AUBURN

46,000 SEE SALEM'S PASSES TURN TILT INTO COMPLETE ROUT

SALEM SHINES AS 'BAMA GOES TO 55–0 ROUT

Later that season, Ed and Mike got letters, and Ed made the Southeast- ern Conference's all-sophomore team. But Ed stayed cool and never let it go to his head. He liked to say, "Don't jump up and down and scream and holla, act like you been there!"

All those years of turning the other cheek in Birmingham—even on the football and baseball fields where he excelled—had taught Ed to always keep his cool.

Ed Salem's people had been in Birmingham just about as long as anyone else's.

The city was established only in 1871, after the Civil War had ended, by developers with a vision of a New South: industrial and powerful. They

named their creation after the manufacturing city in England to hint to
the fates the sort of fortunes they were seeking. Alabama's Birmingham,
after all, was founded in a region rich with iron ore, coal, and lime, waiting to be mined, and at the junction of the coming North and South and
East and West railroads.

The black convicts who were leased to work in the mines kept profit
margins high—they were free labor—but they were not enough. The
demand for workers beckoned whites and newly freed blacks from the
surrounding countryside, and the city grew from 3,000 in 1880 to 38,000
by the turn of the century, earning Birmingham the name the "Magic
City."

People with work and money to spend soon needed items to purchase, so Lebanese immigrants who had already landed in the cities of
the Northeast and the Great Lakes came down to Birmingham, offering
their numbers not to the mines, but for commerce's sake. While blacks,
whites, and other immigrants—namely southern Italians, Scots, and Slo-
vaks—broke their backs working deep in the bowels of Birmingham's
Red Mountain, the Lebanese strapped on their own heavy packs laden
with notions, dry goods, tinware, combs, linens, and laces—and peddled
on foot all over Birmingham and the surrounding hills and fields. They
traded with whites and blacks, speaking little English and using every
penny to raise their large families.

Birmingham was booming, and to shout it to the world, the city com-
missioned a 56-foot-tall cast-iron statue of Vulcan—the Roman God of
the Forge—to be exhibited at the World's Fair in 1904 in St. Louis. A year
later, when Vulcan came home to Birmingham, the Lebanese—who called
themselves Syrians then—started their own Syrian Young Men's Society.
But as fast as the Magic City was growing, it still hungered for more bodies to labor, and in 1907 the Alabama legislature enacted a law that established a commission to promote immigration. They had hoped to attract
desirable white citizens of the United States first, followed by citizens of
the English-speaking and Germanic countries, then France and the Scan-
dinavian countries, and then Belgium.

What they got instead were more Italians, more Lebanese, and their
Mediterranean neighbors, the Greeks. Italians who were not working in
the mines opened grocery stores selling fresh meat, staples, and canned

goods. The Greeks sold fruits and vegetables from stands set up along the city's streets, and the Lebanese peddled some more. By the 1920s, the Lebanese gave up their roaming sales and established shops, some becoming wholesalers and retailers of groceries and produce, while others sold linens and dry goods; most of them lived in the rooms behind their stores. As soon as they could reach the counter, their children were initiated in the family business, working before and after school and on Saturdays.

But they always needed more money. Enterprising Lebanese women opened their windows as they cooked their food, hoping to entice nearby workers who soon started stopping by and paying for a meal. Others sold moonshine and hosted in their back rooms the kind of card games where a man could bet, with one of their children serving as a lookout. If the police managed to sneak in, on account of a child abandoning his post to relieve himself, the Lebanese kept them quiet with heaping servings of their strange food that smelled and tasted so good.

Most of them had come from Zahleh, a town of red-roofed stone houses 3,000 feet toward the heavens on the eastern foothills of Mount Sannine in the Beqaa Valley, and from Wadi al-'Arayish, the Valley of the Vines, at its base. The *wadi* and its vines had been nourished for millennia by the Birdawni River, which flowed from the mountain's womb and through a wooded gorge; to give thanks, antiquity's rulers had erected, not twenty miles away in Baalbek, a magnificent temple to their own Roman god, Bacchus, deity of wine.

Although the ancient columned temple had remained imposing and impressive through centuries, it was but a relic, and the region's sons and daughters had begun leaving by 1870, seeking New World opportunities when the Old failed to feed them and frustrated their aspirations to be free. By 1915, sixty-five families had found their way to Birmingham and its valleys cradled by the more modest—but more lush—slopes of America's Appalachian mountain range.

They made Birmingham their home. The Maronites among them— a sect of Catholics founded by patron saint Maron, a monk from Syria who had died in the fifth century—had established a church in 1910. In 1917, they had formed the Phoenician Club to buy a burial plot in Elmwood Cemetery, and in 1921, the Melkites—another sect of eastern rite

Catholics—had established their own church. The community had also founded an Arabic school to teach their children the language and literature of their homeland.

But there were plenty in Birmingham who did not like the immigrants who answered their call, Lebanese included. They disdained their foreign languages, names, and origins and suspected their dubious racial stock, given their olive skin and darker features. They called these new kinds of darkies *dagos*—Italians from Sicily had been the largest immigrant group, and looked enough like the Lebanese—or *foreigners*, and there were those who challenged their right to use the fountains, bathrooms, or entrances reserved for white people.

To make it worse, these immigrants were *Catholic*, a religion whose adherents many in Alabama believed were loyal only to the Pope, who wanted to make the United States a colony of the Vatican, and for whom there was no place in a Baptist heaven. As for the earthly kingdom, unlike blacks, who knew their place, these foreigners were annoyingly upwardly mobile. But the Ku Klux Klan—which had been revived after 1915 by a former preacher not too far away in Harpersville, Alabama—was there to remind them that their presence was less than desired and carefully watched.

The Lebanese all knew about what had happened to Irishman Father Coyle and still told it as a cautionary tale to their children. On August 11, 1921, Father Coyle had married a white woman to her Puerto Rican fiancé in a secret wedding. Her father, a Methodist minister and Klansman, had refused to officiate, as the Puerto Rican was dark-skinned and a Catholic. Not two hours later, the minister had found Father Coyle on the porch of his rectory and put a bullet in his head for marrying his daughter to Mr. Gussman. The minister was defended by a team of lawyers that included a local lawyer and later Supreme Court Justice named Hugo Black. He was found innocent. That same year, the *Nation* magazine proclaimed that Birmingham was the "American hotbed of anti-Catholic fanaticism." By 1924, Klan membership had peaked, with 115,000 members in Alabama.

The intense dislike of the Catholic foreigners—even when born in America—that so-called native whites felt was hardly discouraged by Birmingham's ruling industrialist class. The more fractured and fragmented their labor force, after all, the fatter their profit margins. And if these groups were fighting, there would be no danger of solidarity with the unequivocally not-white blacks.

In focusing on these foreigners, the Klan helped fuel a growing nativist sentiment spreading across the nation, which advocated for a preservation of America's true racial blood—Anglo-Saxon—from the immigrants who were polluting it.

From Dixie, Alabaman and other southern legislators in Congress warned against the Asiatic and African blood pulsing through the veins of the Mediterranean immigrants who had come to the nation and urged their fellow lawmakers to stem any further arrival. A senator from North Carolina appealed for the preservation of the Anglo-Saxon civilization in America against the "spawn of the Phoenician curse," who were "nothing more than the degenerate progeny of the Asiatic hordes which, long centuries ago, overran the shores of the Mediterranean."

In this nativist time, the federal government began enforcing the immigration statute that had been on the books since 1790, that required those applying for naturalization to prove they were "free white persons." Courts in different parts of the country—from Massachusetts to Oregon to Georgia—struggled with whether or not Syrians—as they were called—were white. Some courts held in their favor, deciding petitioners were considered by science to be Caucasian or were too light to be black. Other courts held that the Founding Fathers had not meant "white" in a scientific sense and that petitioners were too dark to be white. The federal government, however, had no such struggle, and in *each* case opposed the Syrians' naturalization on the grounds they were *not* white for the purposes of naturalization.

Similarly categorical had been a Judge Smith in South Carolina, who had repeatedly denied Syrians citizenship on the grounds they were not white. Syrian Americans from the more established communities in New York City and Boston had petitioned to be heard on the matter, because of a deep feeling that they had been collectively humiliated by being declared unfit for American citizenship and not white. They made two principal arguments: 1) that European Jews, also Semites, had been admitted without question and 2) that as the people of the land where Judaism and Christianity were born, it would be "inconceivable" that the statute would have intended to exclude them, because that would have excluded their ancient compatriot, Jesus Christ.

Judge Smith had quickly dispatched of the first, saying that Jews were European by race and Jewish by religion. As for the second argument, he had been quite insulted:

"The apostrophic utterance that He cannot be supposed to have clothed His Divinity in the body of one of a race that an American Congress would not admit to citizenship is purely emotional and without logical consequence. . . . The pertinent statement rather is that a dark complexioned present inhabitant of what formerly was ancient Phoenicia is not entitled to the inference that he must be of the race commonly known as the white race in 1790, merely because 2000 years ago Judea . . . was the scene of the labor of one who proclaimed that He had come to save from spiritual destruction all mankind."

Judge Smith deferred to what would have been understood by persons in 1790 at the time the statute was passed. He concluded that to the "average citizen":

"All the world was foreign, unknown, and black to him except the American Indians (whom he counted almost as vermin) and the inhabitants of Europe from whence he or his fathers came. He neither expected nor desired immigrants from any other quarter. Certainly not from Syria. . . . His only classification was 'color.' . . . [He] was . . . firmly convinced of the superiority of his own white European race over the rest of the world, whether red, yellow, brown, or black. . . . He would have enslaved a Moor, a Bedouin, a Syrian, a Turk, or an East Indian of sufficiently dark complexion with equal readiness. . . ."

In Birmingham itself, an election handbill circulated in the city in 1920 read:

FOR CORONER

VOTE FOR

J. D. GOSS

THE WHITE MAN'S CANDIDATE

They have disqualified the Negro, an American citizen, from voting in the white primary. The Greek and the Syrian should also be disqualified. I DON'T WANT THEIR VOTE. If I can't be elected by white men, I don't want the office.

But the Lebanese tried not to pay too much mind, and by 1921, the nativists had won anyway. Quotas had slowed immigration from anywhere other than Northwestern Europe to a trickle. Asians—Japanese and Chinese—were completely excluded from coming. By the time of Ed's birth in 1928, only a few hundred Syrians were entering the United States each year.

Ed was born in Tucson, Arizona, while his parents were traveling around on his father's sales route—his sister Helen had been born two years before in California—but in the early 1930s, they were ready to settle down and decided on Birmingham.

They arrived at a time when the Great Depression was draining the city of much of its magic. President Franklin Roosevelt proclaimed Birmingham America's hardest hit city. His New Deal talk of helping workers in general and safeguarding their right to collectively bargain with their employers alarmed Birmingham's iron and coal men. Unions were already trying to organize in their mines, and across racial lines. To deter such dissent, communists and blacks would have to be discredited or otherwise dissuaded. The Klan's punitive eye would have to be retrained.

Ed's father had come from Ramallah in Palestine, and his mother from Chattanooga, Tennessee. Her parents had made the journey from Zahleh, though all that was a world and a half away from what Ed knew, which was Birmingham, Tuscaloosa, and whatever was in between.

His parents had met in Chattanooga at the coffee house his mother's family ran. They had fallen in love, and though his father was Antiochian Orthodox, he married Ed's mother in the Catholic Church. Ed's father spoke little English while his mother twanged her way through Arabic, adjusting her hand-me-down Zahleh dialect to meet his Palestinian one. In Birmingham, the Salems had moved to Southside into a modest house with a big porch, started a rug-cleaning business, and after several miscarriages, had their son George in 1936.

Things began turning around as the country entered the war and Birmingham's steel was conscripted as part of the military effort. The statue of Vulcan was retrieved from the state fairgrounds, painted aluminum, and raised atop a specially built pedestal on Red Mountain, where it could be seen from Southside.

Then in 1942, Ed's father—who had arrived at Ellis Island with the name Yussef Salem El Ankar—died suddenly and was buried under the name he was given in New York's harbor, Joe Salem. Ed's mother's heart was broken. Overnight, at fourteen, Ed became the man of the house, and he started working even more hours in the family business.

But like many other Lebanese boys, he still found time to play baseball and football in Jordan Park. Anyone who ever played with Ed or saw him play knew he was going places. He could hit a ball harder, throw it farther, and run faster than anyone. Unlike other parents in the community who believed in hard work and saw sports as just a means for recreation on a Sunday afternoon, Ed's mother understood that playing ball could be Ed's ticket to a scholarship. Like most of the Lebanese in Southside, they weren't going to be able to afford any kind of college otherwise.

When Ed arrived at Ramsay Public High School, he easily made the baseball and football teams. Ramsay was on the Southside, and a lot of his friends from Jordan Park went there too. Many of the Lebanese had been at Catholic school for the elementary and middle grades; the Catholic high school was still under construction. But just as Birmingham's adults encountered each other when they went shopping downtown, their children—blacks excluded—met when they played the other public high schools on the football or baseball fields.

At those games, Ed learned to keep his cool. Because Ed was dark, he was vulnerable to taunts—the other side would call him *dago* and *foreigner*, and because the Lebanese sold to blacks, they got called *Nigger lovers* too.

His coaches taught him not to react—if he did, he'd surely get thrown out of the game, which is what his detractors wanted to have happen. So Ed learned never to swing at pitches in the dirt. He let it roll off his back, even when others wouldn't. Once while Ed was still a student at Ramsay, he hit a home run far out into the field. As he came around home plate, the other team started hissing, shouting out, "Greasy Greek! Greasy Greek!"

Before Ed had time to respond, the entire Ramsay bench emptied, Coach included, and they brought their bats. While the umpires rushed to stop the brawl, Ed called out matter-of-factly, "I'm not Greek, I'm Lebanese!" In reality, though, Ed spoke Alabama much more than he spoke Arabic.

The same sort of tactics followed him to the University of Alabama—opposing team's fans called him names as he came on the field, and opposing players tried to provoke him as well, but Ed was cool.

That just was the way Birmingham was. Folks, Lebanese included, looked after and stuck to their own. There were others, after all, who still had it worse in the Magic City.

Football had been good to Ed. He would turn to Ann sometimes and say, "Well, we've come a long way," and they'd share a smile. By the spring of 1963, Ed had opened three restaurants, he had three boys, and he and Ann were looking for a bigger house.

After the game in 1948 against Auburn on Legion Field, Ed went down to visit Ann while she summered with her family in Florida in 1949. Strolling along Collins Avenue in Miami, he turned to her and said, "I think it's about time that we started planning for a wedding."

They were married on February 20, 1950, while Ed was a junior at the University of Alabama and still playing for the Crimson and White. He had always wanted to do two things: play ball and go into business in Birmingham. So in April 1950, together with his mother, he opened a burger joint and called it *Ed Salem's Drive-In*. He was already enough of a football hero around Birmingham that his name on a sign meant people would come, though when Ed saw his name in lights and felt all that responsibility, he said to Ann, "We gotta work hard!" With Ed away in Tuscaloosa, his mother, sister, and Ann labored together to get the business up and running.

In his senior year, he was the Washington Redskins second-round draft pick. Without graduating from the university, he left Alabama to play in the National Football League. Ann joined him in the summer of 1951 in the nation's capital, and their newborn son took his first steps at Mount Vernon. But when Ed had to move to Montreal to play in the Canadian league, Ann declared she wasn't going anywhere colder than Washington. He moved to Canada, and she went back to Birmingham and kept working in the restaurant.

In 1953, Ed returned to their house in Southside; he had a family to support, and a career in professional football was not where the money was. He had also been injured one too many times, and he had other dreams to pursue, namely business and family. And in each passing year since 1948, Birmingham had made those dreams come more and more to fruition. But in 1954, not long after Ed returned, it looked like other things might be happening in Birmingham as well.

A police corruption scandal ousted segregation's inside man, Bull Connor, from the City Commission. One of the city's first acts after his departure was to reverse an ordinance that barred the races from any joint recreational activities—including checkers—so that Negroes* and whites would be able to play certain spectator sports together, like baseball and football. Ever since Jackie Robinson had integrated baseball, Birmingham had been knocked off the pro-exhibition circuit. In a city where sports were like mother's milk, that kind of deprivation was akin to starvation!

The new law was only catching up with what white people were already doing: watching the talented Negro teams. When he was younger, Ed used to scale the fence at Rickwood Field to see the Black Barons play baseball. Their star player from the late forties, Willie Mays, now played for the New York Giants. For Ed a good game was a good game, and he still went to watch the Negro high school kids when they played their football matches at Legion Field. Ed knew the transcending possibilities of sports—he had lived them. Progress seemed inevitable.

Some diehards in Birmingham, however, managed to get a referendum to re-segregate sports on the ballot. The plan looked like a long shot. But just before the city's citizens were to cast their vote, on May 17, 1954, the U.S. Supreme Court handed down a decision in *Brown* v. *Board of Education*, which held that "separate"—Birmingham's way of life—was inherently unequal. On the fear that integration was coming too fast, the initiative passed, and Jackie Robinson did not come to town.

By 1963, nine years after segregation had been ruled unconstitutional by the highest court in the land, Birmingham—sports and all—was still segregated, and things were tense. The Klan had found new life, terror-

---

*"Negro" was the respected term for African Americans at the time and so I have used it in this chapter.

izing Negroes clamoring for civil rights, and in the previous eight years, there had been twenty bombings in Birmingham. The Magic City was now known as the Tragic City or Bombingham.

Two governments were also both currently trying to run Ed's city in 1963. In early April, Albert C. Boutwell had narrowly defeated Bull Connor, becoming mayor as Birmingham attempted to change from a commission to a mayor-city council form of municipal government. Connor blamed his defeat on a Negro voting bloc and refused to give up his office as commissioner of public safety.

The entire state, in fact, was bucking the federal government's proclamations that segregation had to come to an end. George Wallace had been elected governor and sworn in that January. He had made it perfectly clear the way things would be in Alabama when he delivered his inaugural address, crying, "Segregation now! Segregation tomorrow! Segregation forever!"

Ed thought discrimination was wrong—the same people that cooked in his kitchen couldn't eat in his restaurant—but politics were not for him. He tore up checks when he knew people couldn't afford a meal, whether it was whites or Negroes who came to the back door to get their orders to go. And he and Ann made sure to vote, but otherwise they stayed out of the matters of downtown and City Hall. Ed knew that getting involved in any of it could ruin a business, and even ruin or cost a person his or her life.

It hadn't been too long ago in Ed's memory that the Lebanese community had felt the sting of Birmingham's discrimination because of their foreign origins and their attempts to move up, but with time things *had* gotten better. Ed was proud of who he was and what he had accomplished, and he focused on his children feeling the same rather than dwelling on the past. Ann was a real partner to him in those efforts. She always reminded their boys of their origins, telling them that they were "a quarter Lebanese and a quarter Palestinian," and of course "half redneck" as well. She also learned how to roll cabbage, stuff grape leaves, and make her own yogurt like Ed's people did.

Though, of course, all-American fare like burgers and fries, and not Arabic food, was on the menu at his restaurants, which were keeping Ed too busy to get involved in politics even if he had cared to. He was working long hours at the original drive-in on 26th Street North: the sports memorabilia–laden restaurant was open from 6 A.M. until 2 A.M. One week Ed would have the day shifts and the next, the nighttime ones, alternating with his mother's husband, who was also Ed's partner.

With Ed always at the restaurant, Ann was in charge that spring of the hunt for a new home; Ed's only restriction was that they not move to a neighborhood where he would have a long commute. Just as she began looking for their new house, in April, Martin Luther King, Jr., the civil rights leader, arrived in Birmingham. King was on a mission to end segregation in the defiant city and thus see passage of a federal civil rights law. His Southern Christian Leadership Conference (SCLC) was organizing with the Alabama Christian Movement for Human Rights under the Reverend Fred Shuttlesworth. Meeting at the 16th Street Baptist Church, they rallied those in Birmingham who were willing to risk their livelihood and their lives to challenge the city's strict segregation. Together they staged a series of nonviolent direct actions, including lunch counter and library sit-ins, marches on city hall, and a boycott of downtown merchants. Ed's restaurants were never targeted.

On Easter Sunday, the Negroes even attempted to celebrate the resurrection at white churches, seeking to integrate Birmingham during America's most segregated hour. Not targeted were the congregations of Southside's Lebanese churches, whose rites had been birthed in lands much closer than Alabama to where their common savior had lived, preached, and died.

The real estate agent showing Ann homes around Birmingham shortly after took her to a house over the mountain in Mountain Brook, where Ann thought people felt they were better than everyone else. But the house was real nice, and she let the agent know.

Later that same afternoon, he called. "Mrs. Salem," he said, "I cannot sell you that house."

"What's the problem?" she asked, realizing he had likely learned to whom she was married.

"I just looked at it, and it's in a restricted area," he said.

"What does that mean?" Ann pushed him.

"You know, you don't want to live over there," he said. "Where nobody wants you to live."

Ann yelled at him, "Who the hell is it restricted to?" and hung up the phone.

That evening, she told Ed about the phone call. He called the real estate agent himself and jokingly said, "Me and my boys will stay down here, and my wife can live up there, over the mountain. Would that be okay?"

He shrugged it off to Ann. "If they don't want me, I don't want them."

As spring gave way to summer in 1963, Ed, Ann, and their boys moved into their new house in Forest Park, a neighborhood with many professionals where other Lebanese already lived. The boys would soon be out of school. The community's Cedars Club was set to open its own swimming pool, so their children would have a place to keep cool in Alabama's summer swelter, without having to test how comfortable those over the mountain would be swimming with Lebanese in their pools.

Birmingham looked poised to head in a new direction. King had been right; Birmingham's brutality—put on nationwide display when Bull Connor set mad dogs on peacefully demonstrating Negro youths—stirred President Kennedy to act. With his intervention, the SCLC and the downtown Birmingham business community signed a desegregation agreement that included pledges to desegregate public accommodations, to ban discrimination in hiring practices, and to maintain public communications between Negro and white leaders to prevent further demonstrations. Though announcement of the agreement was answered with the bombing of the hotel where King and the SCLC leadership were staying and subsequent rioting downtown, President Kennedy moved 3,000 federal troops into position near Birmingham, sending a clear signal that progress was going to happen this time.

The Alabama Supreme Court also settled the matter of who led Birmingham, siding with Mayor Boutwell and the new City Council. In June, when Governor Wallace tried to block desegregation of the University of Alabama by literally blocking the door of the enrollment office, he was forced to yield the very next day, when President Kennedy federalized the

National Guard and deployed them to the university to force its desegregation. The president also sent a federal civil rights bill to Congress.
Then in July, the City of Birmingham finally repealed its segregation ordi-
nances.

The momentum generated by the campaign in Birmingham seemed
unstoppable. On August 28, 200,000 people converged on the nation's
capital in the March for Jobs and Freedom. Fresh from Birmingham, King
spoke to the crowd from the steps of the Lincoln Memorial. He delivered
a speech in which he gave a nod to where he had spent the spring and
summer.

"I have a dream that one day, down in Alabama, with its vicious rac-
ists, with its governor having his lips dripping with the words of 'interpo-
sition' and 'nullification'—one day right there in Alabama little black boys
and black girls will be able to join hands with little white boys and white
girls as sisters and brothers."

But there were those in Alabama who continued to abhor King's vision
for their state. As primary and secondary schools opened in September
for the new school year, Governor Wallace again attempted to block the
doors of an Alabama schoolhouse. President Kennedy answered by feder-
alizing the National Guard. In Birmingham, as schools began to integrate
protesters demonstrated—though not at Ramsay—and a prominent
Negro attorney's house was firebombed two weeks in a row.

Four rogue Klan members decided to come up with a scheme of their
own, one that would slow down those clamoring for integration in Birmingham. They decided to carry out their big plans on Sunday, September 15.

On Sunday mornings, most of the people of Birmingham—the
City of Churches, as it liked to call itself—were scattered throughout its
enclaves in prayer. The Lebanese congregated on that day of rest at either
St. George's Melkite or St. Elias's Maronite churches. The Divine Liturgy
started at 10:30 A.M. at both places of worship.

Ed and Ann took their boys every Sunday to St. George's, where the
mass was said in Arabic. Nothing of the church's modern exterior revealed
its origins, but inside, there was no mistaking the Byzantine style of its
iconography. The faces of Adam and Eve, archangels and saints, Madonna
and child were all painted in brown hues with the gaunt, almost sad fea-

tures of the East's understanding of the Bible. They looked nothing like the blond cherubic figures in paintings in the Western churches. No pastels were to be found, their hungry figures swaddled in jewel tones and their heads wreathed in brilliant gold, all against a backdrop wall of Mediterranean blue.

The priest, like the one at St. Elias's, was from the Old Country, very formal and very strict. He never preached about affairs in Birmingham, and he refused to give communion to women if he thought they were too immodestly made up or dressed. But Ed appreciated the church's ability to help the children—and the adults—stay connected to their parents', grandparents', and great-grandparents' culture.

Services had just begun for Southside's Lebanese that Sunday morning when, downtown, a massive explosion roared through the 16th Street Baptist Church, a congregation of the Birmingham Negro bourgeoisie. The living were bloodied, injured, and traumatized. Four girls who had been primping in the ladies room near the bomb's epicenter after Sunday school and before the 11:00 A.M. service were killed by the blast, one of them decapitated. It was the church's inaugural Youth Day.

By evening, word of what had happened at the Negro church made its way to Southside. People were stunned. This was the first bombing to target a church, to happen in broad daylight, and to exact any deaths. If nothing were sacred—children's lives, churches, and Sunday morning—they could turn around and do it to anybody at any time. Ed, his family, and the Lebanese community mourned for the girls, for their families, and for their city. It was wrong that children should die for nothing, that parents should bury their offspring, and that they should all be caught in the middle.

The bundled sticks of dynamite had been set in the early hours of that morning. The conspirators had each spent their Saturday evening living life as they would on any other weekend. The getaway driver, Tommy Blanton, Jr., took his girl, Jean, out on a date. Toward dusk, he had picked her up in the same white-on-blue '57 Chevy that had later been spotted ominously close to the 16th Street Baptist Church. Before heading up to Vulcan's base atop Red Mountain to park, they had gone out for dinner on 26th Street North at a popular drive-in spot with great burgers and fries named *Ed Salem's*.

On Friday, November 22, 1963, President John F. Kennedy was assassinated in Dallas, Texas. Vice President Lyndon B. Johnson assumed the presidency that very afternoon. Days later, President Johnson addressed Congress, urging lawmakers to heed his predecessor's legislative agenda, placing the greatest importance on Kennedy's civil rights bill.

By the next summer, both the House and the Senate had passed a much stronger version of the bill, and on July 2, 1964, Johnson signed the Civil Rights Act into law. It was the most comprehensive and far-reaching legislation of its kind in American history. The act's provisions prohibited segregation and discrimination in public places, in schools, in employment practices, and in housing contexts. The law also authorized the federal government to sue in such cases.

President Johnson took his defeat of Republican Barry Goldwater in the 1964 presidential election as a mandate to carry out the legislative reforms that would further the cause of his Great Society agenda. He signed into law the Voting Rights Act on August 6, 1965, which gave the federal government authority to suspend barriers at the state and local levels that prevented African Americans from exercising their right to vote.

On October 3, 1965, again under the auspices of the Great Society, President Johnson signed into law another of Kennedy's legislative causes, the Immigration and Naturalization Act of 1965. With the events in Birmingham having given the nation's march toward equality more urgency, the discriminatory nature of the immigration system, which since 1924 had favored Northern Europeans, no longer fit the new way America was imagining itself.

The signing ceremony was held on Liberty Island in New York Harbor. With the decaying and atrophied buildings of Ellis Island making for an evocative and symbolic background, he announced: "This bill we sign today is not a revolutionary bill. It does not affect the lives of millions. It will not reshape the structure of our daily lives, or really add importantly to either our wealth or our power."

His sentiments reflected those of Congress; the principal purpose of the law was to reunite families that since 1924 had been separated by the ocean, and to facilitate the immigration of professionals such as doctors and engineers. Lawmakers envisioned that these professionals would come from places like the UK and Germany.

But the new law, in fact, ended up changing the whole course of American immigration history, opening America's doors to émigrés from nations that had been severely restricted after 1924 and from countries that had previously not sent people in any kind of numbers. Declining birthrates and a much improved standard of living in Western and Southern Europe meant their hunger to emigrate did not match that of people who wanted to come from Asia, Africa, the Middle East, and Latin America.

In 1965 and 1966, 6,490 people emigrated to the United States from the Arabic-speaking world, compared to 1963–1964, during which 4,683 people came under family reunification schemes. But word that America was now open to skilled professionals had only begun to trickle out.

Across the globe, the majority of Palestinian refugees were still looking for a way back home, nearly twenty years after their dispossession. Egyptian President Gamal Abdel Nasser's message of pan-Arabism as the solution to all the problems of the Arab world—particularly the plight of the Palestinians—still resonated, and he played a major role in encouraging the founding of the Palestine Liberation Organization (PLO) in 1964. Many in the Arab world believed that the Palestinians would inevitably return to their homes, possessions, lands, and cities inside what had become Israel, and they believed Nasser would deliver this future.

Home

On June 7, 1967, Luba Sihwail rode with the windows down and the radio on in her blue Buick sedan. Spring always reminded her of home. Even though these outskirts of Baltimore City were nothing like her faraway village, she thought Maryland was nevertheless quite pretty.

Luba had left her husband George's rug installation shop and had given herself fifteen minutes, just enough time, to reach her daughters' elementary school. Each day she would vary her route, taking a different tributary that connected the two major roads, Hartford and Belair, between which her life was contained. With its nicer houses—fully detached single-family structures—Hamilton Avenue was her favorite. Luba liked to pick a house—always one with a wraparound porch—and fantasize she lived there instead of in the tiny apartment they rented, just a few streets away, that overlooked the vast cemetery on Moravia Road.

Outside her window, the trim and manicured lawns, full of verdant green grass, were so different from home, where the terrain was rugged and allowed to remain wild. The land there was interspersed instead with dirt, rocks, and plants that thrived in a climate where it did not rain for half the year. Americans seemed intent on bringing the earth in line, smoothing Maryland's modest crags into even rivers of asphalt, along which Luba now drove. The houses that stood at perfect attention along the roads were made of uniform bricks cast in a die or siding completely level. Each house was so like its neighbors but for some variation such as the color of the shutters, the location of the driveway, or the hue of the roof's shingles. Back home, the houses reflected the needs and means of the individual families that built them and were constructed with hand-chiseled stone, each one an echo of the flicks of the wrist that had formed them.

But it was spring now and spring anywhere always reminded Luba of Ramallah, her village in Palestine. There, when the winter rains finally gave way to the unadulterated blue skies that lasted all spring and summer long, Luba, her sisters, and the neighbors' boys—the three sons of a Palestinian father and a German mother—would race the two miles to the top of one of Ramallah's hills and shout across the valley. The boomerang of their voices' echo would delight them. They would then run down into the low field separating the hills, turning over the rocks on their path to watch what scorpions, little snakes, and centipedes they could find. They picked wild anemones, tulips, narcissus, and cyclamens before returning home. Upon seeing the frenzied bouquets, Luba's mother would admonish her children for bringing more flowers than she had vases before filling pots usually used for cooking with water and standing the blooms upright.

How was her mother now? Luba wondered.

Since Monday, Luba had kept the radio on constantly—at the house, at the store, in the car. A new war close to home had erupted in the Middle East, and each evening she and George watched it unfold on American nightly news.

In a strike meant to preempt what the Israelis claimed was an imminent Egyptian offensive, Israel had on Monday, June 5, 1967, launched an air attack against Egyptian airfields, destroying dozens of planes parked on the runways and killing dozens of Egyptian pilots. In retaliation, Syrian, Jordanian, and Iraqi planes had attacked Israel. Israel responded by bombing Syrian, Iraqi, and Jordanian bases, quickly winning air supremacy. Its ground forces had also crossed into the Sinai, defeating Egyptian troops along the way. Then on Tuesday, Israel had wrested control of Gaza from Egypt. And much closer to Ramallah, fighting between the Jordanians and Israelis had yielded control of Palestinian cities Hebron and Bethlehem to the Israelis.

Luba had convinced George to put off buying a house here in Baltimore so they could one day—when the time was right—return home. But they always seemed to be waiting for the time to be right, and nearly ten years had passed since they had first arrived in Baltimore. With this new war, Luba was starting to panic that things would never be good enough, stable enough, prosperous enough for them to return home.

In Ramallah, they had gotten used to conflict bringing change to their lives. The creation of the state of Israel had seen Palestinian refugees, like George and his family, pour into Luba's village. Many, like George's family, had walked for days and arrived on foot with what little of their belongings they could carry. The amputation of the Palestinian cities, towns, and villages that became part of Israel, the destruction of many others that were cleared to make way for the new state, and the subsequent Jordanian domination of the West Bank meant economic hardships for them all.

But to Luba, it seemed that life-threatening violence came only accidentally to Ramallah. In 1948, an errant bomb intended for the nearby headquarters of the Arab Legion had instead crashed down on her family's house, forcing them out into the midnight darkness in their nightgowns and robes. The explosion had shattered all the glass panes in the house and annihilated two large peach trees and one fig tree. Where the trees had been, they found only craters. When Luba's mother went to retrieve her baby Isa from his crib, she found a puddle of shards and a big piece of sharpened glass balancing on the blanket that covered his body—mercifully his exposed face and head were unscathed. Throughout the 1948 Arab-Israeli War, they had kept their suitcases packed and waiting by the door, should a truce never happen. When it finally did in

April 1949, a kind of normalcy had descended, with both sides menac-
ingly entrenched.

Yet despite the fact that the conflict might not be resolved anytime
soon and that Ramallah might always be ringed by trouble, Luba believed
it was bound to forever remain free from Israeli control. Maybe that
should be good enough reason to just return home.

For now, though, she would be traveling only in Baltimore, and mostly
between house, store, and school. With school soon to be out, that routine
would at least change, and Luba would shuttle their children to dance,
baton, and piano lessons instead. Even if she and George did not have
enough money to take a proper vacation, the girls would have a full summer indeed.

Luba pulled into the parking lot of Gardenville Elementary and saw
her daughters Sana and Mona waiting—as they did every day—at the
school's entrance. Sana had her great-grandfather's blond hair, cropped
short, and Mona's auburn hair sported the two braids that Luba wove
each morning.

Sana jumped up front; it was her turn to sit next to Luba. Luba quizzed
them about how their day had been and what homework they would be
working on once they got back to the shop.

"Mom," Mona interrupted from the back, before switching to Arabic.
"I went to the teacher today, and I told her 'Mrs. Dishler, I don't like how
you're doing your hair.'"

Luba looked at her in the rearview mirror. Mona's teacher was an older
woman who always wore her long blonde hair neatly pinned in a bun.

"I told her," Mona continued, " 'You should do it differently. You
should let your hair down.'"

"You did not tell your teacher this!" Luba exclaimed, trying not to
laugh.

"Yes I did!" Mona retorted, quite serious.

"Mona, you don't talk like this to a teacher," Luba admonished.

"Well, she would look prettier," Mona responded. "What's wrong with
that?"

On the radio, the music was interrupted with a special news report.
Luba hushed the girls.

Violence had escalated in the Middle East. Israeli forces had captured the Old City in East Jerusalem, Sharm el-Sheikh in the Sinai, and several Palestinian villages in the West Bank. Hundreds of thousands of Palestinians were fleeing into Jordan.

Luba needed to hear precisely *which* villages in the West Bank had been taken.

Jericho had fallen.

And Ramallah—Ramallah was now under Israeli control.

Luba let out a heaving scream before moaning "Not Ramallah, not Ramallah!" She wanted to take her head in both hands, but she caught herself and instead banged the steering wheel repeatedly.

Sana and Mona immediately fell silent and stared, startled, at their mother.

Luba's mind quickly traveled to her parents, at home in their house in Ramallah, and she fought the terror of the Deir Yassin massacre creeping into her head. The mere thought of it still sent a chill down her spine.*

What would happen to her parents? Would the Israelis steal anything? Would they bomb anywhere? Kill anyone? Luba panicked that she would never see her parents again. Would she ever go home now? Would there ever be peace? She began to sob.

"What's wrong, Mom?" Sana asked.

Everything was wrong, and Luba could barely see the road in front of her. She wiped at her tears with her sleeves and the backs of her hands.

Sana looked up at her and asked, "Is it your headache again?"

Luba strolled side by side with George in the British Protectorate of Aden in the early months of 1958. The whispering of the calm waters of the

---

*In the period between November 29, 1947, when the United Nations partitioned Palestine into Jewish and Arab states, and May 14, 1948, when the British Mandate ended and Israel declared its independence, fighting between Jewish and Arab forces for control of Palestine had intensified. Deir Yassin was a small Palestinian village that had remained neutral during the fighting and had even entered into a nonaggression pact with the Haganah, the organization that would eventually become the Israeli Defense Forces. Yet in April 1948, right-wing irregular Jewish forces attacked the small village, killing over a hundred villagers. Those who survived were loaded onto trucks and displayed during a victory parade through Jewish quarters. What happened in Deir Yassin caused panic in 1948 among many Palestinians, who were fearful that the same would happen to them, and caused many to flee their homes.

Gulf, fed by the Red and Arabian Seas, kept them company as they chatted and waited for the Abayan Development Board car to return. The British cotton company for which George worked in the remote village of Ja'ar had arranged for them to travel to Aden so that they could fetch the groceries not available in the village. They had finished quickly, but the driver would not be back for them for another two hours.

Abayan Board had hired George just months before as an accountant. Founded with a substantial loan from the British government, the company had put in place a series of major irrigation works to convert the land in Abayan for cotton cultivation. With earnings from cotton exportation, the Abayan district had grown into quite a community, with roads, running water, and electricity.

Great Britain had been in Aden since 1839, when it invaded the strategic port—over which both France and Egypt wanted control—because it provided a western approach to India. Now, Aden had become one of the busiest ship-bunkering and tax-free shopping and trading ports in the world, second only to the port of New York City.

But by the mid-1950s, Britain's presence was under constant attack by Radio Cairo, which broadcast the Voice of the Arabs, and other revolutionary Arab nationalist centers. British exploitation had become a nationalist issue, and the native rulers were being portrayed as imperialist tools. In a nod to those demands, Abayan Board had gone to Jordan to recruit Arab workers. George had sat for the accounting test and with two other Palestinians was offered a job—if he would be willing to relocate to Ja'ar.

Luba and George had been newly engaged, though there were objections in both families. Her parents thought he was not ready for marriage, and his family questioned what kind of girl Luba could be, having been sent by her father to university in Beirut, where she had lived as a single woman. But because George was allowed to bring a wife to Aden, and because the British protectorate at the tip of the Arabian Peninsula was so far from Ramallah and George's family, Luba let go of her misgivings. She quit her job as a mathematics teacher at the Quaker Friends School, and they married hurriedly in Ramallah on October 12, 1957, arriving in the British protectorate south of the Kingdom of Yemen on October 14.

They had come to Ja'ar, a village on top of a mountain surrounded by a lush forest populated by birds and trees Luba had never seen before and could not name. Abayan Board provided them with a fully furnished apartment alongside those of the other expatriate workers. The company even hired a boy to come and sweep the house of all the dust that would accumulate from the frequent sandstorms that beat at the flat's wrap-around balcony. Besides the Palestinians and two Greek couples, the rest of the employees were British. The native villagers lived down the mountainside and away from the foreigners.

Luba loved their newlywed life together. George would bring her morning coffee in bed, and she would always have dinner ready when he came home from work, the table fully set with a tablecloth, formal flatware, and folded fabric napkins. In the evenings they would take walks together and discuss their future. Should she get a job with Abayan Board? What kind of house would they buy in Ramallah with the money saved from working a few years in Aden? How many kids would they have? Luba declared on one of these walks that if they could not conceive she wanted to adopt—Palestine was full of orphaned children—and George readily agreed.

But then, very quickly, the tensions that were nipping at Aden became part of their lives.

One evening in November, not long after they arrived, George and Luba had made their way to the social club in the expatriate section at the top of the mountain. They socialized with their neighbors and George's coworkers and those they would see around the neighborhood when they took their walks. Luba chatted with the British women about how often they went into Aden and how they got there. They liked feeling as if they were part of a community.

The next day, a British man approached George at work. He informed George that he and Luba were not entitled to come to the club because "You and your wife do not belong to the elite."

Luba and George were shocked and never returned there. At Christmas, when its halls were lit with a large celebration attended by all the expats—save for the Palestinians and the Greeks—Luba watched with longing from outside. She and George instead spent a lonely evening with the elder of the Greek couples.

Then shortly after Christmas, George joined in a soccer match down the mountain with the villagers. He was a passionate player whose skills had made him popular in Ramallah. When a British manager saw George running in the dirt with the Adenese, he pulled him out of the game and reprimanded him. George was *not* allowed to mingle with the natives.

Now as Luba and George together discussed what they would cook with their groceries, they came upon a building labeled American Embassy.

Luba turned to George. "Let's check it out," she said playfully.

George was also curious. Back home in Ramallah, going to America was a dream. People put their names on the quota list and waited years for a visa.

Inside they were greeted by the consul—an eager, handsome, and blond American. There was no one else inside; there appeared to be no other staff, not even a secretary.

The American asked how he could help them.

"We would like to know," Luba asked, "what are our chances to go to America?" knowing there was little if any chance at all of getting a visa.

"Where are you from?" the consul asked.

"We are Palestinians," George responded.

The consul seemed confused. "Where's that?" he asked.

Luba and George explained that Palestine was in the Levant and bordered by Jordan, and that parts of it had become Israel.

The American remained confused and brought out a map. Luba and George showed him where Palestine was, even though there was no such name written across any of the colored divisions of nation-states.

The consul then gave them forms to complete, asking basic biographical information. After filling in the required details, Luba and George bid the American good-bye and left.

Two months later, Abayan Board gave George notice that his services would no longer be needed. After only five months of work, George and the two other Palestinians were fired. Syria and Egypt had merged as the United Arab Republic and had then federated with North Yemen; pan-Arab nationalism clearly had British rule in Aden in its sights.

They could not leave immediately—as required by their visas— because Luba had become pregnant. Instead they were granted an extension by the British, moved from Ja'ar, and took jobs in the city of Aden.

Luba was quickly hired to teach math to both the Adenese and the British girls at the British-run schools but shortly got herself in trouble when she complained that the girls were being given drastically different curriculums and that, unlike the British girls, the Adenese girls did not have enough books. The principal threatened Luba, "Keep your mouth shut or you will be fired." As soon as Luba could travel, they left Aden.

Luba and George returned home to Ramallah years earlier than expected and without the money they had hoped to make. At first, they struggled to find work for George and a place to live; both of them moved back into their respective parents' homes. But within a few months, Luba returned to the Friends School to teach, George found work in Jordan, and they were able to furnish their own apartment. Sana was born that October, and after only twenty days' leave, Luba was back at work. She loved the school where she herself had been educated and was a frequent teacher's pet. The stone contours of the school and its gardens were like a second home to Luba, and she loved especially the tall, sky-blue irises Samaan the gardener grew, better than anyone else in Ramallah.

Luba was teaching at her favorite school, she had a new baby girl she adored, she was a neighbor to her parents, and she and George had finally—*finally*—begun to feel settled. But then one morning in the spring of 1959, while Luba was at home a letter arrived that would change everything. She opened the envelope and read its contents.

How could this have happened? she wondered.

According to this letter from the U.S. Embassy in Jordan, waiting there in Amman were two visas for them to emigrate to America. George would be in Ramallah by lunchtime for the weekend. He spent the workweek in Amman at his job and came on Fridays to be with Luba and Sana. Luba decided she would tell George then about the letter.

He arrived early that afternoon, and they examined the letter together. Because George was a Palestinian refugee registered with the United Nations Relief and Works Agency for Palestinian Refugees in the Near East (UNRWA), they would be given visas and their trip would be paid for by the agency provided George turned in his refugee rations card.

George was thrilled. Two of his brothers already lived in the States and were finding financial success. Luba's sister Evelyn was a graduate student in English literature and library science at Columbia University. Her brother Aziz had studied at Harvard for his master of laws degree and was married to an American woman.

But Luba was settled in Ramallah and committed to a life there. She had forgotten all about the embassy on the beach and the blond American with the blue eyes.

Luba decided to seek her father's counsel. Her parents' stone house was just a dusty walk down the Shari` `Ayn Misbah—the street named for the spring where the community filled their jugs with water when it was scarce. Her parents had built the house in the early 1930s in an area surrounded by small orchards of fruit and few houses.

As she approached her parents' house, she found them already seated on its front balcony. Her father, Saliba, had stopped working ten years before, when his illness had forced him to retire at age forty-five.

Luba told her parents she and George had been granted visas to immigrate to America. "What should we do?" she asked her father.

"Don't go," Luba's mother, Zahia, interrupted. "America is for the Americans, not for the Arabs! Look what it did to your father."

Saliba had himself gone to America in 1923, already married and with two children. He had spent eight years separated from them, and the money he had earned peddling had built their very house. But Luba's mother wasn't convinced that money should be a reason to leave the homeland. "God always provides," she would tell her children.

Zahia also blamed America for her husband's illness. His time in America had been during Prohibition. Though he was undiagnosed, something had attacked Saliba's nervous system, and Luba's parents believed it was the wood alcohol that he had drunk in the country's dry years. When he returned from America in 1931, his little finger had begun to feel numb and with each year, the illness had progressed a bit further into his body.

Saliba nonetheless always spoke with admiration about American progress and the opportunities America provided. He wowed his children with stories of American pharmacies, where one could buy not only medicines, but chocolates and ice cream! America was also where he had decided on Luba's name, long before she had ever been imagined. There he had rented a room from two Russian sisters—Nadya and Luba—and he had promised them that if he ever had more daughters, he would give them the same Russian names.

"Let them try it," Luba's father said to her mother. "Don't stand in their way."

Luba looked to her father, whom she believed could guide her.

"Look, go try it. If you like it, you can stay," he told his daughter. "If you don't, come back." He shrugged. "But if you don't go, you might always regret it."

In 1967 Baltimore, Luba walked into the store with the girls.

"Why are you crying?" George asked, startled. "What happened? Did you have an accident?

"It's about Ramallah," Sana answered before her mother could say anything.

"What about Ramallah?" George asked.

Luba was surprised he didn't know. "Listen to the news!" she snapped.

George turned on the radio they kept on the desk. Luba again thought of their parents in Ramallah and started to cry. George had also begun to cry. Luba understood the news had awakened in her husband memories, ugly memories that he would rather not remember.

They decided to close the shop, though it was still hours before seven, and go home. George drove in his truck and Luba followed with the girls in the Buick. Like a funeral procession, they caravanned the short yet eternal road back to their apartment.

As soon as they were home, they turned the television on and waited for the evening news. Phone lines to their village had been cut, so they looked to the television for any information about what had happened and if—God forbid—anyone had died.

Israelis were flocking to the Western Wall to celebrate the capture of East Jerusalem. Luba always felt the Jordanians had been wrong to prohibit Israeli access to the Wall. If Luba wanted to be able to worship at her holy site, the Church of the Holy Sepulchre, she thought the Jews ought to be able to visit theirs as well. The country had enough room for both the Palestinians and the Jewish immigrants.

Now, watching the news, Luba hated their celebration.

In addition, thousands of Palestinians from West Bank towns were fleeing for Jordan proper, dispossessed of even more of their homeland.

But what of Ramallah?

And then Luba found herself staring at images coming from Ramallah. The townspeople were shown waving white handkerchiefs or carrying white pieces of sheets bound to sticks, having put up no fight at all.

Luba felt personally demeaned watching these old women and men made so submissive, submitting to the will of Israeli teenage soldiers, so easily, so quickly.

"Where are the Arab countries?" Luba exclaimed. "Why did they forsake us?" she said, trying to justify the surrender of these people.

Luba didn't care if Israel took all of Syria and all of Egypt, but not her home. Ramallah was off-limits! She felt loss, failure, desperation, hopelessness. Ramallah is mine, mine! How dare you take it!

The girls were hungry, so Luba rose to make dinner, but throughout her preparations, she and George exchanged phone calls with their relatives who also lived in America. They asked each other if anyone had heard a word about their families in Ramallah. "Why can't we get through?"

Though none of these calls gave Luba any solace, she held on to the one comforting piece of news coming from the TV. There were no casualties in Ramallah.

Between her tears, Luba managed to feed the girls.

Finally, they asked her, "Why don't you stop crying? What's the big deal?"

Luba explained that the Jews had taken her hometown, had taken Ramallah.

Both Luba and George had sought to keep the girls connected to their homeland. He insisted the girls speak Arabic in the house, and she always read them the letters from their grandparents. When Luba called her mother and father, she would put Sana and Mona on the line, and they chattered away about their school and friends.

Sana, who had been born in Ramallah and had often listened intently to her father as he watched the news, seemed to understand. Mona could not care less.

"What's wrong with the Jews?" Mona asked.

Luba was frustrated. Mona's questions demanded explanations. They could not be swatted away or easily answered.

"Well, the Jews have been taking Palestine little bit by little bit, and now they reached Ramallah and they took it," Luba said. "Now all Jerusalem is with the Jews and now it is Ramallah's turn to be taken," Luba explained. "And that's why I'm crying, and that's why I want you to shut up and stop asking questions!"

But Mona continued, "The Jews, aren't they human beings? Aren't they people?"

"Yes, of course they are human beings," Luba responded. "They're people like us."

"Then why can't they be in Ramallah?" Mona demanded.

"Mona, this is your house, do you want your neighbors to come and tell you to get out, take your house, and then they live here. Is this right?" Luba asked her.

"Yes, they're people," Luba continued, "but Ramallah does not belong to them."

The taxi driver beeped his horn, signaling to Luba and George, *Time to go!* They were standing on her parents' front balcony, saying good-bye on a crisp morning in August 1959. It was not yet eight in the morning but Ramallah's sun and her people had long been awake, and Luba's parents were already dressed to see their daughter off. Luba herself had been up for hours, anxious about the trip and spending time bathing, feeding, and changing Sana.

The driver had agreed to make a quick stop at Luba's parents' house. Her father could not make the trip down the street the night before when everyone came to formally send them off. And even though George's parents had been there last night, they had stopped by earlier in the morning, to say a last good-bye.

Passersby on the street, already headed to work or to run their errands, yelled out to them:

MA `ASSALAMA!

BON VOYAGE!

GOOD LUCK IN AMREEKA!

COME BACK TO YOUR COUNTRY!

KEEP IN TOUCH!

As Luba said good-bye to her parents, she feared she might never see her father again. After each separation, Luba returned home to find him sicker—his legs less able to carry him, his eyes less able to focus, though his mind was ever sharp and intact.

She embraced her father.

"Go with my blessings," he told Luba. "Maybe we will see you back again next year."

Her mother clung to Sana, crying.

People on the street shouted out comfort: *Wish them luck and they'll be OK! They're going to a good place!*

Luba's mother hurriedly handed Luba packed sandwiches of mortadella and snacks of precut apples, plums, cucumbers, and tomatoes. Luba's father snuck a KitKat bar in the provisions for the road.

The driver sounded his horn again, briefly. Reluctantly, Luba took Sana from her mother and turned toward the car. UNRWA would pay for their voyage to America and had provided the driver to transport Luba and George from Ramallah to Amman and then to Beirut, from where they would travel to America by ship. With their luggage in the sedan's trunk, they unfolded the portable crib they had brought for the journey in the back seat, where Luba sat with Sana, while George rode in front.

They drove in silence through Ramallah, leaving town by the road to Jericho. George's eyes bore the glimmer of tears while Luba wept openly, turning her face away from the buildings that lined the streets that she knew so intimately.

Have we made a mistake? she wondered.

The road to Jericho curved through rocky hills broken down and terraced to bear grape vines and olive trees. Held in the hills' embrace were other villages of white limestone—a church steeple or mosque minaret often the highest peak—that would appear to keep them company for a few blinks of their eyes as they wound their way toward Earth's lowest point. Held motionless by the planet's core pull, the Dead Sea glistened like moving water nonetheless, in the desert surrounding Jericho. Amman would not be much farther now.

They spent a night in the Jordanian capital before continuing to Lebanon. They arrived in Beirut by early afternoon the next day, spending their last night in the Levant in the coastal Mediterranean city.

The next morning they made their way to the port of Beirut, where they were met by the agent contracted by UNRWA, who gave them their tickets. He lead them to the Greek ship on which they would travel from Beirut to Port Said in Egypt before continuing to Piraeus in Greece. On board, a Greek sailor escorted George and Luba three levels below deck. The floors were dirty and the smell of stale, sweaty air filled Luba's nostrils. The sailor told Luba and George that they would be in separate cabins because for those traveling in third class, the Greeks segregated men from women in the sleeping quarters.

They had been swindled! The Lebanese agent had been given money by UNRWA to buy them second-class tickets, not third-class passage. George ran back up to the main deck and tried to chase the man down in the crowds. He was, however, long gone.

When George returned, they were each shown down a narrow corridor to different cabins. Inside each windowless box, there were two pairs of wooden bunk beds. Luba was assigned one of the top bunks that hovered right below the ceiling.

"I cannot keep Sana with me," Luba exclaimed. "There is no room for her here," she said, eyeing the scant distance from her bunk to the wooden ceiling. She turned to George. "She must stay with you."

All around them, Luba and George heard only Greek, a language neither of them could understand. George did not feel safe having Sana with him in his cabin with unknown men. They would have to find another solution.

They returned to the main deck as the ship soon pulled out of port; the journey to Port Said would take just one day. As Lebanon's mountains receded behind them, Luba began to feel nausea swell inside her with the dizzying undulating of the ship as the Mediterranean jostled it toward Egypt. She was soon shuttling back and forth to the bathroom to vomit, and Sana developed a rash.

As night fell, George found a wooden bench across the corridor from Luba's cabin. He decided he would sleep there. He tied Sana's crib to his bench using clothes from their luggage, securing her makeshift bed to his.

Luba flung herself onto her top bunk above a snoring Greek woman. In the darkness, Luba could hear Sana crying, but could not rise to soothe her without losing herself again to the nausea.

When people in Ramallah learned that George and Luba had been granted travel visas to America, some said they were fools even to hesitate. The creation of Israel had forced many Palestinians from their homes and ancestral lands, and most sought to heal the wounds of the displacement by forging a future elsewhere. Those who didn't receive a visa to America traveled to Canada or Australia instead, but it was American opportunity that many idealized. But Luba did not think she could make it.

When they arrived in Port Said the next morning, Luba told George she could travel no farther. They decided she would return to Ramallah and come to America by plane instead of weathering the nearly one-month trip by sea.

Luba was granted special permission to disembark in Port Said. She went to the Egyptian immigration office, taking only her purse and leaving Sana with George until she secured her passage back to Ramallah. Luba at last could breathe fresh air, air not contaminated by sweat, breath, and urine. She walked into the dilapidated office in the port, relieved to be returning home.

"I want to go home," she told the officers. "I am sick, and my daughter is sick, and I cannot go on like this." She asked for their help in getting to the airport.

The Egyptians searched through her purse, examined her passport, and interrogated her. None of their questions seemed to Luba to be relevant to getting her and Sana from the port to the airport and home. She wondered what on earth the Egyptians could possibly suspect her of being or doing, but answered their questions nonetheless. They then asked her the same questions again. Finally, she realized they did not believe she was truly sick.

"You know what," she said, "I don't want to leave. I'm going to stay." She decided that remaining any longer with the Egyptians might be worse for her than the ship.

Luba left the immigration office as quickly as possible and told herself, "What will happen, happens."

One of the officers slipped out of the room and followed her out. When he caught up with her, he advised her to go to the pharmacy and buy a certain medicine good for seasickness.

The Egyptian turned out to be quite right. For the next two days, the rest of the trip to Greece, Luba was able to spend the days on the deck. At breakfast, she was able to sit at the long table where all the passengers ate together. The table was always set with forks, knives, and spoons, though all they were given to eat was bread and olives, to be washed down with tea already sweetened. Each time Luba would mutter, "Why do they bother to give us these utensils?" She was also able to help George set up the crib by the bench each night, and now when she heard Sana cry, she would rise and leave the room to tend to her.

Finally, three days after leaving Beirut, they arrived in Piraeus. There they boarded an Italian ocean liner, the *MS Saturnia*. It was much larger than the Greek one and capable of crossing the rougher waters of the Atlantic Ocean. This time they had second-class tickets and George, Luba, and Sana had their own cabin with a shower and toilet included. For meals, the tables were draped with white linen, and at dinner, there was always a bottle of wine waiting. Luba felt she was in heaven.

The journey to America would last two weeks. From Greece they traveled toward the Strait of Gibraltar. On the day they finally came upon the Rock of Gibraltar, George snapped a picture of the famous island, whose name was derived from the Arabic *Jebel Tariq*, Tariq's mountain, after Tariq bin Zayad, the general who had invaded Spain in the eighth century. In school in Ramallah, they had been required to memorize verses from the speech he gave upon arriving at the island.

Luba again mouthed these words from memory as she looked at the towering mass of land that jutted out of the waters. "Where are you going?" Tariq had proclaimed to his troops, after burning all his ships to prevent his army from retreating. "The sea is in front of you and the enemy is behind you!"

Where was she going, Luba wondered. She was impatient with the waters ahead of her; she wanted the trip to end and to see what America was like. She thought of their apartment in Ramallah, their furniture, the rhythm they had established for their life together. Would she have the same in America? Surely they would, she tried to assure herself; everything in America was better. She imagined the flowers and gardens of New York City—they must be stupendous! But then she worried about George's English, whether either of them would find work, and how expensive America must be.

Then, a month after they had left Ramallah, they arrived at their first port in North America, in the Canadian city of Halifax. After crossing the Atlantic, they finally walked again on land for a few hours. Luba liked the small, orderly houses that formed neat rows, with their gardens full of geraniums and climbing roses. America was not far.

They reboarded the *Saturnia* for their final day of travel. Tomorrow, they would at last arrive in New York City.

The next day, Luba dressed Sana nicely, in a dress with matching socks, shoes, and ribbon for her hair. Instead of wearing her regular jeans, Luba put on her white sandals and her favorite dress—a sleeveless, orange A-line with white polka dots, cinched at her waist with a white belt. She wanted to impress George's family and greet America looking her best.

By late afternoon, the ship began approaching Ellis Island, and Luba and George watched the city appear from the main deck as the Statue of Liberty grew closer and closer

As they pulled into the port, Luba was surprised by what she saw. The buildings, tall as she had heard, seemed dark and dirty and nothing like the shiny pictures she had seen in school of the White House and the Grand Canyon.

The ship finally docked, and Luba and George made their way down a ramp toward the immigration building. When their turn came, they approached the immigration officer and presented their passports. He asked them:

"Do you have a place to live?"

"Are there people here to pick you up?"

"Did you bring any food with you?"

Luba answered for them both.

"You speak good English," he told Luba, and he stamped the passports.

"Thank you!" she replied.

"Welcome to America." He smiled at them.

Luba and George were each handed their Green Card—a small piece of plastic the size of a credit card that was indeed green—the color of moss.

Outside Luba and George immediately found their family. Finally, Luba embraced her sister Evelyn, whom she had not seen in seven years. As they hugged and kissed each other's cheeks, the trip's details spilled out of Luba, and looking at all that surrounded her, she asked Evelyn, "Is this America? Is this it?

"I want to go home," Luba told her sister, "I want to go home."

In Baltimore in the fall of 1967, Luba's feelings were unchanged from that first impression. Her old neighbor and friend Bernice would later tell her that because Luba's American home was on a street named *Providence* Road, God was looking out for her.

Almost four months had passed since the Israelis had invaded and occupied the West Bank. Times had become very tough for Ramallah. Tourism was over, the banks had closed, and rich and poor alike found themselves with no money and no work. Expensive Israeli goods had replaced the affordable Arab products on the shelves in stores; hospitals were low on medicines. A few thousand of the refugees who had come to Ramallah in 1948 fled again, and Israeli personnel had set up residences and offices in people's homes.

Luba had no hope that the United States would intervene—who had given the Israelis their arms, after all? As for the United Nations, Luba had no faith in the international body. True, the international community had been quick to condemn, and the UN had held several emergency sessions and called on Israel to allow the displaced to return, to ensure the safety of civilians, and not to jeopardize the status of Jerusalem. But how many times before had the UN denounced what Israel had done? Since 1948, nothing had come to pass of any of it. And the Arabs? After the crushing collective defeat of the war in June, which had ended in six days, Luba realized her dreams for Palestine's future must be sown in fields elsewhere.

Luba and George discussed almost daily whether they should go back home or stay in America. The stories they heard coming from Ramallah always set off another volley of the same pros and cons they had been listing since they got their visas all those years ago. But now the Israeli invasion had given them several new realities to consider, as the conflict had very much arrived on Ramallah's doorstep.

Luba's uncle in Baltimore told them about what had happened to his daughter back home. The Israeli military had beat on her door and had forced her, her husband, and their son to get out, telling them to move in with the family living on the first floor, while the soldiers took over her second-floor flat as quarters.

Luba's cousin and her family had spent three nights huddled with their downstairs neighbors. When they returned to their house above, after the soldiers vacated, they found it a mess. Instead of toilet paper, the soldiers had used her curtains. She immediately changed them, as well as the mattresses, sheets, and towels, all of which had been soiled.

Then Luba's parents told her over the phone how three Israeli soldiers had banged on her mother's door. Zahia had opened it to find three teen-age boys, each with a gun, demanding to use her bathroom.

She had answered defiantly, "No, you cannot use my bathroom."

One of the soldiers then poked her chest with the butt of his gun. "Yes," he told her, "we are going to use your bathroom," and pushed past her into her home.

When her parents told her this story, Luba felt her face flush in humili-ation and fury. Why am I not there? she asked herself. If I were there I could have protected her. Her parents were living one day at a time, unsure what would happen next. I could comfort them, Luba thought. Having their granddaughters close could ease their anguish, she chastised herself.

Luba and George questioned why people in Ramallah—their families, their friends, their countrymen and -women—should suffer every day, while they lived in a place called Baltimore, in a country that had given them citizenship, safety, and some security. Why are we here and not there?

But then Luba would think of Sana and Mona and the educational opportunities available to them here. It was also for the children that they had decided to acquire American citizenship the year before, in 1966.

They had both had misgivings then about becoming Americans; it had felt like an acknowledgment that they were not going to go back home. But Luba had reasoned citizenship would make it easier for the girls to find scholarships or grants for their studies. Yet though they had been in America for more than eight years and more than a year had passed since they had acquired citizenship, she herself still did not feel like an American. She was an Arab living in America. And America is for the Americans, America is not for the Arabs, Luba believed. Where did that leave her daughters?

America was also a country that Luba felt did not understand the place where she came from. After the Israeli invasion and occupation of the West Bank, Luba had heard from the media one unending narrative about the situation: Israel was a modern David to the Arabs' primitive Goliath; Nasser was to blame for the conflict; the Israelis were stoic individuals, the Arabs irrational masses; and the survival of the state of Israel must be assured.

Luba wanted to know, what about the survival of Palestine? She did not hear voices in the mainstream media lamenting the loss of *her* country, of its cities, its traditions, and its existence upon this same land now so easily assigned to the Israelis. She wanted to know, would anyone remind Americans that a nation had been made refugees not twenty years before, in 1948, its homes and their belongings lost to Palestinians and taken by new arrivals from other shores? Did it matter that its collective heart had been broken once already? Did anyone share her horror now as it happened *again*, as further dispossession tore at the already tattered fabric of its society, and did anyone care that Ramallah was Luba's and that this time, it was her own chest that might explode from this pain?

It was so simple for the Americans, she believed. Israelis were like them, and Arabs were so different. Most significant, Arabs seemed incapable of suffering, and so they could be ignored.

It had been nearly ten years since Luba and George had arrived in New York City, since Luba had sat lonely on a bench, watching Sana play, in Forest Hills in Queens, where they had had their first American apartment. Wanting to make just one friend, Luba had wished someone in the tall and stifling housing complex would just return a smile or say hi.

That day, a woman with a daughter almost the same age as Sana had sat next to Luba. Luba smiled at her, and offered a "Hello."

They exchanged their daughters' ages, which floor they lived on, and what they did. When the American woman told Luba she was a teacher, Luba felt an instant connection.

The American then asked Luba where she came from.

"I'm an Arab from Palestine," Luba said.

The woman was excited. "How do you like living in an apartment after living in a tent?" she asked Luba.

Luba was taken aback, shocked that a teacher, no less, thought such things and knew so little. Luba wanted to impart as much knowledge as she could. In America, Luba felt constantly cooped up in their one-bedroom apartment on the sixteenth floor of a red-brick apartment building that looked out on only more red-brick apartment buildings.

"If you knew the house I lived in!" Luba responded. "We lived in a big stone house, stone chiseled by hand, with spacious rooms, and balconies, running water, and a toilet. We had a garden with olive trees, grapes, and peaches."

The American woman flushed. "I'm sorry. But this is what we are taught about the Arabs." She changed the subject before leaving shortly.

Since then Luba felt compelled to explain to Americans that Palestine and Pakistan were not the same place and that Jerusalem was a city of Christians and Muslims as well as Jews. And now in the wake of the war, she was reminded daily how little Americans understood about her homeland.

Luba felt an obligation to educate Americans and share the Palestinian side where she could. She confessed to her neighbors that though the situation now was bad in Ramallah, she felt even more of a pull to go home, especially now.

Some of her neighbors thought that was crazy and asked her, "Why would you want to go back *there*?"

Others would acknowledge, "The homeland is always homeland."

The Tupperware representative across the street whose husband loved Luba's Palestinian cooking just baked them sponge cake and brought it over when she heard Ramallah had been taken.

Luba and George felt they had to do more. They began attending meetings in Washington, D.C., mostly organized by the American Ramallah Federation, founded in 1959 for those Americans who could trace their origins to one of the founding brothers of Ramallah. Telegrams were sent to President Johnson, Secretary of State Rusk, Congress, and other political figures urging the United States to be fair to both sides and true to its own values in safeguarding the rights of Palestinians. The federation also insisted that the property rights of Americans who owned land and houses in Ramallah be protected. Money was collected for food and medicines, and grief, anger, and indignation were readily shared.

But Luba felt only frustration in these meetings. It seemed all they could do was raise money for relief efforts. She felt they should be writing articles and speaking on TV and radio, but not only did they have no access to such outlets, they were also afraid of what might happen to them if they spoke out too much or dissented in their adopted country.

George still struggled with whether they should return, and one night he banged on the kitchen table, yelling "This is not fair!," referring to the fact that people were dying and fighting for their homeland in Palestine, and he was in Baltimore. "This is not fair," he said.

Luba told him then, "Just go," and she meant it. "See what you can do there." She could see how tortured he was. Though she felt the same, she could not stay miserable in front of the girls. She did not want the girls to be nurtured on what was gnawing at her insides. She convinced herself she could hide it. For the girls, for their futures, she could abide the loneliness and the guilt of staying in America.

George gave her a look to say, how can I leave you and the girls? They did not even own their house.

Though George talked about it nearly every day, he did not go back.

This split-level house off Providence Road was the third one they had visited. They had begun searching for a house to buy in late summer, and the real estate agent had already shown them two other houses. The first had an underground basement, which for Luba ruled it out—to be in that basement was to be in a grave. The second house sat too close to the street, and Luba wanted the girls to play in safety.

This house off Providence Road had several picture windows that let in the sun's light. Luba loved the trees in the neighborhood, especially the evergreens that would stay faithful in the winters and the magnolia tree that steadfastly stood outside and in view of the window above the kitchen sink. These houses had been built in 1958, and Luba could see many children running in the cul-de-sac they formed, children with whom she imagined Sana and Mona could play. A new elementary school had opened within walking distance, on the other side of Providence Road, and another Arab-American family, Lebanese, already lived up the street.

For $28,000, this house off Providence Road would be the house they would buy.

This house off Providence Road was where Bernice promised God in Baltimore—far away from his and their Holy Land—would look out for them.

Americans spared little attention for the war in the Middle East; after all, U.S. troops were fighting another war in Vietnam. By July 1967, there were a total of 675,000 U.S. ground forces in the Asian country. American troops were also deployed in the homeland, as racial unrest saw American cities such as Detroit and Newark go up in flames in 1967. Other cities, like Baltimore, would burn the following year, after the assassination of Martin Luther King, Jr.

But the Arab world remained stunned by the defeat of the combined Egyptian, Syrian, and Jordanian armies. Arabs in America and Americans of Arab descent had also been bewildered by the incredible defeat; the occupation by Israel of East Jerusalem, the West Bank, the Gaza Strip, and the Golan Heights directly affected them, their families, their property rights, and their homelands. They were similarly confounded by the complete absence of any Arab or Palestinian perspective from the mainstream American discourse and foreign policy discussions. It begged the necessity for a national presence, organized around far more than just religious or fraternal concerns.

In 1967, the Association of Arab American University Graduates (AAUG) was formed as a nonprofit educational and cultural organization to promote better understanding between Arabs and Americans. Largely as a response to the unchallenged influence of the pro-Israel lobby in U.S. Middle East policy, the National Association of Arab Americans (NAAA) was formed in 1972.

In the Arab world, one of most significant consequences of the June defeat was that it destroyed the credibility of the nation-states that had sought to be the patrons of the Palestinian people, and it weakened

Nasser's power significantly. He soon died, in 1970, and was replaced by his vice president, Anwar al-Sadat.

The way was opened for Yasser Arafat, who advocated guerrilla warfare and who successfully sought to make the PLO a fully independent organization under his control. The PLO's base of operations was Jordan, effectively establishing a state within a state, until September 1970, known as Black September, when King Hussein cracked down on and expelled the PLO. The PLO reconstituted in Lebanon, and continued from there to carry out its cross-border attacks on Israel.

At the Summer Olympic Games in Munich in 1972, a militant splinter group that used the name Black September, and had mostly focused its efforts on attacks against Jordan, carried out its most infamous operation. The group infiltrated the Olympic Village in Munich, taking members of the Israeli team hostage and eventually killing eleven of them.

In response to the events in Munich, President Nixon launched Operation Boulder on September 25, 1972. It was headed by Secretary of State William Rogers and involved the State Department, the CIA, the Immigration and Naturalization Service (INS), and the FBI. The initiative targeted Arabs living and studying in America. They were interrogated, photographed, and fingerprinted by FBI and immigration officials. Their families, friends, neighbors, and employers were interviewed by FBI agents. Their visa applications were subjected to a mandatory waiting period while they were checked out through United States, Israeli, and European intelligence sources. Profiles of community activists were developed, and Arab—especially Palestinian—political and nonpolitical associations, such as the AAUG, came under heavy surveillance.

The intimidation resulting from these efforts discouraged many Arab Americans from participating in any kind of lawful, organized community-building activities.

In 1967–1973, political upheaval throughout the Middle East hastened emigration, and 59,035 Arabs chose to immigrate to the United States. Palestinians and Jordanians were well represented at 14,504, as Israel had annexed and occupied areas in which they lived. It is important to note here that after 1967, U.S. immigration figures included

Palestinians in Jordanian totals, and they account for the majority of those figures. Israel also seized Egyptian territory, which, combined with the pessimism felt after the defeat and death of Nasser, helped persuade 13,529 Egyptians to immigrate to the United States. While many though not all of the 22,398 Lebanese and Syrians in this period came under the rubric of family reunification, Egyptians had not before immigrated to the States in numbers and came under the provision for skilled professionals.

In this same period, 5,127 Iraqi immigrants arrived, including Iraqi Christians joining family members who had immigrated in the years prior to the 1965 immigration law change, as well as skilled Muslim and Christian professionals. Political upheaval also occurred outside the context of the Israeli-Arab conflict. In late 1967, South Yemen gained independence from Great Britain and quickly began experiencing the growing pains of nation building. Of the remaining 3,477 Arab immigrants to come, most were Yemenis.

Many of those who came were drawn by the freedoms and opportunities the United States offered, at the same time that they disagreed with U.S. policies in their homelands.

Early in 1973, the Vietnam War came to an end. But the 1967 war in the Middle East was not yet resolved; Israel still maintained control over the territory it had annexed during the war. The UN Security Council had called for the return of Arab territories occupied by Israel, but six years had passed. Diplomatic means had failed to return the land on which Israel had already begun to build Jewish-only settlements. In the United States, the desire to have a more active role in affecting U.S. Middle East policy began to bring the different waves of Arab immigration together into one larger community that transcended national origin and religious lines.

© DR. ALBERT-ABDALLAH ROSSETTE HARP

Dissent

On the Monday afternoon of July 24, 1967, as Alan Amen and his pals Sammy and Johnny rode in Sammy's '63 blue Plymouth Fury down Michigan Avenue in Detroit, all Alan could think was, this shit is crazy.

Alan and the boys had come up from their neighborhood in the South-end of Dearborn to see for themselves what was going on in the city. In the early hours of Sunday morning, Detroit cops—tipped off that a black uprising was about to set fire to their town—had raided a blind pig (speak-easy) in a black neighborhood. An informant had passed the word, for 50 cents, that the after-hours club was where the havoc was being hatched. Though the police had found nothing of the sort when they arrived, they decided to arrest everyone there. While the cops waited for paddy wagons to transport the more than 80 people they were detaining, a crowd of nearly 200, angry and frustrated, had gathered to watch.

By the time the sun had risen, the looting and rioting had begun. Those who had gotten up and gone to church that Sunday morning saw stores, homes, and cars on fire, and some even thought Judgment Day had come. Black leaders considered to be moderate, like Congressman John Conyers, offered to help police calm the situation, but calm was not to be had. Even Detroit Tigers left-fielder Willie Horton, still in uniform after his game, had driven on Sunday through the riots, stood on a car, and pleaded for peace. But the crowd stayed angry.

Alan had watched from home on TV on Sunday as a hundred city blocks retched in turmoil. Fires had hollowed out brick houses from the inside and lit them up like jack-o-lanterns, and firemen like his uncle Don, who were trying to extinguish the flames, had to be protected by cops and guardsmen from rioters pelting them with rocks and debris. That evening, as night had fallen, Governor Romney mobilized the Michigan National Guard, and soon the first of 3,000 mostly white and heavily armed men with little training in crowd control arrived to patrol black neighborhoods. Before 8 P.M. curfew had been instated, but thousands were on the streets, made darker by the guardsmen and cops who, jittery with rumors of snipers, had nervously shot out the streetlamps.

Horton's team, the Detroit Tigers, scheduled to play Monday and Tuesday at Tiger Stadium, had their games moved to Baltimore. The baseball team was Alan's favorite of all the Detroit sports teams, and their stadium had better be all right.

Driving now along Michigan Avenue, Alan, Sammy, and Johnny slowed to peer down 12th Street, the heart of the riot, before speeding up to make sure Tiger Stadium was still standing. Relieved to see that it did not seem in danger, they turned the car down Trumbull.

From the back seat of the car, Alan stared out his open window as they careened no faster than 25 miles per hour down the center of the streets, the sides blocked with burned-out or burning cars, furniture, and debris. Buildings still on fire sent up a thick black smoke, and the sound of fire crackled from behind broken windows. Stores had vomited up their merchandise, what was left of it, onto the streets. Residential neighborhoods were lined with roofless, gutted homes, only their masonry facades still standing, and their possessions—furniture, clothes, toys—lay mutilated on the sidewalks in front. The place looked like the ruins of a civilization long gone.

Tons of people were on the streets. The Westinghouse Warehouse was being looted just as Alan and the guys approached it and the radio began reporting it. A crowd of people ran back and forth from the warehouse to the street, grabbing their loot and passing it off to people in cars before the cops got there.

Sammy steered the car to Milwaukee Street toward Woodward Avenue. As they drove down Milwaukee, they began to see more and more cops. They were approaching General Motors Headquarters—*Jeez*, Alan thought, they were everywhere all of a sudden, where they had been scant just a minute before. People were running across the street, and the police were grabbing black men by the shirt collars and throwing them in cop cars.

Alan and the boys decided to get the hell out of there. In the Southend, there were two things you had to learn growing up: how to fight and when to run. They didn't want to be anywhere near the cops or the cops anywhere near their business. Sammy and Johnny were regular tough guys, and Alan had had a run-in of his own with the police one night when he got pulled over for jibber-jabbering with a lady in the red-light district.

As soon as there was open road, they sped their way back to Dearborn.

Later that Monday afternoon and at Governor Romney's request, President Lyndon B. Johnson sent Detroit 4,200 paratroopers—some of whom had just come back from Vietnam. They went into the city with unloaded weapons, swelling the number of law enforcement men to 17,000.

Monday night, Alan decided to keep his distance. He watched Detroit burn instead from his family's front porch in the Southend, the poorest neighborhood in Dearborn, where three square miles of modest homes stood hidden in the shadow of the Ford Rouge Plant and its Big Eight rising smokestacks.

This madness might be new, but for Alan the shit had been hitting the fan for a while now.

It had all started when the government took his older brother Ronnie and sent him to Vietnam.

In 1963, Ronnie had graduated high school and started college, getting a deferment from the draft and the Vietnam War. To pay his way through school, he had taken a full-time job that summer in a steel-fabricating plant that supplied Ford Motor Company. Ronnie had worked the steel-shearing machine, which cut large pieces of sheet metal the right size to punch out a car door. While working his shift in the summer of '64, a bar gauge crushed his hand, shattering bones, severing tendons, and bursting open his palm. He underwent several surgeries to put his hand back together and lost a year of school recuperating. In June of '65 he was able to reenroll in school as a full-time student to start that September. Then in July, he was drafted.

Ronnie went straight to the draft board with proof of his college enrollment and all his medical documents; he was still scheduled for one more surgery. The lady there reassured him that he was due to be called up in October and that his college deferment would be reinstated by then. Instead, he received orders a few weeks later to report to Ft. Wayne. He showed up as ordered, but with several pounds of medical documents and with only 30 percent usage of his crippled hand.

At his physical, as Ronnie stood there in his underwear, the doctor listening to his lungs asked how long he had been smoking.

"Never once in my life," Ronnie told him, learning only then that growing up in the embrace of the Rouge plant meant its waste had been deposited in his lungs and, he guessed, in the lungs of every other kid who had ever grown up in the Southend.

But it had not mattered; eight hours later, Ronnie had walked out the back door onto a bus to Fort Knox, Kentucky, to start boot camp.

From there, they sent Ronnie to Aberdeen, Maryland, for advanced training; he stayed on and become an instructor. After his training, he had come home on a weekend pass and married his girlfriend, and they returned together to Aberdeen. She soon had gotten pregnant, and a few weeks after his daughter was born, Ronnie was given orders to go to the Mekong Delta.

Before Ronnie had gotten screwed by the government, and Alan was left living every day with the thought "Where the hell is he at?," Alan had planned to boost his draft as soon as he graduated high school in 1965. Their uncles had served in the air force and the army, and Alan was proud of them.

He had truly believed that when the United States fought in a war, it was on the side of good; after all, the country had fought fascism in World War II only after a despicable sneak attack by a terrible, vicious, and evil enemy. Now we were under attack by a new enemy, Alan believed, and if we all didn't fight the Commies over there, the fight would end up here.

But it didn't make much sense to Alan that a guy like Ronnie with a busted hand should even be in the army, let alone in Vietnam. So he had started reading about Vietnam and had taken a sociology course in college, and by the time Ronnie got to the Mekong Delta earlier that year, Alan already thought the whole thing was bullshit.

And Ronnie made it clear to Alan what he thought of the war. Ronnie had written that he didn't know what the hell he was doing in Vietnam or what the hell the Army was doing there. He had told Alan not to let them draft him. If he got drafted, he should go to Canada, where they speak English. Ronnie had told his little brother, "If you end up in Vietnam, I will shoot you myself."

Nevertheless, it felt strange to Alan that Ronnie was off fighting somewhere now and Alan was not getting his back, a lesson he had learned early when he got a whipping from his father when they had been kids.

Walking back from Salina Elementary School a decade before, a kid had come up to Ronnie and told him he wanted to fight him. Ronnie had handed Alan his books and told him to take them home. When Alan got there, his father, who worked the midnight shift at Ford as a janitor, was waiting as usual, wearing his slippers, smoking his cigarette, and having his coffee in his Ford Motor Company cup.

"Where's your brother?" he asked Alan.

"He's going to fight a kid," Alan shrugged.

Without changing into shoes, their father ran out and came back with Ronnie in tow, smacking him with the slipper as they came in the back door.

Their father then looked at Alan, and said, "Come here."

"What?" Alan protested. He knew he was going to get it. "I didn't fight!"

He then had gotten it worse than Ronnie.

"Don't you ever let your brother fight and you leave him alone!" his father had said. "Now get up in your room."

In the Southend, they were all like brothers, and they all had one another's back. It was the kind of place where if one of the guys came into the pool hall and said someone was about to jump him, the other guys would go—no questions asked. When Alan had visited Ronnie at boot camp—the first time they had ever been separated—he had realized that, *Jeez*, Ronnie was on his own, he didn't have anyone.

Alan had gotten Ronnie's letter telling him to go to Canada if he were drafted that June, around the time the *other* war was happening in the Old Country, between Israel and the Arabs. Their mother was always railing against the Vietnam War. "What the hell are we doing in Vietnam?" she would say. During the June fighting in the Old Country, she had also complained, "Look what they're doing to the Arabs. Again! They are not going to be happy until they have all the Middle East!"

At first, in Alan's family, they thought maybe a war of liberation had begun there, and that the Palestinians would soon get their land and houses back. Then, as Alan watched the Israelis dancing on the Syrian Golan Heights, he felt immediately dejected, and he hated their celebration.

Alan had watched how the American networks covered the war in June on channels 2, 4, and 7 and then switched to channel 9, which came from Canada, across the Detroit River. Something about the Canadian coverage seemed different to Alan; U.S. news talked about Israel defending itself while the Canadian outlets reported Israel seizing territory and killing civilians. Alan was confused. Weren't we—Americans and Canadians—more or less the same?

And earlier, in July, he had just received another letter from Ronnie, written a month before in June, telling him the scuttlebutt was that his helicopter gunship outfit might be getting shipped out to the Middle East, on the side of the Israelis.

As if it weren't bad enough that they had taken Ronnie to Vietnam, the idea that they would take him to make war on his own people really bothered and confused Alan. Things kept catching him by surprise, and he was sick of being ignorant; he wanted to know what all this crap was about.

Alan now sat on the porch, facing Detroit just a few blocks away. Their neighbor from across the street, Millie—an Italian from Brooklyn who had married a Yemeni guy—was there with her son Tony. Alan's sister Sandra kept coming in and out of the house, and Alan was sitting next to Ronnie's wife Alice on the porch swing. Alice had been picnicking the day before at the state fairgrounds, enjoying the summer Sunday afternoon with about a hundred other people from the Shiite mosque when they received word the riots were spreading. She hadn't been able to make it back to her mother's in Highland Park, so she had come to Ron's parents' place instead with her young daughter.

Together they now watched the orange glow of the dusk sky; twenty-nine fires were out of control that night in Detroit.

Is this what Ronnie saw in Vietnam? Alan wondered. It sure looked similar to the newsreels they watched in the States.

They stared as the black smoke rose from the building casualties. The dark haze hovered above Detroit much more ominously than the smoke the Ford Rouge Plant puffed into the Southend every day.

The Rouge sat not 300 yards behind their house and 100 yards behind the elementary school all the neighborhood kids attended. This was the Southend. Alan wanted to get out of here, finish college, and buy a nice house in a neighborhood where you didn't have to tape your windows shut to keep the soot from coming through or where if you left your car outside, it wouldn't turn a rusty brown from the fly ash.

The Old Man himself, Henry Ford, had built the town of Dearborn, carefully planning who would live where. For hourly workers, there was East Dearborn, while West Dearborn was reserved for management. For blacks, Ford created what he imagined to be a model town. He named it Inkster. For the poorer new immigrants who had come from across the ocean and the hillbillies who had traveled across the Mason-Dixon, there was the Southend, so close to the factories that they could walk to work.

Ford Motor Company had brought them all to this neighborhood, the Southend. It lay on the wrong side of a few tracks of the Ford Railroad, and from the west, where management lived, it was completely obscured from view by the Rouge. The Southend was a neighborhood full of immigrants, their children, their grandchildren, and even their great-grandchildren. They had all come on the promise of a job and pay. They were varied nationalities; Italians, Poles, Romanians, Serbians, Armenians, and Syrians were among them. The Syrians came mostly from villages that in 1943 had become part of the newly formed Lebanon. But only after Lebanese actor Danny Thomas got his own TV show with a Lebanese character did they stop calling themselves "Syrians" and become "Lebanese."

Yemeni merchant marines who had worked ships that had traveled from Aden to Detroit's port came to worship at the Sunni mosque on Vernor on their liberty days. Some eventually stayed, and now 10 percent of the Southend had origins in the Arabic-speaking world. But those Yemenis were single men or had wives in Yemen whom they were supporting. Alan and the other Lebanese socialized with them mostly only in the coffeehouses on Dix Avenue.

To get jobs at Ford, many had anglicized their Arabic names, given their children English names, and hidden their "Husseins" and "Muhammads" in their middle names. So "Amin" became "Amen," and "Ronnie" and "Alan" were used, instead of "Ali" and "Abdel Hassan," which their parents stopped using even at home once their children started school. And so here they were.

Alan's father was in his twenty-sixth year as a janitor at Ford; Ronnie had sheared steel for Ford car doors for a year before his hand got crushed, and Alan had signed up with the company in the summer of 1965, during Senior Week. He had already worked three days by the night of his prom.

Even though the job was meant to just last the summer, Alan had thought he would never last two days, let alone be working his third summer now. He had wanted to quit after the first day, but there was no way to do that and still live in his father's house.

That first summer, Alan had worked eleven hours a day, six days a week, on the assembly line in the passenger trim section. It was miserable—unbearably hot and noisy. His station was right below the bake oven, where a car's metal shell was cooked after being spray painted. When it was 90 degrees outside, Alan would watch the floor thermometer hit 123. There were no scheduled water breaks, which did ease the fact that there were no bathroom breaks either. What they did have was eleven minutes off in the morning and nineteen in the afternoon, and the relief guy who took over Alan's job during those breaks timed it to the second.

So if Alan had a thirst that needed to be quenched at any other point during the shift, he would have to shave eight seconds off the sixty-three seconds he had to do his part on the cars as they were coming down. That gave him just enough time to run to the fountain, drink, and make it back for the next car. Above the fountain, there was a sign reminding the workers—who didn't have time for water built into their schedule—to take salt tablets, which were available in the dispenser by the fountain.

In Alan's first month, he saw a man drop dead. Alan had been headed to Gate 4 to say hello to his father, who came on when Alan got off. Alan came out of the plant and found the day blazing hot; a guy in front of him fell all of a sudden, hit the ground, and began convulsing. Rouge paramedics—the plant had its own ambulance and fire department—rushed over, placed the guy onto a stretcher, and worked on him. Alan watched them cover the man with a sheet and was horrified as they pulled it over his face.

That day Alan ran all the way to Gate 4, and when his father saw him, he had immediately asked, "What's wrong with you?"

"They're dropping dead here," he panted. "I gotta get out of here!"

His father had laughed and told him to go home.

At least with these riots now, they didn't have to go into work!

But just like how Ron had disappeared, the Southend was disappearing from beneath him in more bullshit, called Urban Renewal. More like urban removal, Alan thought. The city was quietly buying up their low-income houses and clearing them so they could convert the Southend into an industrial zone. Dearborn's Mayor Hubbard wanted a buffer between Dearborn and Detroit, or rather Detroit's black folk. Besides, plenty of Dearborn's good people already thought the Southend *was* Detroit and didn't really care anyway what happened to the greasers and their factory rat children.

But it would all be moot, Alan thought, if blacks came in and burnt the Southend down all around them, as Mayor Hubbard was warning. Hubbard, who called black folk "niggers" and blamed the riot on Martin Luther King, had put the fear of God in them all. On the porch, Alan was afraid of what would happen to them in the chaos.

Hubbard had run for mayor on the promise that no blacks would ever live in Dearborn. He was now in his twenty-fifth year in office. Just two years ago he had been indicted under a federal civil rights statute for allowing Dearborn police to stand by while a crowd stoned the house of a resident who was mistakenly believed to have sold his property to a black family. When the jury acquitted him, Mayor Hubbard treated them all to a steak dinner.

Alan had had his own run-in with the mayor in 1965, as a senior in high school. For social studies class, Alan had invited a Student Non-violent Coordinating Committee (SNCC) representative to come discuss voter registration efforts in the South. Unbeknownst to Alan, his social studies teacher wasn't as cool as Alan had thought. He actually invited Mayor Hubbard to come in and give the other perspective. The day the mayor came to their class, the teacher made Alan go greet the mayor at the door of the school.

As Alan escorted the mayor to the classroom, the mayor asked Alan his name and when he was born. Then in the classroom, Mayor Hubbard had presented the case for segregation. Alan had been disgusted. He had also received a birthday card from the mayor every year since.

But Alan was still afraid that in this impending mayhem, the mayor might be right that something could happen to him, his family, his girlfriend, or his neighborhood. The Southend, after all, bordered Detroit, and they were separated only by an invisible force field that ran along shared arteries like Dix Avenue.

And of course Alan wouldn't be surprised if blacks hated Dearborn. Blacks who worked at the Rouge—nearly a third of the employees—knew not to even think about living in Dearborn; in fact they went well out of their way to go around Dearborn to get home after their shifts, rather than drive through it.

Hubbard had said he wasn't going to let anyone come in from Detroit and harm Dearborn. But Alan wasn't going to count on Hubbard to help the Southend; if anyone came near his house, or family, or girlfriend, *he'd* be the one to give them a fight.

As Alan swung lazily back and forth on the porch swing, a loud BOOM! made everyone jump up.

"A gunshot! A gunshot! They are firing!"

Alan found himself bumping into the others in the dark, trying to get into the house first. Alice shoved her daughter into the arms of Sandra, who was already in the house, and screamed at her to protect her.

Before he got in the house, Alan remembered himself. "I'll go check and see what it is," he declared.

The women pleaded with him, "Be careful!" "Be careful!"

Around back, Alan saw what had happened. Their neighbor had dropped a heavy chest of drawers as he attempted to move it.

Goddamn, Alan thought. Why should I feel scared? He was sick of stuff sneaking up on him.

Alan decided to head over to his girlfriend Karen's house, about five blocks away. She lived with her mother, her sister, and her brother-in-law, but they were all away on a vacation. Alan's family pleaded with him not to go, but he wanted to make sure Karen was safe. And he relished being able to spend some time with her in an empty house!

He arrived at Karen's house to find her startled: someone had come by and banged on her door. She was also not alone; Ruby, her best friend, was there as well. Karen, who knew how to shoot, wanted Alan to load up her brother-in-law's 12-gauge over-and-under shotgun.

He set up the rifle for her and hung around for a couple of hours, but Ruby wasn't going anywhere so he headed up to Dix Avenue, the main drag in the Southend.

When Alan got up to Dix, as night crept to midnight, he found at least a hundred other guys standing around on the street, as they did on any warm summer night. Alan joined up with a bunch of his friends standing in front of the pool hall, where the older guys hung after they graduated from the spot in front of the drugstore next door.

Guys were smoking and shooting the shit. The National Guard had been bivouacked in and were stationed at Patton Park, right up on Dix, but on the Detroit side. Across Dix—a boulevard of several lanes—two guardsmen Jeeps were parked.

Some of the toughs decided to light up some firecrackers.

Ba ba ba bum! Ba ba ba bum, the firecrackers crackled.

The Jeeps wheeled around and came over. "What are you guys doing?" the guardsmen asked, machine guns pointed. "What's going on?"

The Southend guys hollered back:

"Don't worry about us."

"All's fine here, go back where you came from, *boys*."

"Go back to your tents!"

"We can take care of ourselves."

On October 6, 1973, Egypt, Syria, and Israel were at war. Again.

Today, on October 14, 1973, Alan and the others were doing something about it.

It may have taken only six days to fight the last one over there, but in Dearborn they had spent the last six years obsessing over it. They had discussed it, dissected it, and deconstructed it from every angle while hanging out in coffeehouses on Dix Avenue. They condemned Israel for being colonialist and expansionist; mourned Nasser and his failures; proclaimed Jordan's King Hussein a sellout; excoriated the Saudis as decadent monarchs who were morally repugnant; and idolized the *Fida'iyyin*, the Palestinian guerrillas who had decided no Arab government could deliver them their rights. They had to count on themselves.

It was a kind of group therapy.

Neither Alan nor any of the others were going to sit this one out, like they had six years ago, when they had been stunned, confused, and shamed by the defeat, the American official reaction to the war, and the portrayal of the Arabs. They had been no better than schoolboys then, silent, only raising their voices in shock among one another, but not sounding much more than a whimper outside.

But things had changed since the summer of '67, when both the Middle East and Detroit had last burned. This time Alan planned to do more about it than just take a joy ride around the ruins.

Detroit had not recovered from the violence. The city's population had dropped by 200,000; nearly 2,000 retail businesses were gone; and over 50 million dollars in property had been destroyed. Even Motown Records—Motown!—had quit Detroit in 1972.

Ronnie had come home in August of '67, so darkened by the Vietnamese sun that Alan had walked right past him at the airport until Ronnie had hollered out, "Where the hell you going?"

Alan himself was married and had a child now. He and Karen had gotten engaged right after Ronnie had come home. When Karen's mother heard the news, she told her daughter that if she didn't get married by a Catholic priest, she wasn't going to come.

When Alan told his parents, they responded that if he didn't get married by an imam, as a Muslim, not to bother inviting them.

So in the summer of '68, they eloped in Dearborn, honeymooning for a few nights at the Ramada Inn off I-94. They had never spent a night together before.

And in the Southend, urban renewal/removal had been brutal. Since 1967, the city had razed another 486 houses. In his thirty-first year as mayor, Hubbard had forced Southenders to sell their houses to the city of Dearborn by using a variety of tactics. The city had refused to grant residents permits to upgrade their homes; had classified any building less than sixteen feet from the rear lot to be substandard, regardless of the condition of the house; had required the installation of items not required by the building code; had actually contributed to the pollution in the area by selling property to the Levy Asphalt Company and Mercier Brick Company; had not placed city-owned lots back on the public market as done in other parts of Dearborn; and had put signs on the vacant houses that read "Free at Your Risk; Take Any Part of the House."

Alan had never had illusions about Hubbard being a racist, but in the last six years, Alan had a much clearer understanding of what Hubbard thought of his "white niggers" in the Southend.

But Southenders had started to fight back. The multiethnic residents came together as the South East Dearborn Community Council, an organization in which Alan's mother, Katherine, had already become involved. Katherine, who was born in Dearborn, came from a long line of strong women.

Her grandmother and grandfather—Alan's great-grandparents—had emigrated from Lebanon to Mexico and had started a family there. Around 1910, they had decided to move to the United States. While pregnant with her second daughter, Katherine's grandmother, Bazaar, came alone ahead of her husband and his brother to set up a home in Highland Park, Michigan, where Ford built his Model Ts and As. She soon gave birth to Zainab, Katherine's mother—Alan's grandmother.

The men had followed shortly from Mexico by train. Once inside the States, somewhere in Texas, bandits had boarded the train, shooting the men to death and stealing their Ottoman gold coins. On account of the coins, the newspaper had reported their deaths as the murder of two Turks. Alan's great-grandmother never missed a beat. Her daughter, Alan's grandmother, gorgeous and wild Zainab, had children by three men and divorced two of them. And it was Alan's mother who long ago had taught him it was just fine to question authority.

In seventh grade, Alan had come home and asked his mother, "What is a Mohammedan?"

"Why are you asking?" she had replied, stopping her cooking.

"I'm doing my social studies homework," Alan had said. "And I think I'm a Mohammedan."

"No, you're not one," his mother had answered sternly. "You worship God and only God, not his prophet. Your textbook is wrong."

In those days Alan believed his teachers, and textbooks were infallible. The truth about Mohammedans had disturbed that reassuring order to his world.

Alan's father, on the other hand, never got involved in the Southend activities—he was the kind of person who believed you couldn't fight City Hall. Thus Katherine had instead conscripted her son Alan in 1967, taking him to meetings so he could find out what was going on and so he could start helping. The following year, he had become treasurer of the community council, and he had been president since 1970.

Then in 1971, the Council had sued the City of Dearborn in federal court. Alan's mother had been the named plaintiff in the case *Amen v. The City of Dearborn*. Many others were afraid to have their names associated with the case because of fear of Hubbard's retaliation. Their office, which Alan was paying for with his unemployment check, had already been burned down. The mayor had also finally stopped sending Alan birthday cards.

Just two months ago in August, the court had announced its decision that the city's tactics *did* constitute the taking of property without due process of law. It had ordered the city to halt any further acquisition of property in the area and to allow the more than 300 homeowners to sue for the difference between the price paid by the city and a price later determined to be the fair market value of the property.

The city was already working on its appeal, both in court and in public opinion. Hubbard's people were telling the rest of Dearborn that the Southenders were both sabotaging good city planning and about to cost them all millions of dollars.

Alan and the council countered by meeting with church groups and civic associations outside the Southend to explain what was happening to their neighborhood. Before the court decision in their favor, no one would listen to them or help them in their fight. Inside the Southend, they were educating people about filing claims and getting their money back.

Alan had no hopes of actually *saving* the Southend—Ford Motor Company had designs on the land and Hubbard was nearly invincible. But if they were going to get tossed out of the place that for many had been their only home in America, then he wanted fair treatment and a little bit of justice.

Alan wanted it enough that when his employer, an accounting firm—headed by a good friend of Hubbard's—gave him the choice to give up the Council or his job, Alan chose to give up his job, and his paycheck. The three of them—Alan, Karen, and their four-year-old son Sam—were living off Karen's salary as a nurse. Alan didn't feel too good about that.

At the same time the Council was suing the city, they were also working on getting one of their own—a Southender—elected to the city council. Alan was convinced they needed to have a voice at city council meetings. Begging them all these years to do the right thing had been pointless. No one had the guts to disagree with Hubbard.

They had decided to run Helen Okdi Atwell, the outspoken secretary of the South East Council and a divorced mother of eight. She was also a Lebanese, and Alan was her campaign manager; she had already cleared the primaries.

And since 1967, the Southend itself was changing as it was disappearing. While some folks were moving out to Detroit or wherever else they could find housing, many more Arabs had arrived. By 1973, there were 85,000 Arabs and Arab Americans in the Detroit area; the vast majority were citizens.

Turmoil in the Middle East—namely the Israeli occupation of the Gaza Strip and the West Bank and the fight for Yemeni independence—meant Yemenis and Palestinians had been pouring into Detroit and Dearborn. The metropolitan Detroit area was a natural place for them to come, not only for its Arab-American community, but also for all the factory jobs available in the wake of young American men being sent to Vietnam.

For the new arrivals—many of whom spoke little English, were in a state of trauma, and had little bearing in this new place—the Southenders, who looked like Arabs but spoke with the flat Midwestern accent of a native, taught them how it worked here.

But it was what the new arrivals had that Alan and many other Arab Southenders wanted: information—firsthand experience of what had happened in the Middle East in '67, and a way to believe in pan-Arabism even after Nasser's promises had proven empty. Few knew for themselves the villages from where their ancestors had come, few spoke Arabic, or publicly used their Arabic middle names, but everyone in the Southend had their Old Country—whether it was Poland or Italy or Romania—and that tortured part of the world was theirs.

And those who came from Palestine told a very different story from that told by the American media about was happening in their homeland under occupation. On Michigan campuses, Arab student organizations showed movies, held teach-ins, and invited speakers, trying to educate both Arab Americans and Americans as to what their reality was like.

Through this exchange of information he experienced while hanging out at Kamel's restaurant, the coffeehouses, and the pool hall on Dix, Alan had been learning his heritage and his history right. Since '67, Alan and the others had been getting educated.

So when this latest war happened, meetings were immediately called and the ad hoc Arab-American Coordinating Committee was formed. The committee pooled together different Arab organizations in the metropolitan area, including the National Association of Arab Americans, Iraqi-Chaldean Association of Michigan, Jordanian Club of Detroit, Arab-American Congress for Palestine, United Holy Land, various student groups, and Islamic groups. They met at the hall of the Hashmi Society, which had been founded by the immigrants from the Tibnine and Bint Jbail villages and which used to serve as the Shiite mosque before the new one on Joy Road was built in 1962.

Just five days before, on October 9, the groups had called a press conference. A local television broadcast had announced that there was "no reaction" from the Arab community over the war. At the press conference, the groups had let Detroiters know they did have a reaction and exactly what it was.

They had denounced the U.S.'s unconditional financial, political, diplomatic, and military support of Israel. They had deplored the media's rabid anti-Arab slant and its characterization of the conflict as one between "Arab" and "Jew." To them, this was overly simplistic and designed to obscure the political and economic basis of the conflict—namely the Palestinian dispossession of their homeland, making them stateless refugees. They also had proclaimed that the Arab nations were engaged in a fight to get back *their* territory, occupied by Israel since 1967.

The next day, a teach-in was held at Wayne State University.

But it was today's action, organized by Alan and the others, that he believed would have the most impact.

Right before this latest war began, community activists had discovered that in 1967, their local branch of the United Auto Workers (UAW), the largest local and home to 15,000 Arab and Arab-American auto workers, had bought $330,000 worth of Israeli bonds. The decision had been made without rank-and-file approval, but with the money raised from their own dues. Additionally, the UAW as a whole had bought over $750,000 worth of the bonds. Moreover, their yield was minimal and had essentially constituted a long-term loan to Israel.

The committee had decided that some of their actions in response to this new war would have to focus on the bonds and call out the UAW. Through leaflets and word of mouth, they got the word out to Arab auto workers. Many of them were already ready to rumble, as it had been a hot summer of wildcat walkouts in the plants, led by black workers. And word had spread of the death of Nagi Daifullah. A Yemeni farm worker, Daifullah had been killed by a sheriff in California because of his work with the United Farm Workers organizing the many migrant Yemeni and Mexican grape pickers.

So when they called for this afternoon's rally, nearly 2,000 people showed up at the parking lot of the headquarters of UAW Local 600 on Dix Avenue, right across from the Hashmi Hall and Kamel's, to protest the purchase of the bonds and to support those fighting in the war. Poor Arab auto workers joined with more affluent professionals, and people came from the Palestinian, Iraqi, Syrian, and Lebanese-American communities, their Chaldean, Melkite, Maronite, and Orthodox churches, and their Sunni and Shiite mosques.

From the Local, they marched seventy abreast through the Southend. The numerous stores, coffeeshops, and restaurants had closed in solidarity. They carried banners in English and Arabic:

NO VIETNAM IN THE MIDEAST.

STOP U.S.-ISRAELI TERROR AGAINST ARAB PEOPLE

ISRAEL WANTS ITS PEACE—
A PIECE OF JORDAN, SYRIA, LEBANON, EGYPT!

They chanted:

> *Break our back? No you can't! We will get our homeland back!*
> *Nixon, Nixon, don't forget, Agnew fell and you will yet.*
> *Keep your bomb, keep your jet. No more aid, for your pet!*
> *Free of taxes, Israeli bonds, to purchase arms, to kill my people.*
> *Phosphor bombs, napalm bombs, tax-free bombs, to kill my*
> *people.*
> *We must scream, we must thunder, No, no, Nixon, no more*
> *bombs!*

They continued to the American Moslem mosque on Vernor Avenue. Religious and civil leaders addressed the crowd, speaking from the elevated steps of the mosque. They urged support for Arab efforts to regain territories taken by the Israelis. They demanded that the United States remain neutral and "not cause another Vietnam" by continuing arms support for Israel. And they called on U.S. newspapers and TV stations to report the dispute between the Arabs and Israelis objectively.

Abdeen Jabara, the lawyer who represented the South East Dearborn Community Council, urged the UAW members present to circulate petitions among fellow workers asking the union to divest its Israeli financial holdings.

When Jabara said, "Arab liberation cannot be won through manipulation but only through struggle," cries went up: "You speak the truth!"

As the leaders spoke, Alan and the guys up front decided to pass a cardboard box for contributions. People threw in what they could. Some contributed money; many Yemeni auto workers—among the poorest—signed over a whole week's paycheck, while others took their gold wedding bands off and tossed them in. By the end of the afternoon, they had raised over $30,000.

————

The wind whipping up the wide Detroit River settled in Alan's bones as he picketed, shivering, in front of downtown's Cobo Hall on November 28, 1973.

With 2,000 other auto workers—Arabs, blacks, and whites—they were going to show the UAW they were serious about those Israeli bonds. Continuing to ignore them—the workers—was no longer going to be possible.

Tonight the UAW leadership would be arriving in their tuxedos, with their wives in long gowns, for a dinner sponsored by B'nai B'rith. The American Jewish organization was going to honor UAW president Leonard Woodcock with the award for "Humanitarian of the Year."

Some of the more prominent attendees included the GM chairman, a Michigan Supreme Court justice, a former Michigan governor, and the Detroit mayor. They were joining several state university presidents and a thousand other guests of Detroit's liberal establishment.

Alan was sure the dinner would be fancy, but Woodcock would have to cross a picket line of auto workers freezing their asses off to get to his hundred-dollar-a-plate dinner. And the workers were going to make sure those dining would not be able to ignore them.

Things weren't good these days for the auto industry or its workers. On October 17, three days after Alan and thousands of others rallied in front of the UAW Local 600 and the mosque on Vernor, eleven Arab oil-producing nations announced they were reducing oil production by 5 percent every month until Israel withdrew from occupied Arab territories and the rights of the Palestinian people were recognized and restored.

During the twenty days of fighting, which ended with a ceasefire on October 26, it seemed to Alan most Americans had not given the war much thought. The oil embargo, on the other hand, had forced Americans to pay more attention. While in 1967 the war had been "over there" and out of mind, Americans were now waiting in line for gas and not getting any. And a lot of them, from politicians to newspeople to regular folk, were blaming Arabs for it.

Even before the war, the United States had already been facing an impending shortage of oil; in the last six weeks, the country as a whole was feeling the pinch.

Earlier that month, President Nixon had addressed the nation in a televised speech. He urged Congress to create an agency that would be given more funding than the Manhattan Project to develop enough domestic petroleum, nuclear, solar, and other energy resources to make the United States self-sufficient by 1980.

In the meantime, he had ordered public utilities and other companies to stop shifting from coal to oil as fuel. Commercial flights had decreased by more than 10 percent because of reduced allocations of jet fuel for aircraft. The president had called on Americans to turn their thermostats down to 68 degrees and urged managers of offices, factories, and stores to reduce energy consumption by 10 percent, by either using less heat or cutting down work hours. Additionally, he had asked governors to reduce speed limits from sixty to fifty miles per hour.

Then on Sunday, November 25, the president announced that as of January 1, 1974, rationing of home heating oil would start. He also asked gasoline stations to close on Sundays.

Because automobiles were accountable for 28 percent of the nation's petroleum consumption, the shortage was altering how much Americans were willing to spend on their love affair with cars. Car sales in October had fallen 11.4 percent. And because cars had built Detroit as much as Detroit had built cars for nearly seventy years, the Motor City was feeling the nation's pinch even more.

What had made the car companies so rich was the full-size car. Models like the Chevrolet Impala, Oldsmobile 88 or 98, and the Buick got 10.5 miles to a gallon of gasoline in city driving. European and Japanese cars got better mileage because American-made full-size sedans weighed 4,000 pounds, half a ton more than what they drove in Europe and Japan. In the last month, sales of smaller cars, which got around twenty miles per gallon, had gone up 10 percent while sales of standard-size cars had fallen 25 percent.

This was bad news for Detroit. Small cars were inherently less profitable than the big ones, because they cost about as many man-hours of work but procured a much smaller selling price.

Auto workers were feeling it. A couple of weeks before, General Motors had laid off 137,000 workers. At Ford, 150,000 workers were facing layoffs. Arab workers, often among the last ones hired, found themselves to be among the first ones laid off.

For Detroiters, it was a bad cycle—there wasn't enough gas to fill up their cars, let alone fuel the cars that many of them made for a living. And for Arab Detroiters, there were those who turned around and blamed the people in Dearborn for what they were all suffering together.

When Alan addressed groups all over Dearborn about the Southend lawsuit and explained why the neighborhood was viable given the influx of immigrant workers, he would sometimes get asked, "Why do you people want to come here if you hate America so much?"

Alan would respond, "People would love to be here. And the ones who are here love being here."

Others would ask, "Why are you guys doing this to us with the oil?"

Alan would tell them, "We're not all oil sheikhs," or "I don't have a pump in my backyard, nor is there a special pump for Arab Americans," explaining that he was suffering too from the shortage.

Others didn't bother to ask anything. They just started calling the Arabs rag heads and towel heads—based on the new caricatures popping up everywhere—in addition to old-school sand scratchers, camel jockeys, and desert niggers.

But the Arab and Arab-American auto workers were not going to drop their demand that *their* union divest all its Israeli bonds; they ultimately believed in the American sense of right.

After the Local 600 demonstration in October, they realized that they needed their own workers' caucus—like blacks—to facilitate their own organizing and advocacy in the factories as well as to be able to take their issues to the other workers. After all, not only did they need their support, but as workers on the line, their interests were often the same.

They formed caucuses in all of the plants, and Alan briefed the workers on how to make their case with their colleagues. He told them not to get involved in discussions about the Arab-Israeli conflict but to focus instead on the dues workers were paying. The emphasis, he explained, had to be on the fact that their dollars were going to a foreign government to help foreign folks in their foreign countries. Their money, Alan believed and had argued, should stay in America to help *American* workers in Dearborn, in Detroit, or wherever their neighborhoods were. For example, the money could be used to build playgrounds for workers' kids, where many had none, or at the very least buy them sneakers and balls.

In addition to using the caucus to spread the word about tonight's show-down at Cobo Hall, they created leaflets in Arabic and English. They tried to run a full-page ad based on the English version in the *Detroit Free Press*. The header of the ad read: From Bonds to Bombs to Bondage. The paper ran it only as a quarter-page ad and after changing the wording. It appeared as a half-page ad in the black newspaper *The Michigan Chronicle*.

To encourage Arab auto worker turnout, the leaders of the Arab churches and mosques called for a day of mourning for the Arab vic-tims of the October war, nearly 20,000, and asked that Arab workers be excused. Others took vacation time or called in sick. For those who hadn't heard or showed up at work that afternoon during the shift change, they were greeted by community members encouraging them to come to Cobo Hall instead. They had been there picketing in the cold since late in the afternoon.

Other Detroit Arabs who weren't auto workers were attending memo-rial services at the churches and mosques at the same time.

And this was un-fucking-believable, Alan thought; they shut down both lines of the afternoon shift at Dodge Main! They probably cost Chrysler hundreds of thousands of dollars of lost production. For the first time since the black workers' caucus was founded in 1968, a politi-cal action had stopped production at the largest Chrysler plant in the world.

They were able to pull it off because so many of the other workers—non-Arabs—had walked off in solidarity with them.

Alan was elated. Detroit was the Big Three (General Motors, Chrysler, and Ford), and they had just rattled their cage. It meant they had some power. The union would have to pay attention to them now, see that they had been wrong, and have to agree to change their ways.

And though it was the union's attention they were trying to get, it sure felt good to give it to the Big Three. Alan hated Ford for what they had done to Ronnie. When his brother came home from Vietnam and applied for a job at Ford—to be able to support his wife and daughter—the doc-tors at the Rouge told him he was a liability to the company with his hand like that. "I wasn't a liability to my country!" Ronnie had yelled back. Alan had been so angry that day that he had declared he was going to quit, until Ronnie pulled him back and told him not to give up his pay.

And though Alan was off the line now, just thinking of it, he still could feel the heat on his skin, hear the drilling and hammering as if it were in his skull, and smell the burning oil as if it lined his nostrils. For all the other guys who still had to get permission to go to the bathroom and listen to the foreman tell them to work faster, it felt pretty good to have stopped the lines.

Now Woodcock, the head of the union that was supposed to represent them, the workers—who weren't eating any hundred-dollar-a plate dinners—was coming to one in his fancy tuxedo.

As a few dinner guests watched from the huge plate-glass windows at Cobo Hall, Alan and the others circled slowly on the pavement, carrying signs, and chanting in English, "No more bombs, no more bonds" and in Arabic, "Oh my people, fight on, fight on until we liberate Palestine."

Signs read:

> DON'T ABUSE WORKERS' DUES.
> BONDS MURDER BLACK BROTHERS IN SOUTH AFRICA.
> JEWISH PEOPLE YES, ZIONISM NO.

They waited for Woodcock until finally a cop came and told them that the UAW president had taken a back entrance and was already inside, enjoying his dinner. Someone ran in to see if it was true. It was, so the crowd moved on to Kennedy Square for the scheduled rally.

Afterward, a few of them headed back to Stanley's Bar on Dix in the Southend for a drink. Alan didn't think he could get warm without one.

Alan sat tensely at a makeshift negotiation table in the Hashmi Hall.

The UAW Local 600 had finally agreed to meet with them, a meeting Alan had been trying to get ever since the Israeli bonds had come to light. Only after the stunt at Cobo Hall had the union paid them any attention.

Alan realized that they hadn't been given the meeting because there was moral legitimacy to their point, but rather because they had kicked them in the teeth with the walkout. Just like with the Southend lawsuit, what was right didn't seem to matter as much as a showing of some force, whether it was by legal or labor action.

The picketing had taken Woodcock by surprise; that night, he stated that the UAW had purchased the bonds in 1966 and 1968 and promised not to buy any more. He reiterated that the union had nothing against the Arab people, and added that the UAW was in fact working with Arab-American senator James Abourezk from South Dakota to contact Egyptian union leaders.

Emil Mazey, the secretary-treasurer of the UAW, had been less kind. He had both told reporters and written in the December issue of *Solidarity*, the union's magazine, that the Arab-American Coordinating Committee was guilty of "distortions" and "outright lies." It was the U.S. Communist Party, he said, that was "agitating union members of Arab descent in an effort to alienate them from their non-Arab brothers and sisters," adding that the Soviet Union was the only country that benefited from turmoil in the Middle East. He had also said that "We believe the state of Israel has a right to live. It is the only democracy in the Middle East."

Walter Dorosh, the UAW Local head, had been directed by the national leadership to meet with the Arab organizers of the walkout. He would momentarily be coming across the street from the 600's headquarters to meet with Alan and the other representatives in the Hashmi Hall. They set up a table in front of the stage and took seats on one side. On the other were two chairs, one for Dorosh and one for his financial secretary.

Alan didn't want to have to go up against these guys; the union had been pretty good at advocating for them as workers. Alan came from a union family; they went to the union Christmas party at Solidarity House every year—the union was their home. Alan also knew that the car companies had likely busted the union's chops over the wildcat walkout. The union leadership was supposed to control their guys, and Alan and the others had just undermined them.

Dorosh arrived. He was a slightly stocky, fair-haired man who looked mean when he scowled, and Alan never saw him not scowling, even when he strutted up and down Dix, which took nerve for someone not from the Southend.

Perfunctory greetings were exchanged. Alan thanked Dorosh for the meeting.

Yeah yeah, all right. "What do you want?" Dorosh asked.

"We have a list of demands," Alan said, passing them over.

The demands included divesting of the bonds; agreeing to send no more money to any foreign country, including Israel; supporting the Arab Workers Caucus; and voting and transparency on how their dues were being spent.

Dorosh read the demands silently, then handed them to his financial secretary. They nodded at each other.

Dorosh put the list down in front of him.

"That it?" he finally asked.

Yes, that was it. Alan felt like an idiot. They hadn't asked for enough.

"All right, let me tell you something," Dorosh said, very slowly and deliberately. "Don't you ever fuck with the union again."

Dorosh made it clear they were playing with fire; these guys didn't make idle threats. Alan understood that "Don't you ever fuck with the union again" was the official UAW line, and he worried for the Arab guys working at the plants. He also worried that they had alienated someone they would rather have as an ally.

But what were they supposed to do, Alan wanted to know. The way he saw it, here was this institution that espoused the greatest sentiments of workers' rights, of liberating the oppressed, providing security for its workers, sticking its foot up their asses by taking their dues, and arming the country that was killing their people.

The more Alan thought about it, the more he decided he wanted out of street politics. They had to get a candidate on the city council. They had to break in. Helen had lost in the general elections. She had been the wrong candidate to run; she was too easily irritated and the woman was already fiery! But Alan was not ready to give up and had already decided they would try again in the next election.

Once Dorosh left, Alan finally let his breath out again.

That fall, Motown—now based in L.A. and a world away from the Motor City—released a hit record on its Tamla label by Stevie Wonder called *Higher Ground*. To a funk beat played on his synthesizer, Stevie encouraged folks to keep on trying, even though the powerful would ignore them and even work against them. As bad as things seemed, he promised, it wouldn't be forever, and one day soon they would all reach a higher ground.

Though the oil embargo had been called off by March 1974, it had a lasting effect in that it changed the bigotry Arabs in America encountered from a general xenophobia to a specific prejudice stemming from geopolitical events. This was most readily seen in pop culture portrayals of Arabs. Before 1973, movies and television often showed Arabs as a lascivious and primitive people. These stereotypes were rooted in French and British colonialist imagery and were often interchanged for different racial and ethnic groups. After 1973, however, a stereotype specific to Arabs became popular, that of the oil-rich sheikh intent on world economic domination. Throughout the 1970s, this stereotype was expanded to eventually give way to that of the Arab as terrorist because of the kind of tactics used by the PLO or affiliated groups.

Both of these stereotypes haunted Arab Americans in the States. First of all, Arab Americans were not already present in the American consciousness the way other ethnic groups were, such as Italian Americans. That is, the assumption that Arabs were not also Americans, or part of America's immigrant tradition, was prevalent. The representations of Arabs that were present, in addition to always positing them as foreign, were also extremely negative. Fictionalized and generic Arab terrorists began to frequent the plots of films, TV shows, and books.

The actual PLO in the meantime continued to operate out of Lebanon, much to the chagrin of those Lebanese who did not want to see their country drawn into the conflict with Israel and/or did not want to host an exiled state within their state. Clashes in the spring of 1975 between PLO fighters and Lebanese militia sparked the civil war that would for years consume the country and churn out émigrés to Canada, Australia, Europe, and of course the United States. In the spring of 1978, in reprisal for a Palestinian attack into its territory, Israel launched a major invasion of Lebanon. Israel occupied Lebanese land as far north as the Litani River before withdrawing by summer. Instead of handing over the territory in southern Lebanon to the United Nations Interim Force in Lebanon (UNIFIL), Israel left control with its proxy, the Christian South Lebanese Army. Many of the Shiite Lebanese from the south began leaving for the west, and many came to the United States, where a considerable Lebanese Shiite population already lived in Michigan. In the years 1974–1979, 27,867 Lebanese immigrated to the States.

The hard-line Likud Party won its first Israeli election in the summer of 1977; until then, the left-wing Labor Party had dominated Israeli politics. Likud ideology focused on extending Israeli sovereignty over the West Bank and the Gaza Strip by intensifying Israeli settlement activity in those territories to create facts on the ground and to prevent any future territorial compromise over the areas captured in 1967. The entrenchment of the occupation and the difficult conditions under which Palestinians lived pushed many of them to seek their futures in the countries of the West and the Arabian Gulf. Another 16,660 people emigrated from Jordan (again, reflecting mostly Palestinians) to the United States.

Egyptian President Anwar Sadat stunned the world by making a speech to the Israeli Knesset in November 1977 and became the first Arab leader to recognize Israel, only four years after launching the October 1973 war. In September 1978, Egypt and Israel signed the Camp David accords and concluded a bilateral peace treaty in March 1979. The Sinai Peninsula, which Israel had seized in the 1967 war, was returned to Egypt. Egyptian yearly immigration to the United States, however, remained relatively consistent between 1974 and 1979; 13,604 Egyptians arrived.

A total of 80,197 Arabs immigrated to America in these years.

Significant players came to power in the region in 1979; first, Iran, a non-Arab country in the Middle East, declared itself a theocracy in April after its Islamic Revolution. Second, in July, a man named Saddam Hussein came to power in Iraq.

© WAEL KAWASH

Driven

In February 1979, Mohammed Dasoqi needed a new name. His bell-boy uniform for the Oxford Hotel in downtown Chicago would not be complete until his name tag was engraved. He imagined the sound of his name said out loud—flagging him instantly as foreign to everyone—and worse, he imagined the effect it would have on the tips he could make. With his fair skin and green eyes, an American name would leave everyone to guess his origins. European maybe? A different name would give him a fighting chance at passing for something less alien. Besides, their tongues here dwelled excessively on vowels, and there was no thirst to their Hs. The way they pronounced *Moe-aaa-med* was hardly worthy of a great prophet, let alone a skinny little piece of nothing like himself.

He had no idea what name to choose. He had walked into the hotel

81

just days before, looking—practically begging—for a job. He had got it in his head that this was where he was destined to work. The hotel was just down the street from the city college at which he had also decided, on the same day, that he was destined to study. He had come through the revolving door, formulating his plan for finding a job here, when he had caught a glimpse of the most gorgeous golden-haired girl behind the desk. She looked like the heroines on the American TV shows he had seen back in Jordan, but he had known his chances were, as they said in Arabic, only as good as the devil's of getting into heaven.

He had never been in a hotel in his entire life before that day. Walking into the lobby, he had not known what to expect. Even though the blonde looked to be his age, eighteen, she was standing behind a big oak desk, and people entering the hotel had gone directly to speak to her. He had decided he should ask her for a job.

He walked straight through the lobby, past a little shop with newspapers and candy to the girl with the wavy long hair and blue eyes. He wanted her to see and know every piece of him, to fathom what the last eighteen years had been like; if she could just know what he had been through, he thought, she would give him a job immediately. At the desk he leaned in toward her so she could begin to surmise this—*God, she smelled good*—and also just in case, so she could hear it in his voice. With his best English, he said, "I look for a job, please. Anything I do, I carry bag, open door, clean room maybe, anything. I look for job, I need job."

She looked at Mohammed; he was wearing the only winter coat he could find for one dinar at Um Ahmad's thrift shop in the refugee camp where he had grown up in Jordan. It flared below the waist almost like a skirt, and on his 5'10", 155-pound frame, he was swallowed in its embrace. His thick curly hair was long, yet resisted gravity, growing outward. They called it an Afro here.

She smiled at him and said politely, "I don't think they're hiring."

"You the manager?" Mohammed asked.

"No," she answered.

"Manager, can I see the manager please?" Mohammed persisted.

"Why don't you have a seat?" she told him.

Mohammed took a seat on the couch in the lobby and watched the office and elevator doors for the appearance of the manager, all the time stealing a few looks at her.

The manager soon arrived and introduced himself as Sal. He was Pakistani, and later Mohammed would learn his name was actually Suleiman. They had this exchange:

"What do you want?"

"I want work."

"What do you do?"

"I do anything you need me I do."

"Where are you from?"

"Palestine. Palestinian from Jordan."

"Palestine! Do you know Mido? Mahmoud?"

Mohammed knew a few Mahmouds; which Mahmoud, nicknamed Mido, Sal was talking about, he had no idea. But he had the feeling that his getting a job hinged on his knowing this Mido. "Yes," Mohammed had answered.

"I think we need a bellman."

"I can bell man, no problem."

"You'll need a white shirt, black pants, and black jacket."

Mohammed nodded, but where the hell was he going to get a suit?

"Go talk to Fred. He's the head bellman."

Fred, Mohammed had discovered, was also the only bellman. He also discovered that Fred was Assyrian.

"A Syrian?" Mohammed thought he heard him say.

"No, Assyrian. *Ashuri.*"

Tigris and Euphrates Rivers, Mesopotamia, that *kind* of Ashuri? Mohammed thought the Ashuris had become extinct with their ancient empire; instead he quickly learned from Fred that there was a big community from Iraq living in the city.

Fred helped him secure a jacket—guests sometimes left clothes and never reclaimed them—and explained a bellman's duties: come to the front when guests arrive, get a cart, put the bags on the cart, take the guests to Kathy—*so her name was Kathy*—she'll give you the key, go up to the room, unload their bags, they give you money, you come back down.

"That's it?"

"That's it."

That's easy, Mohammed had thought. He had been working in construction since he was ten, cleaning paint droppings, digging trenches for sewers and electric cables, mixing and pouring concrete into discarded five-gallon ghee containers. How hard could being a bellman be? he had wondered.

So here he was just days later, at the Oxford Hotel, a bellman with his very own uniform. They were about to make him his very own name tag. All he needed now was a name.

He approached Kathy, thrilled to have an excuse to talk to her. He asked her for the most common name in America, reasoning that Mohammed was extremely popular in Arabic.

She rattled off a few. He stopped at the name John, English for *Yahya*. St. John the Baptist was also a prophet in Islam. Because the name was ordinary and existed in Arabic, he chose it.

When he came into work the next day, his name tag was ready. There it was—JOHN—in declarative black letters on gold plastic. The first time he pinned it to his black jacket, he gathered too much fabric, and it lay crooked. He unfastened it, straightened it out, and checked himself in the big framed mirror in the lobby. He looked at the name ИНОᵗ on himself. He felt as if he had been stamped and branded like cattle. Here was a different name, a Christian name, a different him. He started to feel guilty, like he had betrayed his upbringing and his status as *ibn al-mughayyam*, a son of the refugee camps. Many looked down on them, but it was a badge of honor for him.

But he could never forget where he had been, what he had been through, and who was depending on him. I am just *using* this name, he told himself, to get better tips. Besides, the only person they knew in this country with his name was the boxer Muhammad Ali, the champ of champs, but nevertheless a black man. Mohammed knew about *Amreeka*, he had seen American TV—blacks were second-class citizens; he wanted to be accepted. After all, he had come here to make something out of his life, to succeed in America. Putting another name on a piece of plastic was no skin off his back.

Before he left the refugee camp in Jordan, his mother had asked him to promise two things: one that he never swim, because she had foreseen that if he swam, he would drown. And second, not to change his name, not to become one of Them.

On November 20, 1978, when Mohammed was leaving for America, his mother, sisters, and some twenty other women and girls cried as if they were putting his body in the ground and burying it there forever. For days, fellow mourners had been streaming in to offer their condolences to his family. They were received in the asbestos sheetrock shack where he lived with his parents and six siblings, in the UN-operated Baqa'a refugee camp for Palestinians in Jordan. He was going to America with no money, no job, no family, no friends, and not even a return ticket. He was euphoric.

Those who wept, however, thought that Mohammed's traveling to the city of gangsters and Al Capone meant they would never see him again. It was easy to foretell: if the Mafia didn't kill him in Chicago, Mohammed himself would be driven to do something crazy because of the misery of being poor where he knew no one. And then he would die. Any scenario where he went to America ended in his death.

But Mohammed felt he was already dead if he stayed in this refugee camp. Today he was feeling for the first time liberated, hopeful, and happy. Today he would be leaving for *Amreeka*. He shed no tears; after all, he wanted to get the hell out. Why should he stay here?

Baqa'a camp, where he and his family had arrived when he was eight years old, was not home, though Mohammed was not really sure where home actually was.

Until 1948, home for his parents, their parents, theirs before, and so forth had for centuries been Tel al Safi, a small village of 1,500, named for its location at the top of a hill and for its pure air. But in that summer of 1948, its elders had decided the villagers should all seek refuge for a few days in nearby al Khalil, Hebron, to keep safe from the danger they feared would arrive with the advancing Israeli militias.

Mohammed himself did not know what Tel al Safi looked or smelled or sounded like, though his family's yearnings for its breezes, rolling hills, and simplicity of life, passed through story and memory, had long become his own. Did it matter though? Like his parents, he was forbidden by the Israelis to ever return.

Mohammed's birthplace meant nothing to him. He had been born near the Palestinian town of Jericho in 1960 in Aqbat Jaber, a refugee camp where his parents had landed in 1948—traumatized, newly poor, and reeling from the changes on a map that told them to shut up and forget their lives as they had just been. Yet, his parents had still believed the separation from their home—they knew where home was—could not last forever.

As for this glorified chicken coop that gave him shelter when he put his head down to slumber, it was hardly a house, let alone a home.

He hated this place, Baqa'a. Fate had spat them out and forgotten them here in March 1968, after a long journey of nine months that had begun on June 7, 1967. On that June morning, Israeli jets had screeched in the skies above Aqbat Jaber. People had scrambled for cover as their camp did not have a bomb shelter. An Israeli military vehicle with speakers had announced in Arabic that they, the Palestinians in the camp, were to clear the area immediately. They had had no time to pack anything, few real possessions though they had to pack. Mohammed's father had grabbed his bicycle, loaded it up with some food and cooking utensils, and Mohammed, his siblings, parents, and grandmother had set out from Jericho to Naour, a village on the East Bank of the River Jordan and a two-day journey by foot.

They walked with other fleeing Palestinian refugees and Jordanian soldiers who had been given the orders overnight to retreat. They took care not to walk in big clusters so they wouldn't all get killed at once from the falling bombs. Two of his family alternated walking in the rear with his grandmother, one on either side to support and help her.

Along the way they saw much death. Mohammed, only seven years old then, was too young to recognize it right away, but he realized what it was once he heard his father begin to recite from the Koran, *Ya ayyatuha 'l-nafsu 'l-mutma'innatu 'irji`i ila rabbiki.* What was the worst thing they saw? The abandoned dowry chest that had retched onto their road a wedding dress, jewelry, and some girl's dreams? The old couple, sitting in a truck while other family members loaded their possessions into the back, who suddenly caught fire from a bomb they never saw, frenetically alive in its flames until they died trapped in the cab? Or maybe the dying woman who was trying to breast-feed her baby, to whom they stopped to give water? No, no, it was leaving the baby behind after its mother died. Mohammed heard it crying as they walked away, his father again reciting *O thou comforted soul! Return unto thy Lord.*

By the time they arrived at Naour, his grandmother's soles were bleeding and his plastic sandals had worn away. Their feet finally found some rest when a farmer on a tractor took them the rest of the way to his aunt's house in Salt. They stayed for a few months before following the opportunity of work to the Jordanian village of Karameh. They were there six months when in March of 1968, Israeli forces, in retaliation for PLO attacks against Israel, carried out a raid on fighters based in the village. The PLO and the Jordanian Army fought side by side, and the Israelis retreated at the end of a day's battle, though they destroyed most of Karameh and took hundreds prisoners.

Again Mohammed and his family had to keep moving. Word had already reached them of a new UN camp for Palestinian refugees at Baqa'a. They had no other alternatives and journeyed anew with the hope that some of their prayers for a temporary solution might be finally answered.

They had arrived to find a flat area of less than a square mile surrounded by onion fields and lines and lines of weary people. They waited their turn, and were finally given a tent with stakes to drive into the ground and rope to secure the canvas. And blankets, they were allotted blankets as well. Mohammed's family looked for anyone from Tel al Safi or Aqbat Jaber so that they could be near people they knew. Once they decided on a plot, they cleared it of onions and pitched their tent. When unfurled, the canvas covered an area of 12x15 feet and provided permeable shelter. The winds swept up under the tent and sent shivers through Mohammed's body as he slept on the ground; the mattresses they eventually bought were always a little bit damp in the winters. Some 26,000 refugees lived like this alongside them.

There were communal showers in a building made of corrugated metal siding with the same for a roof; a card granted them access to a shower only once a week. Their showers were timed. The toilets were also communal, holes in the ground and housed in open buildings near the garbage dump. Since no one collected the garbage, it was set on fire when the pile became too high. Water was also communal, and families had to bring their own containers to collect the water they would need to wash and cook.

In 1971, the UN replaced the tents with 8,048 prefabricated shelters—uninsulated chicken coops—thanks to special contributions from West Germany. Because the shelters could be so easily dismantled, Mohammed's parents reasoned that they would still, in time, be returning home. Once they had saved some money, Mohammed's family, like others, built an accompanying room of concrete. Being allowed to use materials more permanent, they began to understand that return might not happen in their lifetimes.

Mohammed had known other children lived differently. While he had taken several buses to travel short distances, he had seen beautiful cars whiz by him with little boys and girls sitting in their own seats. He had seen children wearing patch-free clothes that had not been bought in a secondhand store. He had seen school buildings and had discovered that not every child went to school in a tent. He had walked past restaurants where he could smell meat roasting and realized that there had to be families who could afford to eat in such places—why else would they exist?

No, he was not going to shed any tears over this place; he had been trying to escape all his life. For years, he had thought members of the foreign press could be his ticket out. Ever since he was ten years old, journalists would come through every once in a while to film them in "camp life" or to get the perspective of "the camps." To him they had been proof that there was an outside world. His older sister, who had been studying English in school, had been teaching him what she learned. It had been important for him to learn the language so that he could communicate, no matter how rudimentarily, to these tall foreigners without their Jordanian minders understanding what he was saying. He couldn't just come out and say in Arabic, "Hey, we're getting screwed here," otherwise those minders, who were really *mukhabarat*, the secret police, would have visited his family in the middle of the night. But Mohammed had wanted these foreigners to know, to get the message out, what the hell the Palestinian refugees were going through. He had listened sickened, as adults, the appointed interviewees, had given the standard line: they were hopeful, particularly under the leadership of King Hussein.

Hopeful? Mohammed would have told them the truth. They were hungry, they were thirsty, they had hardly any clothes, they were forgotten.

He had also fantasized that a foreign journalist would take him away. When they came through Baqa'a, he would look as cute as he could, wearing bright colors and T-shirts with English words on them, which he got at the thrift store. He had wanted them to see that he was so adorable that they would have to adopt him and take him away to the outside world. Or they would see how smart he was and say, "Come study with us." As he had gotten a bit older, he dreamed that some female journalist would fall for him and ask his parents if he could leave with her.

When no one ever took him away, he understood he would have to take matters into his own hands.

Others went to Syria, to Turkey, to West Germany, to the USSR—wherever they were granted scholarships to study. His parents told him they would not allow him to travel to the godless Soviet Union. But there was only one place that he wanted to go: *Amreeka.*

His mother hated *Amreeka.* Every second of every minute of every hour, she blamed the United States for what had happened to them. She never forgot that the United States was the first country to recognize Israel and the country that armed Israel. She always said, "The Israelis are not our problem, our problem is *Amreeka*; without *Amreeka*, there would be no Israel." She also despised and loathed the Arab leaders—leaderless leaders—emirs, kings, and robots all executing policies that had been their destruction.

But his mother knew Mohammed would never be able to get the American visa, so "Go" she would tell him. Because he was the fairest of her children, she would say, "You look like them anyway."

Deep inside, Mohammed had known he *would* get the visa. He had been accepted to college in Jordan but refused to attend because he had known that his parents would pressure him to graduate before attempting to go to the States. But he had stayed faithful, knowing the visa was within his grasp. Buying time, he had gone to a two-year UN college where he studied math and English while saving money from his construction jobs to pay for the required papers for a visa. Finally the day arrived, and he went to the U.S. Embassy. Everyone else said it would be an impossibility.

They had been right. He had not gotten the visa. When the Palestinian intermediary at the window of the U.S. Embassy in Jordan handed him back his papers and told him he had been rejected, Mohammed had started to despair. His best shot in the camps was to become a teacher, make 100 dinars a month, and hope that 500 years later he would have enough to build a house and buy a car. Mohammed's eyes started to tear.

"Why are you crying?" the man had asked.

"I'm not crying," Mohammed had said. "I'm just so frustrated. This rejection means I'm stuck. I really want to succeed and make something out of myself. I have no other way. Now I'm trapped."

The man had asked Mohammed if he could see his papers again and then had disappeared behind a door. At last he returned. Inside Mohammed's passport—a Jordanian passport that made it clear he wasn't a real Jordanian, but a Palestinian—was the American visa.

Now the day was finally here and he was leaving. Many of his school friends came to say good-bye. As he made his way to the taxi to begin his journey, neighbors gathered by the car, and all started advising him at once. *Be careful! Enjoy! Take us with you!*

His mother, his brother, and his older sister piled into the cab to accompany him to the Amman International Airport. He had never been in a cab before; they had always taken the public buses, and he knew this ride would set his family back for a month.

A song came on the radio about losing loved ones and longing to see them, and his mother and sister again began to weep. He rode silently.

What madness was this that he was doing? they cried.

Mohammed was unfazed by the fact that he had no friends or family where he was going. He would depend on himself. He was also angry that they did not believe in him.

"I can't believe how hard your heart is," his sister said. "Why do you have to do this? You can still stay here and go to school."

He was not going to go to school here. He had watched how the camp kids would spend three hours taking buses to travel the ten miles to the university. That would not be him.

"*Qasi!*"—Hard!—his sister uttered, as they neared the airport.

In the airport, he went through the processes of showing all his identification and getting the exit stamps required to leave the country—another five dinars. His family meanwhile remained behind the counter, where they were not allowed to cross. He could hear them still crying, and finally he turned to them, "*Bitshufu! Bitshufu!*" You will see, you will see.

He left without saying all that "I love you" business. He would *show* them how much he loved them, how much he cared, how hard his heart wasn't.

After traveling from Amman to New York City, he switched airports and finally arrived in Chicago. Standing outside O'Hare Airport in the dark and drizzle, he watched people be greeted by those waiting for them. He recognized Palestinians and Jordanians who had traveled on his flights from Amman hug and kiss their friends and families and was stunned to see whole Palestinian families here.

He had not been by himself since leaving. On the plane, in the airports, he had been surrounded by people. Now, he was alone, really alone. No one here knew who he was, who *his* family was, how smart he was, how hungry he was. And now he couldn't even go back; he had come on a one-way ticket. He wondered, what the hell had he been thinking?

As the other Palestinians began to stuff their bags into the trunks of waiting cars, and steal a few more warm embraces from people who had missed them, who loved them, Mohammed started to cry.

To hotel employees, to hotel guests, to Kathy, and to Americans—especially white Americans—he was John, and he left his origins to people's imagination. Though his accent signaled he was foreign, no one ever guessed he was Arab or Palestinian, unless they saw him with others who were.

To the Palestinian, Arab, and Iranian guys who had become his friends, he was Mohammed.

At O'Hare back in November, he had approached one of the Palestinians he had met on the plane from Jordan and who was being greeted by his friends; Mohammed had swallowed his pride and asked if he could go with them. The Palestinians were a group of friends who were all studying and working in the States. They welcomed him and gave him a place to stay.

One of them had a one-bedroom apartment in the part of Rogers Park the police avoided. The place served almost as a halfway house for new arrivals while they each established their own rhythms in the United States. During Mohammed's stay in November 1978, there had been five or six other guys as well, depending on the night, alternating who slept on the couch and who on the floor. They were all students working to put themselves through school.

Mohammed had left after a few days to go to River Forest and the English Language Center at Concordia University. When he arrived at the campus in the Chicago suburb, he met foreign students from the world over. The terms of their visas required that they enroll in a language program. The agency that had prepared Mohammed's papers for the visa in Jordan had told him that he should spend nine months at the center, but he had used all the money he had saved to pay for the agency's fees and the plane ticket, and had only enough left for one month of lessons. Maybe the rich Arab kids from the Gulf states could afford to stay there for months, learning English on *Baba's* dime, but Mohammed was down to his last 100 dollars. His plan was to start his regular schooling and work at the same time; the agency in Jordan had arranged for him to enroll for classes at the community college in Danville, Illinois.

He asked around and heard that Danville was a rural area—they had horses out there, someone told him. That would be a disaster for Mohammed. He needed to be in a city so he could get a job. He didn't have money for tuition. The other foreign students that he had befriended told him about the city colleges in Chicago, where the tuition per course was much less than at the University of Illinois. What they intended to do was to take two years of classes in the city college system before transferring to the university to finish their degrees. Loop College downtown was where many of them went, so Mohammed decided to check it out for himself.

He took the El from River Forest, along the way learning about the fortunes of each area he passed through based on who got on and off the train at each stop. That same day that he had checked out Loop, he had walked into the Oxford Hotel. It had made perfect sense to him. He would spend less time commuting between work and school and more time working and learning, which is what he had come to America to do. When the time came to leave the Concordia dorms, he moved back to Rogers Park with three other foreign students into a one-bedroom apartment.

They had been living together since February. The other guys had taken jobs at the Jack in the Box near their apartment, where the manager was an Iranian, and word-of-mouth among the students provided a steady supply of employees for the restaurant. By working five days a week at the hotel, Mohammed was making the most money. To liven the place, which he was a dictator about keeping clean, he had bought for the apartment an old 1950s Zenith TV, which looked more like a fireplace and produced a grainy picture at best, and only on a day that was clear, sunny, and windless.

Now in the spring of 1979, he watched it late, after midnight when he returned from the hotel and to keep him company as he did his class assignment. The television had several dials and required patience in exchange for any kind of reception. Several times he picked up the channel of some Iranian faction, often demonstrating and chanting in Farsi. He had no idea who they were or what they were saying.

Mohammed did not know much about Iran, except that a few months before in January the Shah had gone into exile, and the opposition leader, the Ayatollah Khomeini, had returned from his own exile in Iraq and France. Before coming to America, Mohammed had never known any Iranians.

Here he met several who were also foreign students. Some supported the Shah while others were for the revolution. The pro-Shah ones seemed to have more money, dressed in slacks and pressed shirts, spoke much better English, and had come to the United States on their own terms. The most attractive Iranian women hung out with them.

The pro-revolution ones were poor like Mohammed and had to work to pay their way through school. They also dressed similarly, in tight jeans, army green jackets, and a *kaffiyyah* around their necks. They had unruly waves and curls atop their heads and a healthy amount of stubble on their faces. They were all studying to become engineers; they had found that their third-world educations in math and science were first rate by American standards. Mohammed was going to become a structural engineer—after all, he had seen the innards and guts of buildings all his life.

Like Mohammed, they all felt a long way from home and had come
to Ahm-reekah, as they said it, believing they had nothing and nowhere
to return to.

In one stark way, the revolution had reversed their fortunes; the pro-
Shah Iranians found themselves suddenly in instant exile while those who
favored the revolution felt they could return and help build a nation more
equitable than it had been under the deposed leader.

Mohammed watched the Iranian channel and the events with interest. He remembered that back in the camp in Baqa'a, people did not like
the Shah, whom they understood to be oppressive and a CIA lackey,
which reminded them of many of the Arab leaders. Though he never had
much use for religion—Mohammed certainly wouldn't want to live in an
Islamic state—he did want some kind of revolution to spill over into the
Arab world. He wanted all Arabs, who were watching Palestinians' slow
death, to feel his agony.

He wanted *them* to walk till their feet bled; to feel the aches of a body
always working; to suffer the elements and feel the filth on their skin,
the cold in their bones, and the heat in their lungs. He wanted *them* to
wrestle the nightmares, to feel the guilt of abandoning a baby in the arms
of its dead mother, to lose their home and homeland and be a refugee in
the dirty and muddy camps. Why should he alone know the misery and
shame that had been his loyal companions all his life?

Mohammed wanted to learn more, so he asked his Iranian friends to
explain what exactly he was watching on the TV late nights.

As they explained it, the Shah's regime had been oppressive and ille-
gitimate. The Shah had ousted the democratically elected and popular
Mohammed Mossadegh, who had nationalized Iran's oil industry. They
believed the CIA was behind the change in power. The Iranians also told
Mohammed of the SAVAK, the feared secret police, who sounded to him
a lot like the *mukhabarat* used by the Arab dictators.

These Iranians had been ecstatic that the Shah had been forced from
power, but now they were angry that America had frozen their country's
wealth and refused to hand the Shah over to the new government for
prosecution. Though these guys were not refugees like him, Mohammed
recognized that they, too, were locked in their own struggle. But since
none of them in Chicago were actually fighting their revolutions, they

held demonstrations instead for their different causes and each went to the other's in solidarity.

To pass the time and to numb the pain of being so far away from the ones they loved, they also ventured into Chicago's bars and discos and shared a beer in solidarity. On good nights, they even met cute girls.

But Mohammed's focus was always on his mission to succeed, which to him meant getting an education. Not only would failure at school restrict his life options, it would also mean being forced out of this country, and he did not want to leave. He had come to love Chicago, even as he found it dangerous. Of all the places fate could have tossed him, this time he had landed in a place he found awesome and majestic. As a city, he loved its logic and infrastructure. He admired its trains and buses that always ran and could take him anywhere; the city had everything and anything that someone who was broke, alone, and a stranger in a strange land needed to find his way around. He loved the changing of its weather, from the snow to the sandy beaches that were easily in reach. And Mohammed loved its architecture, the tall buildings that represented success, industry, and power. He took particular pride in the John Hancock Center and the Sears Tower; the structural engineer who had designed them, Fazlur Khan, was Muslim too.

Chicago was also exciting for its different kinds of people. He found Americans to be honest and straightforward. As Mohammed's English got better, he gained access to more and more of them. He was becoming one of them. Then on November 4, 1979, in Iran, students stormed the American Embassy in Tehran, took fifty-two Americans hostage, and changed his life across the globe in Chicago overnight.

As soon as the standoff at the American Embassy in Iran began, Mohammed was asked: Why do people like you take Americans hostage? What the hell are you doing here? Why don't you go back to where you came from?

Yelled out at him were the names foreigner, camel jockey, sand nigger, fucking Persian.

He discovered all the places a person could be hated: the grocery, classroom, bar, restaurant, street, soccer field, dentist's office, shopping mall.

He learned the ways revulsion could be communicated: in a glare, a tone of voice, a shudder, a menacing invasion of his space.

He had not known this pain before.

Every day the news reminded everyone in America that Americans had been taken hostage in Iran. At the bar in the hotel, at home, on televisions everywhere was the image that came to represent the crisis—a blindfolded captive with Iranian students standing behind him. Talking heads speculated about Khomeini's motives and his effect on regional politics, Israel, and U.S. interests in Iran. There were also reports about Iran under the Shah and how wonderful life had been then for Iranians. Sunday morning news shows were dominated with surrogates from the Carter and Reagan campaigns debating how and when the hostages would be freed. Some way or another, the hostages were always, always on the news, with a reminder of how many days it had been since their capture.

Mohammed also heard news that didn't make the news. President Carter issued directives to the Department of Justice and the INS regarding Iranian students studying in the States. Around the country, Iranians, or people perceived to be Iranians, were being verbally and physically assaulted. In Chicago, Iranians who drove taxis were sitting targets, their cabs frequently vandalized, as was an Albanian mosque in the suburbs. And "Nuke Iran" graffiti could be seen on bridge abutments.

And much closer, many of Mohammed's friends and acquaintances were spat upon, unable to rent homes, or lost jobs. The Jack in the Box where his friends and fellow foreign students worked under an Iranian manager became the scene of frequent friction. Patrons threw bottles, urinated in the restaurant, though not in the bathroom, started a fire in the Iranian manager's car, yelling, swearing, and shouting variations of *Iranian fucks, go back home, you fucking camel jockey.*

One night, three guys came into the Jack in the Box, looking for some Iranian ass to kick. They found instead Mohammed's friend Jamil, a Palestinian who had grown up in Bethlehem after his parents had fled the same village that Mohammed's parents had left in 1948. The American guys jumped Jamil and beat him unconscious.

It did not matter that Jamil was not Iranian. What did matter was that he was darker skinned, spoke English with an accent, and hadn't had the good fortune of being born in this country.

Overnight, at school they—the foreigners—were isolated, ignored, and excluded. Angry Americans leveled accusations against Mohammed about the crisis. It didn't matter that he wasn't Iranian, that he wasn't a religious fanatic, or that he wasn't actually one of the hostage takers! They were all the face of the hostage takers, who, like them, were Middle Eastern, Muslim, and students.

When Mohammed engaged in dialogue to give a voice to the face, to explain that he was Palestinian and not Iranian—not as an excuse but to inform—he was disappointed. There were people who didn't need to know anything about him other than he was Middle Eastern and Muslim; with those bits of information they could confidently surmise everything they needed to know about him even though most of them could not place on a map where he came from. Americans seemed to not really know, care to know, or even try to know who they—these foreigners— were, where they came from, what circumstances had brought them here, or what role their own American government's policies might have played in their coming here.

Mohammed was shocked. America's knowledge was so technologically and scientifically vast—Americans were exploring the moon—yet they knew so little about the people with whom they shared this planet. He found it so frustrating that this one-of-a-kind country that he so admired was basically illiterate about anyone else's history and current reality. Even while Mohammed and his friends wanted to be in America and be part of the country, they recognized that outside its borders, and especially in the Middle East, the American government played by a different set of rules. But they still wanted America, knowing this. Some of them hoped one day it would live up to its ideals. What dumbfounded Mohammed was how on the part of many Americans there was zero acknowledgment of this reality and how many were willfully unaware of all the places the country's policies directly impacted and how.

Mohammed learned to be self-conscious about what he knew, thought, or felt, and he held back in conversations. He learned to study his environs and the audience, waiting for some action or reaction to indicate whether it was safe to speak up. He had to tread lightly and make it as easy and painless as possible for Americans to hear his truth.

As a group, he and the other foreign students made sure to frequent only places where they were known, and they tried not to advertise where they were from. It was fairly clear they were foreign, though, and the girls in the discos and bars—who had thought they were exotic before— turned from them in disgust.

Then on January 21, 1981, Ronald Reagan was inaugurated and the hostages were freed after 444 days of captivity. People stopped talking about the crisis, and to Mohammed it was as if a switch were flipped and everyone went back to normal, with their racism and hate for foreigners safely stowed away. Though after fourteen months of the TV reminding the country what the face of evil looked like, Mohammed took the *kaffiyyah* from around his neck, tucked it under his jacket to keep him warm, and locked the revolution away in his heart.

After the crisis ended, he bumped into Kathy on the El. She had left the hotel nine months before, and he had not seen her since. On the train, she told him she had broken up with her boyfriend from that time. His English was much better and inflected with that Midwestern accent he had been perfecting. So John asked her out, and they made a date.

On the day of both the hostages' release and his inauguration, President Reagan announced that fighting terrorism would be a foreign policy priority. This would lead the United States, under Reagan, to give Iraq military and logistic support in its war with Iran, as well as to sell arms to the Iranians in an effort to free hostages held by Shiite groups in Lebanon. The latter was unbeknownst to the American people.

The hostage crisis also added another dimension to the terrorist stereotype plaguing Arab Americans. Though the Palestinian struggle had been predominantly secular (and unrelated), the Islamic nature of the Iranian Revolution expanded the caricature of the militant Middle Easterner to incorporate religion—Islam. The negative representation had heretofore implicated Arab Americans—who were mostly Christian—because they shared the same ethnicity as the Arabs populating the American nightly news with little context. With the inclusion of Islam in the stereotype, Muslim Americans of other ethnicities began to similarly be included in its harm.

In February 1980, the story broke that in 1978, the FBI had begun a high-level undercover sting operation—code-named ABSCAM— meant to catch corrupt congressmen and organized crime members. The FBI operation consisted of agents posing as Arab oil sheikhs and bribing several members of Congress on video. The FBI created a front (Abdul Enterprises, Ltd., hence, ABSCAM) for these purposes, and eventually six congressmen and one senator were convicted of bribery and conspiracy charges in 1981.

But no Arab or Arab American had ever been accused of bribing an American politician. For Arab Americans, ABSCAM's unquestioned use of the "Arab sheikh" indicated that the stereotype of the slimy, wealthy, and corrupt foreigner lived not only in media and pop culture, but at the highest levels of U.S. power as well. They saw these omnipresent portrayals as creating the perception in the United States that anything Arab was almost inherently bad or anti-American; therefore Arabs, Arab Americans, their speech, or their perspectives were easily dismissible and politically risky.

For South Dakotan senator James Abourezk—the first Arab American ever elected to the Senate—ABSCAM was the last straw. Having voluntarily left the Senate in 1978, calling it a "chickenshit outfit," Abourezk founded in May 1980 the Arab-American Anti-Discrimination Committee (ADC), a Washington-based organization with chapters across the country, to counter the racial stereotyping.

Because of the strong presence of the stereotypes combined with the near absence of the Palestinian and Arab narratives of major geopolitical events that occurred in the Middle East, Arab Americans remained in many cases critical of the coverage of the major events of this period, which were numerous. However it was events in Lebanon that saw ADC's membership swell to 22,000.

In June 1982, Israel invaded Lebanon, ostensibly to wipe out Palestinian guerrilla bases near Israel's northern border; Israeli forces, however, continued to push all the way to Beirut, where the Palestine Liberation Organization (PLO) and its leader Yasser Arafat were then based. In the course of the invasion, 30,000–40,000 Palestinians and Lebanese were killed, 100,000 were seriously wounded, and half a million were made homeless. On August 30, 1982, Arafat and the PLO leadership were allowed to leave Lebanon for exile in Tunisia, leaving behind the Palestinian refugees, many living in the squalor of refugee camps. Just weeks after the PLO's departure, anywhere from 800 to 2,000 civilians were massacred by the Lebanese Christian Phalangist militia in the camps of Sabra and Shatila. At the time, Israeli troops were in control of the area, and eventually, in February 1983, an Israeli commission would find then–defense minister Ariel Sharon responsible for the massacre for failing to act to prevent it.

In the wake of the massacre, ADC and other organizations broadened their activities to include organizing demonstrations, marches, press conferences, and other public events aimed at protesting the inva-sion and exposing Americans to the Lebanese, Palestinian, and greater Arab narratives of what was happening on Lebanese soil.

Israel eventually withdrew in May 1983, largely because the con-tinued incursion into Lebanon was unpopular within Israel itself, but it left enough of its army behind to occupy the southern third of Leb-anon, a heavily Shiite area. In response, Hezbollah, a mainly Shiite organization, was founded. With Lebanon already destabilized by civil war, the 1982 invasion set off a period of increased Lebanese immigra-tion to America: in 1980–1985, 17,192 people immigrated.

At the same time ADC and Arab-American leaders were also tak-ing note of the use of anti-Arab stereotyping and rhetoric to preclude Arab-American participation in academia and American politics. In academia, several cases were noted of university centers or professors at institutions being silenced or harassed by the labels "pro-Arab" or "anti-Semitic" or "anti-Israel" for focusing on the Arab world, receiving funding from Arab sources (even though the sources had no influence on curricula), or offering any narrative of the Arab-Israeli conflict that was either critical of Israel or sympathetic to the Palestinian plight.

In politics, at a time when the PLO was perceived only negatively, Arab-American candidates were baited as "PLO sympathizers." And for non-Arab-American candidates, donations from the community carried political risk. Political contributions from Arab Americans were returned at both the local level and the presidential level. During the 1984 presidential primary, five prominent Chicago Arab Americans contributed $1,000 each to candidate Walter Mondale. Shortly after, the $5,000 was returned, according to campaign officials, because of a "misunderstanding."

Some 79,524 Arabs immigrated to the United States in these years; notably, in addition to the Lebanese, another 16,369 came from Jor-dan; 14,524 from Egypt; and 6,676 from Iraq.

© BETTMAN/CORBIS

Silenced

W hen the phone rang in the middle of the night in May 1985, Norma Odeh thought she was still dreaming. With the receiver dangling close to her ear, all she heard was music, a melody that sounded to her like mourning.

"It's music," she said out loud, in response to her husband's shifting beside her.

Though she could not make out the tune, when the caller finally spoke, his words were unequivocal.

"Alex is going to die," he taunted her, daring her to not believe him. "And soon you're going to be a widow."

Norma was stunned. She knew there had been calls to Alex's office, and she knew right away this had to be one of *those* calls. But this was the first to the house, and the first she had ever answered. She never imagined they threatened actual death.

Alex took the phone from her. "Are you going to stop this or what?" he asked the caller, even then not raising his voice. "This is my family. Don't call my house anymore." Alex reached over and gently settled the phone back in its place.

Norma turned on the lights. "What is going on?" she asked him. "What if they really mean it, what if they kill you?"

"Don't worry about it," Alex responded.

Norma persisted. "What if they do it again? Why didn't you tell me they threatened to kill you? Are you going to report this to the police, to the FBI?"

"In the morning," Alex said.

Then Norma started asking about all the other incidents that had been happening in the past few years. "Did you report the egging of the car?" she asked.

"Yes," he answered.

"Alex, he said he's going to kill you."

"Nothing is going to happen," Alex tried to reassure her.

"What if they do it on our trip?" she kept on.

With summer vacation about to begin for their eldest two girls—ages seven and five—Norma and Alex were planning a trip to visit their village, Jifna, in the Israeli-occupied West Bank. Alex always promised the girls they would know where their parents came from—a simple place of many steeples and limestone houses, where history's ancient eras, from Biblical to Byzantine to Roman to Crusader, were written in the architecture. This trip would be their first time back since 1981, and Alex had already planned an itinerary that would take the two older girls all across the Holy Land. Norma could not wait to show her mother how much they had grown, and to introduce her baby girl. Even though she loved her home in California, in the village she could let the kids run outside and never worry about them. She could talk to her best friend, Nahla, with whom she had been exchanging letters for the ten years since she had come to America, and Alex could roam his family's fruit groves, eating right off the trees all the apricots, figs, plums, and peaches he desired.

But now, Norma chastised herself for missing the obvious; if someone really wanted to kill Alex, they could easily do it in Jerusalem or Nablus. There, she thought, a Palestinian could be killed and no authority would investigate or prosecute the murder.

For the past few weeks, she had been consumed only with planning the baby's baptism, which Norma was determined to see done in Orange, the town of citrus trees and terra-cotta roofs that they had made home. The older girls were baptized in Jifna, but Norma had had little control over the party thrown afterward at her mother-in-law's house. In California, Norma could do it her way—she would pick the decorations, choose the food, and decide who to invite. As she lay back, letting Alex think she was reassured, she prayed their trip to their village would be a safe one.

For now, though, she took comfort in being in California. Nothing, she told herself, after all, would happen here where Alex—where all Americans—had the freedom to speak their minds.

The calls had started years before when Alex took the job as West Coast regional director of the Arab-American Anti-Discrimination Committee (ADC) in 1981. ADC, a Washington-based organization with chapters across the country, had been founded the year before to counter the racial stereotyping that Americans of Arab descent believed was causing discrimination against them; it was modeled on the Jewish Anti-Defamation League.

One month after Norma had received the threatening phone call, in June 1985, the hijacking of a TWA jet by Hezbollah-linked operatives set off a flood of reports to ADC of anti-Arab and anti-Muslim incidents around the United States. Pipe bombs were thrown into a Houston mosque. Islamic centers were vandalized in San Francisco, Dearborn, and near Bethesda. Centers in Denver and Quincy, Massachusetts, received bomb threats. Since its founding, threats to ADC were common, and Alex was its main representative in California.

He had become a recognizable face in the Arab-American community, intervening on behalf of any who needed assistance. He advocated for women who wanted to wear their head coverings at work, gave voice to the concerns of migrant Yemeni workers who picked grapes on farms in Lamont, invited politicians to come meet their Arab-American constituents, organized concerts with Arab singers, and confronted car dealers who used grotesque caricatures of Arabs to move last year's model off their lots. He also built relationships with community and religious leaders from black, Hispanic, and Jewish groups and was a member of many interfaith and interracial/ethnic groups, including the Orange County Human Relations Commission.

In addition, he was often called on to share the seldom-heard Palestinian perspective on the conflict with Israel. Alex would poignantly describe their own exodus and dispossession as a way to move the region toward peace, which he believed would better the lives of both Jews and Arabs whether overseas or here in America.

The Palestinian narrative, however, was one that did not sit well with the Jewish Defense League (JDL), an extremist group inspired by the teachings of Rabbi Meir Kahane, who advocated that the Palestinians be driven from Israel to make it ethnically "pure," and disowned by many of the Jewish groups in the United States. The JDL's involvement in both threats and acts of violence had put them on the FBI's radar since the 1970s. JDL members often picketed ADC events, heckling attendees, and had even entered a mosque in LA and held a sit-in. They provocatively opened an office down the street from that of ADC—Alex's office—in Santa Ana.

The JDL's constant proximity to Alex's workplace was worrisome, though Alex never talked about the depths of their hostility. With Norma and the girls still in Jifna until the beginning of the school year in September, Alex managed to hide from her what had happened in Boston after he had returned ahead of her from the summer visit to the West Bank.

Across the country on August 17, a bomb was found in a package propped up against the door of ADC's New England office. Police bomb-squad officers removed the bomb successfully, but when they tried to detonate it in a dump in West Roxbury, it exploded in the face of one officer, causing severe burns on his face, arms, and hands; another man was injured. An anonymous caller to the *Boston Herald* claimed responsibility on behalf of the JDL, promising that such incidents would continue.

Alex suspected the threatening calls he was receiving came from the JDL as well, because he often recognized the voice of their leader, Irv Rubin. Alex initially sought to engage Rubin, as was always his habit, telling him, "Let's sit and talk and stop fighting," but he soon realized that those efforts were futile. Rubin's currency was violence, imbuing even the slogans that he coined, such as "For every Jew, a .22" and "Keep Jews alive with a .45." In 1978, Rubin had been charged with soliciting murder when he held up five $100 bills at a news conference against a Nazi march in Skokie and offered them to anyone who maimed or killed a member of the Nazi Party. "And if they bring us the ears," he said, "we'll make it $1,000." Daring anyone not to believe him, he added, "This is not said in jest, we are deadly serious." But after an intense legal battle lasting several years, he was acquitted, astounding even some of his supporters.

Alex believed violence as a way of solving problems was only for animals and that when human beings resorted to it, they themselves became animals. While the threats worried Alex once they became directed against Norma and the girls, he felt nonetheless that he had to continue speaking up on behalf of Arab Americans, whom he saw as easy targets of discrimination, and to try to let Americans know the Palestinian side of what had happened and was happening to their homeland.

Politics, though, had not always been Alex's passion. He had remained relatively less touched than other Palestinians by the creation of the State of Israel in Palestine in 1948. Both his parents were from Jifna, in the West Bank, and as such were not forced from their homes when Israel was created, unlike Norma's father, who, when torn from his home in Jaffa, had had time only to take the worn bed pillow from beneath his cheek. The pillow had remained sacred to her family, and it occupied a spot on her eldest sister's bed even after her father's passing, when Norma was only three years old.

Then Alex's destiny was reborn in 1967, and it would become Norma's as well when she wedded her fate to his with their marriage in 1975. In 1967, Alex had been a college student studying engineering at the University of Cairo. During the war that year, Israel roundly defeated the combined military forces of Syria, Jordan, and Egypt, capturing the Sinai, the Gaza Strip, the Golan Heights, and the West Bank. When Alex tried to go back to his village in the West Bank at the war's end, he was told by the Israeli Occupation that he had to have someone sponsor him to "visit" the land where he was born and where his ancestors had lived for centuries.

Suddenly the consequences of the founding of Israel had come to involve him personally. He was not able to return home until 1972. Years later, Alex told Norma that it had killed him inside in 1967 that he was forbidden to return home. He was hounded: why are they doing this to me?

Needing an answer to this question and trying to make sense of the pain of being denied entrance to his own country, Alex abruptly changed majors from engineering to economics while in Cairo. He then went on to pursue a master's degree in political science at California State University at Fullerton. He taught Arabic at Cal State and at Coastline Community College, where he also taught Mideast history and politics and had been recently elected to the Academic Senate.

But what Alex had loved was poetry, publishing a book of poems in 1983, *Whispers in Exile*. He wrote a few verses in his journal every night, after he recorded his daily happenings. Before sleeping, he would read the verses, written in classical Arabic, to Norma. He translated them for her into dialect or English, and she found them beautiful.

While Alex made justice and equality for Arabs and Arab Americans his life's mission, Norma focused instead on learning all the skills required to provide a loving home for her husband and their daughters. Having grown up in a boarding school, she was not as experienced as most Palestinian girls in chores and cooking. The only food she knew how to make was falafel. Alex helped so much, though, as he promised he would the day he proposed to her: "I want you to be my queen, and I will never do anything less for you than what suits a queen."

Norma hoped to God Alex would get his dream to see an independent and free Palestinian state, but she herself never believed it would happen. How could Alex, one man, stop the internal fighting among Palestinians, who drew lines in the sand between themselves over political and religious differences? How could he make Israel and America see the Palestinians as fellow human beings? Yet Alex never stopped believing, never lost faith, and Norma, who admired his idealism, was determined to support him.

But when the threats started, and the specter of danger haunted their lives, she asked Alex, whom she did not think understood the sacrifice she was making in raising a family with threatened peril hanging over their heads, "Why, why if these things are so important, if you have such strong feelings about Palestine and politics, why would you even consider marriage?"

"Why did you marry me and have us in your life?" she would ask.

On Thursday, October 10, 1985, Alex appeared during an interview on the eleven o'clock news on KABC–TV in L.A. Alex was being asked for a reaction to the slaying that Tuesday of Leon Klinghoffer, a 69-year-old tourist from New York City who, after being held hostage aboard the ship *Achille Lauro* in the Mediterranean, had been killed in his wheelchair and then dumped overboard. The Italian cruise liner had been hijacked by Palestinian militants from the Palestinian Liberation Front, though Israel had accused the Palestine Liberation Organization (PLO) of being linked to the hijacking.

The standoff had come to an end after two days, when through Arafat's intervention, the armed Palestinians surrendered to Egyptian authorities in exchange for a promise of safe passage to Tunisia, where the PLO said it would try the men. The hijackers, however, had initially demanded that they not be handed over to the PLO. There was speculation that the gunmen, who had held the 500 passengers and crew hostage since Monday, had disobeyed orders to carry out an operation inside Israel and hijacked the ship instead. But as an Egyptian civilian airliner was flying them to Tunisia, U.S. Navy fighter jets forced the plane to land at a NATO air base in Italy, where they were detained.

Asked to comment on the events, Alex gave KABC a lengthy interview. During the broadcast, a brief segment was shown. In mild terms, Alex denied that Arafat was responsible for the hijacking, saying, "As far as I know, Arafat did an excellent job, and we commend Arafat for his positive role in solving this issue." He characterized Arafat as a "man of peace," and expressed regret that U.S. action had kept those responsible from being taken to Tunisia for trial by PLO authorities.

When Alex came home, Norma asked him right away, "Why would you say *just* that?" She was terrified; in recent weeks the threats had escalated, and all promised the same thing: "An eye for an eye" and "If a Jew dies, an Arab dies." To Norma, Arafat was seen only as a terrorist in the

United States, and the Palestinian cause as terrorism. Any suggestion of nuance or context would be taken as an endorsement of the man or of terrorism.

"Norma, I said much much more." Alex sighed. "But you know how they cut." Alex told Norma he had condemned the killing of Klinghoffer and had condemned the hijacking as well as terrorism around the world. What he had said about Arafat was that he should not be underestimated, that he could be a man of peace, and that he would do justice to those who committed the murder and hijacking.

"They're going to hurt you over this," she told him, unconvinced that anyone would give his abbreviated words the benefit of the doubt.

The next morning, Norma and Alex shared their coffee in bed while watching *Good Morning America*. When the national network cut to local affiliates, KABC rebroadcast the truncated interview with Alex from the night before.

Alex yelled out, smiling, "Girls, come see Daddy on TV!"

Norma leaned over and whispered in his ear, "They're going to kill Daddy for this."

Alex said nothing.

Since the *Achille Lauro* hijacking, the threatening calls had increased, both to Alex's office and even to their home. Alex again recognized the voice as belonging to JDL head Irv Rubin. Norma and Alex dutifully reported the calls to the Santa Ana Police Department; the police told them each time that there was nothing they could do unless something actually happened.

Whenever Norma tried to scare him straight, as she had just done, Alex would calmly respond, "It will be an honor to die for Palestine." Norma knew he felt the same way about dying for the United States, but she was intent on his staying alive.

"Just think of me and the girls," she would tell him. "I grew up without a father, I don't want our girls to grow up without one too." Norma's father had died when she was three years old. As he lay in the casket, he had a cigarette tucked between his fingers, a last fix her mother had given him to make the journey to the afterlife easier. He had looked like he was sleeping.

"Who will take care of us if anything were to happen to you?" she would ask him.

Alex would respond in the same soft-spoken voice he used in any situation, no matter how tense. "God will."

While he played with the baby, Norma pulled the older girls' long black hair back into ponytails. She put her robe over her nightgown and drove the girls around the corner to school. As she dropped them off, she kissed them both and told them to have fun.

As she drove home, Norma suddenly felt like making Alex a proper sit-down breakfast, something she hardly ever did on the weekdays, when Alex would just drink some OJ on the run. She made him all his favorite foods, scrambling eggs, frying ham, making hummus, and mixing olive oil with za`tar—a spice mixture of thyme and sesame seeds—that she had brought with her from Palestine. She brewed tea and made it Arabic style, sweetening it with a generous amount of sugar and steeping it with fresh mint leaves that she cut from her garden.

"Wow," Alex told her when he joined her in the kitchen, after he had showered and dressed. "You went out of your way!"

As the bowls and plates began to empty and with the baby in her high chair, entertained by the TV, Alex and Norma shared as private a morning as they could, stealing time at a moment usually spent rushing. When the last morsel disappeared, Norma rose smiling and went about returning the kitchen to order.

Alex had lingered as long as he could. He had to make it to work by nine. His assistant, who usually arrived first, had a doctor's appointment, and so it fell to Alex to open the office today. Alex bent to kiss the baby, and as Norma stood at the sink washing the dishes, Alex came up behind her and kissed her on the cheek.

"I love you very much," he told her in her ear. "You know that, don't you?" he said, before turning to leave.

"I love you too," she answered. And then she added, "Be careful." They looked at each other, both surprised at the words she had never uttered before.

Norma had been so innocent when they met. She had been raised in the wholly sheltered and asexual world of the Evangelical Home for Girls; her father's death when she was three had forced her mother, a registered nurse, to return to work. With no one to help raise her four children, Norma's mother had no choice but to send her children to a boarding school for orphans in a village twenty kilometers away. Paying to board them at the Evangelical Home for Girls was still cheaper than having them in the house. During the days, Norma's mother tended instead to the refugees and their children in the Kalandia, Deir Ammar, and Jalazone camps, as a head nurse for UNRWA, the United Nations Relief and Works Agency for Palestine Refugees in the Near East.

Until she was fifteen, Norma had fallen asleep crying every night because she wanted more than anything to be with her mother. She wanted to lie beside her and drift into slumber as her mother stroked her hair; she had always begged not to be sent back to the school during her once-a-month trip home or at the end of her month-long summer vacation.

But by August 1975, weeks after her seventeenth birthday, she did not want to go home at all. On her floor at the boarding house of the school, she enjoyed being by herself, doing what she wanted, with no pressures, no authority, and no one telling her what to do. However, whether or not she went home for the compulsory break was hardly up to Norma, and so she found herself back in Jifna for what remained of the summer vacation.

When she arrived in front of her family's simple one-room stone house to find the door locked, she ran next door to the much bigger home where her mother was visiting their neighbors, the Odeh family, whose eldest son was home for a brief visit from the States, where he was studying. As her mother handed her the keys, she admonished Norma for turning to run off so quickly. "Why don't you come in and greet the people here?"

Having essentially grown up under the care of the American and Scottish sisters and in isolation from Palestinian society, Norma had little idea of Arab social protocol and graces, which required respect and deference on the part of the young toward the old, and warmth and hospitality toward all.

At the prompting of her mother, who rarely had a chance to exercise a parental role, Norma made the rounds of the people assembled, shaking hands, and leaning in first toward the right, touching cheeks and making a kissing sound, and then repeating the same on the left, a perfunctory ritual kiss, placed nowhere but in the air.

When she stopped in front of Alex Odeh, a balding thirty-one-year-old with sleepy eyes and a mole beside his lengthy nose, she hardly noticed him. She had no idea that Alex would never forget the green dress she wore that day and the way it made her chameleon eyes seem so green against her black, feathered hair.

She had no idea that when he bent to shake her hand and kiss her that he had already decided he would marry her. Norma also had no idea what Alex's father meant when he said, "I'm afraid that kiss is going to stick."

After finishing the dishes, Norma got dressed to go visit Therese, a Jordanian woman married to a Palestinian whom Norma had befriended in California.

As had been their habit ever since the phone threats had begun, she phoned Alex to tell him she was leaving the house even though Therese lived only a mile away. The number to his office was busy, and she paused for a moment, but decided not to wait; she would call him when she arrived at Therese's house.

She loaded the baby into the Oldsmobile and picked up one of her other daughters from kindergarten at 11:30, then headed to Therese's for a late morning of coffee and conversation.

When Norma pulled into Therese's driveway, she saw Therese's mother-in-law, whom they all called *Um Habib* (mother of Habib) perched on the edge of the low fence in the front yard. Norma could tell she was crying.

"What's wrong?" Norma asked her as she got out of her car.

"Nothing," she said.

"Did anything happen?" Norma asked her.

"You didn't hear the news?" Um Habib responded, beginning to cry even more.

"If you know something, you need to tell me," Norma insisted.

"There was a bomb in Santa Ana," she said.

Therese then came out of the house. "What's going on?" Norma asked her.

"An office was bombed in Santa Ana," Therese told her. "It might be your husband's office."

"It can't be," Norma said. Then, "Was anyone hurt?"

"Give me the girls," Therese said. "I'll watch them and you can go."

Norma left the girls with Therese. Running to her car, she hoped to God nothing had happened to Alex. She crossed red lights, not caring if the police tried to stop her. Once in downtown Santa Ana, she turned onto the street where Alex's office was located, only to find the police blocking her way; they would not let her go any farther. Norma got out of her car, and even from a block away, she could see shattered glass on the ground everywhere. There was no sign of Alex.

"Please," she told the policeman, "I need to know if anyone got hurt."

"We have no news at this time," he told her.

"Please, I need to know," she pleaded.

"Who are you?" he asked.

"I think it's the office my husband worked in that was bombed. His name is Alex Odeh, and I am his wife," she responded. Norma thought she saw recognition flicker across the policeman's face. She started shaking; Norma didn't think anything like this would happen in America. She began to collapse, falling forward, but the policeman caught her and put her in her car.

From afar, a man named Ahmad recognized Norma. He had a scheduled appointment with Alex that morning, and when he saw Norma he approached the policeman and explained who he was.

"Go with her to Western Medical Center," he told Ahmad. "That's where they took Alex."

As Norma drove, following behind Ahmad, she prayed to God that Alex was not seriously hurt; if he's hurt, she thought, he'll get over it. He'll heal. But please don't let anything happen to him, please God, she pleaded. I don't want my daughters to grow up without a father like I did.

When they arrived at the hospital, she saw Sami, Alex's brother, leaving. Sami's head was down; he looked like he was in shock. Norma could tell from his look that Alex was badly hurt.

"What's going on?" Norma asked him.

"They put a bomb in Alex's office," Sami said.

Norma began to imagine what his injuries must be when Sami told her, "They killed Alex, Norma."

Norma began repeating, "No, no, no."

She was escorted into a room with Sami. People she did not recognize were there as well.

Norma asked to see Alex, that there had to be a mistake, that he was not dead.

"Face it, Norma, he's dead," said a woman Norma would later learn was a social worker.

"No, no, he can't be dead," Norma insisted.

"Yes, he is," the social worker volleyed.

"No, he might be sleeping," Norma retorted, wanting to smack her. "I want to see him," she declared. "Nobody knows him like me, he's my husband," Norma explained, trying to remain calm. "Maybe it's not him, maybe he's sleeping, he might be someone else," she said, offering all the alternatives she could muster.

"Fine," the social worker pronounced to the others. "She won't believe it if she doesn't see him."

Norma, Sami, and the social worker rode in silence in the elevator down to the morgue. There they were met by an orderly who guided them to a stretcher that cradled a black bag cocooned around what looked like a human figure. The orderly pulled on the zipper, revealing only a face, neck, and the top of a chest; he would not let the zipper travel farther.

Inside the body bag, the face was burned and covered by what looked like purple blotches.

Norma stared at Alex. "No," she declared, "he's sleeping. That's how he sleeps." She looked at his mouth, open, its lips parted like when he would lie beside her every night. "Wake him up," she said.

No one moved.

The waiting bomb that had ripped through Alex's office at 9 A.M. was set off by a trip wire attached to the door. The blast had also ripped through the lower part of Alex's body, and the chemicals he inhaled had incinerated his lungs from the inside. The explosion was so strong that seven other people in adjoining offices and on the street were also injured. And when the first person to reach Alex had knelt beside him, Alex had whispered, "Tell my wife I love her and the girls." He had died in surgery later that morning, around 11:30.

Norma fainted. She awoke hours later in Sami's house.

In the days leading up to Alex's funeral, Norma received a continuous stream of mourners wanting to share their condolences at her brother-in-law's house. There were other Arab Americans, regular Americans, anyone who had heard of the murder—people just kept coming and coming. She received them all in total disbelief.

Norma barely talked to anyone, and though she couldn't stop crying, she constantly wondered if what was happening was real or just a hallucination.

Since fainting and waking up in Sami's home, she had gone to her house only to choose clothing to dress Alex in for his burial. She had closed their bedroom door behind her, taking his framed picture from her bedside, holding it to her chest, and asking it, "What's going to happen to us?"

Finally she approached the closet, where Alex's own fingers had traveled often, gliding over all the shirts, ties, and suits that he had been so fond of and had so carefully collected. She retrieved the brand-new suit that Alex had bought to wear to an upcoming ADC *hafla* (party/soiree) in November. She gave it to Sami to take to the mortician.

Norma spent the nights at Sami's house in a room with her daughters, who would plead with her as they all lay in bed together, not to cry anymore, Mommy. She asked them if they understood what happened.

"Daddy went to heaven," they responded. "We're not going to see him anymore."

During those nights, Norma would not let herself sleep; she was afraid whoever had killed Alex would come for her and the girls. Yet every time she began to close her eyes, she would see Alex and be sure he was knocking at the door.

Immediately after Alex's murder, news of his killing was inescapable. Local and national TV news constantly showed images of his disembow-eled office. Blown-out windows revealed interior office contents to the external world with curtains, still tethered to the wall inside, floating toward the sky, while the beige coils of Alex's phone cord reached down toward the ground. Frequently repeated were the comments of Rubin, head of the JDL—the group that Arab-American leaders already were publicly accusing of being behind the attack—who said, "I have no tears for Mr. Odeh. He got exactly what he deserved."

The Anti-Defamation League of B'nai B'rith immediately denounced Alex's murder, calling it "domestic terrorism which cannot be tolerated." Regional presidents of the American Jewish Congress of Northern and Southern California issued a joint statement saying "no political disagreement justifies attacks on those engaged in peaceful and lawful pursuits." An editorial in the *New York Times* accused the JDL of being a "promoter of blatant racism in America and Israel."

But the investigations of the Santa Ana police, the FBI, the U.S. Bureau of Alcohol, Tobacco, and Firearms, and the L.A. police antiterrorist division still had yielded no suspects.

ADC's deputy executive director in Washington chastised American newspapers for running short wire-service accounts of Alex's murder while rightly devoting pages to stories on the life and death of Klinghoffer. She told the *Washington Post*, "This was an American killed on American soil by American terrorists." News accounts told every detail of Klinghoffer's life—he was a retiree, he lived in Greenwich Village, he had high blood pressure, it was his thirty-sixth wedding anniversary. Alex or ADC was identified as everything from an Arab group and its leader to a PLO front to a bomb victim.

At the less-than-gentle urging of the Arab-American community the White House finally issued a statement saying, "The administration deeply deplores this tragic event and condemns in the strongest possible terms the criminal use of violence and terrorism to achieve political ends. To even think for a moment that there exists a justification for such heinous acts does grave injustice to the principles of political freedom upon which this country was founded."

But then, even before the Tuesday funeral, local news had shifted to the Santa Ana winds, the dry warm currents that blow through Southern California every autumn. To Norma, the focus on the weather was as if to say Alex's life meant nothing.

At the viewing, Norma studied the navy suit she had selected for Alex to wear. It matched beautifully the indigo shirt of pure silk and the striped tie of alternating blues that Alex had paired with it in advance of November's big party. He also was wearing the new black Bally shoes he had purchased for the event; he had never worn any of these clothes before.

Norma had always loved how Alex dressed. But she did not recognize Alex in the figure over which she was saying the rosary. With wax and makeup, the morticians had tried to fix the damage to Alex's face and to fill the cavity the bomb had left in his midsection, but to Norma it was all plastic. She told them to close and seal the casket.

The day of the funeral, Sami rented a limousine to drive the family from his house to St. Norbert's Catholic Church and then later to the cemetery. Norma's house, a multifamily bungalow, was just across the street from their church, but she would not turn her face to look at it as they drove on that clear morning through the neighborhood that had been her home for years and through whose streets she had strolled hand-in-hand with Alex. He had brought her here, to California, to a place with weather he loved where he could speak his mind and not be afraid.

Hundreds of cars were already pouring into the church parking lot, and Norma was surprised to see that the police had set up checkpoints to monitor who was coming and going. When the driver got out of the limousine, Norma noticed that under his jacket a gun was holstered to his side and handcuffs were clipped to his belt.

She asked Sami what was going on. Only then did she learn that the church had received threats that a bomb would go off during the funeral. The church decided to close the adjoining school for the day, and FBI agents walked the roof of the sandstone-colored church.

Though the bomb threat deterred many from coming, thousands had nonetheless gathered, and those who could not fit inside St. Norbert's spilled out onto the pavement surrounding the church. Though the doors were closed, speakers allowed those outside to hear the service.

As a precaution should a bomb explode, Norma, her daughters, and her in-laws were led into the crying room, a designated area where parents ordinarily took fussy children so that they could still hear mass without disturbing the service. The crying room was partitioned from the church by glass, a rectangular bubble adjacent to the altar, in front of which Alex's coffin had been placed. Two flags shrouded his casket, that of Palestine—the birthplace he never forgot—and that of the United States—the place he had made home.

Norma looked in amazement at how many had gathered. Then she saw several rabbis in the pews closest to the altar and became angry. How dare you kill him and then come to his funeral, how dare you add insult to my injury, she thought, before she forced herself to acknowledge that they, too, were Alex's friends. Yet Norma could not believe that all this was happening for Alex, how could he really be gone?

Outside, mourners mingled to the sound of eulogies and prayers, and at one point to that of a melancholic *ney*, the Arabic flute, weeping from inside the church. Some wore around their necks *kaffiyyahs* that would hours later flutter in the sky, sharing the breezes with Palestinian flags as cars filled with people made their way to Alex's final rest during the funeral procession, a journey that took them through winding roads and rising hills, to a place that looked so much like Palestine.

Even during the church service, reporters swam through the crowds in front of the church. Asked as to the significance of Alex's death, a rabbi responded with the question, "Who will I speak to now?"

Whenever Norma asked Alex why, if he was going to live a life of politics—one that might jeopardize his very life—why would he then choose to marry her, he always had a simple answer. "It was my destiny to marry you."

Norma wept in the crying room, where she could still hear the service but disturb no one.

Two weeks after the funeral, FBI agents came to visit Norma at Sami's house, where she was still staying. They told her everyone was a suspect, even her. Then they asked a series of questions.

What did she know of Alex's activities?

Did Alex keep cassette tapes of his meetings?

What could she tell them about Arab Americans in Southern California?

Did she know about "any other" activities?

And what might she know about drug smuggling?

Norma asked them, "Where do you come up with these things?" So they could see for themselves what Alex's activities were, she then gave the FBI the leather journal in which Alex wrote his poetry and daily happenings each night. His name was engraved in gold and in Arabic on the front: *Iskander Michel Odeh.*

The FBI told her they were sorry for her loss.

Norma thought, what's the use of you feeling sorry? We kept telling you and you kept doing nothing, and now Alex is dead.

Later, an agent who had been through Alex's things at the crime site brought her a piece of traditional Palestinian cross-stitching that had hung in the office before the explosion. He told Norma, "I'm sure this was valuable for Alex, you should have it." The little tapestry had been made for Alex by Norma's mother.

In early November, an FBI official mentioned to a *New York Times* reporter that the FBI suspected the JDL was involved in the bombing. The *Times* reporter called Rubin for a comment, Rubin then called other news organizations to protest the FBI's claim. The FBI was forced the next day to publicly clarify that though they had established a possible link between the JDL and Alex's death, they were not close to an arrest. Two other bombs, aimed at former Nazi Party members, had exploded in August and September, one in New Jersey and the other in New York; the FBI believed the JDL was responsible. The bomb used to kill Alex was similarly constructed, and the way the bombs were rigged indicated explosive experts were involved.

The JDL members who would later be named as suspects moved to Israel soon after the killing. The suspects, all American-born Americans, did not, however, settle within Israel's internationally recognized borders, instead choosing to live in the state-subsidized settlements built on stolen Palestinian land in the West Bank, not far from Alex and Norma's home town of Jifna. One of them had a 1973 conviction for a bomb attack against a Palestinian in California, and another had a conviction in Israel for shooting at passing Palestinians on the West Bank.

Analysis and coverage of the murder in the press immediately linked the killing to Alex's interview the night before, opining that he died because of what he had said. But it was not Alex's habit to open the office, a task that usually fell to his assistant, Hind Baki, a woman who had emigrated from Syria in 1976. To many, it appeared that the Arab-American community had been the real intended target and intimidation the aim.

Lending credence to such beliefs was the rash of bomb threats, in the aftermath of Alex's death, against the Arab Community Center in L.A. and the Islamic Center of Southern California. Then on Friday, November 29, a deliberately set fire heavily damaged ADC's national headquarters in Washington, D.C., gutting its offices and destroying the food market in the same building on Connecticut Avenue. The flames burned out of control for over forty-five minutes and brought eighty firefighters to the scene.

In response to what appeared to be a pattern of hate crimes aimed at the community as a whole, that following Thursday, December 5, the U.S. Department of Justice announced that it had ordered the FBI to investigate all the attacks against Arab Americans under the Civil Rights Act. And though Ronald Reagan did not visit with Norma and did not hug Norma while Nancy Reagan kissed her, as the president and first lady had done with Klinghoffer's widow, his spokesman did say the president "extended his sincere condolences" to Alex's family.

With Christmas approaching, Norma was sinking further into mourning. She and the girls had finally returned to their home to live, but she couldn't bring herself to buy a tree. Alex's sister then brought her a large pine, and since Norma could not bear to see it all the time, she took it to the girls' room instead. She did not weave any lights through its boughs, or hang glass balls from its branches, or offer any gifts by its trunk.

Two days before Christmas, a man knocked on her door. He was a Palestinian man whom Norma had known as Alex's friend. With him he had brought bags of gifts—almost a hundred different things for the girls. He explained that several of his friends, all Palestinian men, had pooled their money together to buy the toys, books, and clothes.

"I just want you to know we're always here for you," the man told Norma. "And we wish you Merry Christmas." Norma had to pause; the man was Muslim, and in fact all those who contributed the money for the presents were Muslim.

On Christmas Eve, Norma stood outside Sami's house and wept. When she went home that night, she still refused to sleep in the bed that had been hers and Alex's. Since returning home, she had slept on the couch in the living room, though sometimes she slept with the girls in their bedroom. Regardless, she always left the living room lights on through the night, to scare off anyone thinking about bombing her home.

Six months later, with no arrests or indictments in the case, Norma's mother came from Jifna to stay with her widowed daughter. Norma had prepared the bed in the room she had not entered since fetching Alex's final suit; her mother would sleep there. When it came time to kiss each other goodnight, Norma began to approach her daughters' bedroom door.

"No," her mother told her, "come into this one." She pushed open the door to Norma and Alex's room and went in.

Norma hesitated outside the door.

"Come," her mother said. "I'll sleep with you."

That night Norma lay beside her mother, and for the first time since Alex's murder, she slept through the night. The next morning, her mother dressed the girls, pulling their black hair back into long ponytails, and walked them to school while Norma slept in.

Within a year of Alex Odeh's murder, the FBI indicated that four suspects—all of whom had dual Israeli/American citizenship and were JDL members—had fled the United States and were living in the West Bank settlement of Kiryat Arba.

ADC continued to organize on the grassroots level, but Arab Americans came away from 1985 believing that not only would they have to suffer ignorant stereotypes in popular culture and a hostile foreign policy, but also that if they tried to participate in American politics, they would risk death. Many of the post-1965 immigrants, still feeling insecure in their relatively new citizenship, came to believe that there were conditions and limitations on that citizenship; they could dream of financial wealth and success but should not fathom having impact on foreign policy in the Middle East nor influence on how Arabs or Arab Americans were represented in pop and media culture. Many learned this lesson and responded with simmering silence.

While the acts of the JDL extremists had been perpetrated by private individuals, several state actions bolstered these beliefs.

In November 1986, the Alien Border Control Committee at the Department of Justice circulated a document entitled "Alien Terrorists and Undesirables: A Contingency Plan." The plan proposed building a detention camp in a remote area of Louisiana to hold such "undesirables" until they could be expelled. The mayor of Oakdale, George Mouwad, told ABC's Nightline that it would be "good for business." His ancestors had come to the United States from Lebanon.

Then, in the dawn hours of January 26, 1987, in Los Angeles, FBI and INS agents arrested seven Palestinians and one Kenyan for pass-

ing out pamphlets and fund-raising on behalf of the Popular Front for the Liberation of Palestine (PFLP), a secular and socialist organization that formed the second-largest faction in the PLO after Arafat's Fatah. The group came to be known as the LA-8. After a ten-month investigation turned up no evidence of illegal actions, the FBI turned the case over to the INS, which initiated deportation proceedings. The INS dusted off the McCarran-Walter Act, which made it a deportable offense to distribute literature advocating communist principles. (The last of the cases would not be completely over until October 2007. None of the individuals were deported.)

For those Arab Americans who had emigrated from totalitarian regimes where dissent was not tolerated and people were disappeared or imprisoned without cause, the act was a clear sign that they should keep out of politics.

In another indication to both Arabs and Arab Americans that U.S. policy in the Middle East was operating on many levels, President Reagan acknowledged to the American people that his overtures to Iran to free hostages being held by Shiite groups in Lebanon had "deteriorated" into an arms-for-hostages deal, whereby proceeds from secret U.S. arms sales to Iran were used illegally to fund Contra rebels in Nicaragua. The United States, however, continued to support Iraq and its leader, Saddam Hussein, in the ongoing war with Iran.

One victory was to be had. That May, the Supreme Court held in the case of Saint Francis College *v.* Al-Khazraji *that Arabs could avail themselves of the protections of §1981, federal legislation which protects people from discrimination on racial grounds.*

In 1986 and 1987, 29,588 Arabs immigrated to the United States. The largest number proportionally (5,879) came from Lebanon, given the continued war; nearly 6,000 each came from Egypt and Jordan, the latter including those who came from the West Bank and the Gaza Strip.

Bound

I n March 1987, Omar Dajani and some friends at Presidential Classroom thought it would be a great idea to seal their weeklong friendship by smoking marijuana together in one of their rooms at the
Omni Hotel in Washington, D.C.

The whole week had been incredible. Omar had been selected by his
high school in Tyler, Texas, to participate in Presidential Classroom, a program that brought high school students from across the United States to
the nation's capital for an up-close civics education. Over the week, Omar
had met members of Congress and lobbyists and had heard presentations
at think tanks and nongovernmental organizations (NGOs). Even better, he had gotten to know other high school seniors from all around the
country who were going to be attending top colleges like Princeton, NYU,

Columbia, Stanford, and West Point. A lot of them listened to the music of bands like the Violent Femmes and Public Image Limited, bands most of the kids back at Robert E. Lee High School in Tyler didn't really know, though Omar did. Most of all, he was just thrilled to be outside of Tyler and its world.

He really liked the guys he had befriended; there was David from a posh New York suburb, Bub who went to a military academy in the South, and Pedro from Puerto Rico.

Friday was the last night of the program, and their last night together. On Saturday, they would all be returning to their regular lives. David, who had gotten some pot FedExed to him at Presidential Classroom, suggested, "Let's smoke."

Omar had never tried any drugs before and was curious. Earlier in the week, during the mini-seminars on problems in high schools, Omar had lead the session on fighting drug abuse because back in Tyler, as president of the Key Club, he had organized "Say No to Drugs" activities at his school. In Tyler, kids were doing a lot of Ecstasy and cocaine, which scared Omar, but pot just never seemed as bad.

David had rolled a joint, and they were passing it around. Omar was not feeling any effects, but he was having fun. They were singing along to the music and laughing when someone knocked on their door.

David ran to the bathroom and began flushing his stash down the toilet.

Their college-age chaperone had come by to reprimand them about the noise and told them to keep it down. Then noticing the smoke, he smelled *it*, gave them a look, and repeated slowly, "Keep it down."

But on the heels of the permissive college kid, a parental chaperone stuck his head in and asked, "What's that smell? Have you boys been smoking marijuana?"

Omar and the guys looked at one another, but no one said anything. What could they say?

"You need to be honest," the chaperone said. "It's obvious what you're doing." They were then ordered to pack up and head down to the infirmary.

As they gathered their belongings, they hurriedly conferred and decided that while they would have to admit what they had done, they all agreed to say that Pedro had *not* been involved. They had the collective notion that he should be protected because he was *Puerto Rican*—Omar learned only later that Puerto Rico was basically part of the United States.

Down in the infirmary, they were shown seats on one side of a table. Four adults sat across from them; they had been awakened and assembled at 2:30 in the morning for the mini-tribunal.

The adults were angry; this was the first year where there had been no disciplinary incidents whatsoever until this stunt. They wanted to know, "Why would you do something like this?"

David offered, "We love the program, you did so much to link us together, it was hard to say good-bye, and we thought this would be a great way to stay awake."

"Look at Bub," one of them said. "He's not awake, is he?" Bub was in fact falling asleep in his chair, though he had been dancing in his underwear on the heater not an hour earlier.

The adults proceeded to lecture them on the dangers of drugs.

Omar decided to intervene. "I just wanted to say for whatever it's worth, I was chosen to lead the seminar on fighting drug abuse earlier this week." He wanted to signal that he knew how bad drugs were.

"Do you think that's going to help your case?" a woman said.

Neither Omar nor the other guys said anything after that.

The adults took a moment to confer, then announced that they would have to send a letter to each of their parents and principals letting them know what had happened.

"You guys are lucky we're not calling the police," one of them said. "In the past, students have had college acceptances revoked for less than this."

Omar started to panic. Oh my God. My life is over! He had already been accepted to Northwestern University early, and he was planning on attending that fall. Everything he had worked for was finished.

The next morning his uncle who lived in Virginia picked him up. Omar was staying the weekend in town. He decided to call his parents to preempt the letter. He expected his father, who rarely yelled, to scream at him for becoming a drug addict.

When Omar told them what had happened, his father listened, then responded, "Well, you're curious. But," he added, "this was really not a smart decision."

Omar was thrown by his father's calm reaction.

"What are you going to do?" his father continued.

"I don't know," Omar said.

"You have to be proactive and go talk to your principal," his father said.

Omar returned to Tyler Sunday night. On Monday, the first day of "Say No to Drugs" week, which Omar was also coordinating, Omar went into the office of Principal Billy Hall and asked to speak with him.

Principal Hall was a devout Christian who made a habit of measuring students' shorts, making sure that they conformed to the rule that clothing not be more than an inch above the center of a student's knees, lest they suffer punishment. Serious infractions, such as drinking or fighting, could earn a kid a few licks of the paddle his assistant principals were known to wield.

Omar explained to Mr. Hall what had happened at Presidential Classroom.

Sitting behind his desk, Mr. Hall looked at Omar somberly. He said in the accent everyone in Tyler had, except for Omar's parents, "Oh-mar, I wanna commend you for your honesty and forthrightness in talking to me about all of this. But you have to realize that, even though boys can be boys—I know, I have a son myself—this act cannot go without retribution."

Omar felt complete dread.

Mr. Hall continued, "I will have to give some thought as to the appropriate punishment. Come back on Wednesday with your mom and dad."

Omar agreed and began to get up.

"I trust you haven't told anyone else," Mr. Hall added.

"No," Omar responded.

Mr. Hall seemed relieved. "I think it's best you not tell anyone about this."

Later that night at home, Omar and his parents looked through the behavior policy in the school's manual. They read there together that if a student were caught with alcohol, it would result in an automatic expulsion.

His mother's initial calm gave way to panicked exclamations of "Oh my goodness! What did we do wrong?"

Realizing Omar was freaking out himself, she tried to comfort him, "It's okay, *habibi*. You will go to junior college next year and live with us, then the next year you will go to Northwestern."

The last thing Omar wanted was to get stuck in Tyler, even if in the last two years of high school, things had finally taken a turn for the better. Before then, life had basically sucked in Tyler.

Omar was born in Tyler, but six months later, his family had followed his father's job with a Texas-based engineering firm to London, Beirut, and then Athens. Because he had been born in Tyler, he had been known as Omar "Tex" Dajani in the company's family directory, and his father's colleagues had always called him "Tex." Omar had taken pride in the fact that he was *from* Texas. When the family had returned to Tyler when he was eight, Omar looked forward to being where his roots were and fitting right in.

At the elementary school in which his parents enrolled him once they arrived, the students referred to him as the smelly Greek kid. In the following years in Tyler, he had come to hate everything about himself, not just the way he smelled. In fifth grade, he had developed a curl in the middle of his forehead, which had rapidly spread across his scalp. No matter what he tried to make his hair straight again, it stayed frizzy and ridiculous. He hated that his skin was dark and that his nose was gigantic. And when his spindly legs and arms had begun to sprout hair, he had been horrified. He couldn't stand that his name was "Omar," or that his middle name was "Mahmoud." He hated how smelly their food was—he was utterly repulsed by hummus—and hated the fact that somehow he was associated with the bad guys, like terrorists and dictators. As if all that weren't bad enough, his parents refused to show off any of the wealth they had, or fake any they didn't; being rich, or being perceived to be rich, was really important in Tyler, and his parents just didn't get it.

And the reason for all this misery, as far as Omar could tell, was because he was Arab. It messed with his DNA, it meant gloomy foreign visitors to their house, and it was even the reason his parents wouldn't drive fancier cars, join the golf club, or buy Omar the Ralph Lauren Polo shirts that he insisted were way better than the shirts sold at Dillard's. Because his father had been made a refugee from Palestine when he was sixteen and his family had lost all their belongings, he lived with the possibility that it could all disappear again. Although Omar wanted him to lighten up and spend a little, his father believed in saving.

Omar found the whole Palestine thing to be a drag. He really didn't care about Palestine. What was the point of obsessing over and pining for a place long lost? The Arab world seemed stuck and backward to Omar, and he was very relieved to be living here instead. The last Omar remembered of the region was when his family fled Lebanon in 1975, after the outbreak of war, effectively ending his parents' efforts to ever make a home for the family in the Middle East. But he figured he knew what the place was about from having had his cousin, Tayeb, live with them. Only a few years older than Omar, Tayeb had come from Egypt in Omar's freshman year to attend Tyler Junior College—home of the Apache Belles Drill Team!—before matriculating to a better university in the United States.

Tayeb always walked about with a *kaffiyyah* wrapped around his neck, using Arabic flourishes that seemed strangely formal to Omar. Instead of just saying a simple *shukran*, thank-you, Tayeb always had to say *shukran jazeelan*, and he never hesitated to add a *rahmit Allah* or a *bismillah al-rahman al-rahim* when he could. Omar was annoyed by the way he spoke, structuring even his casual conversation into introduction, argument presented, support, and conclusion.

Back in Cairo, Tayeb had been driving since he was twelve, but in Tyler he had to take driver's ed before he could take the license exam. Once he had, he bought a car—not a Mercedes or a BMW, but a Fiat. And the first day Tayeb had the car, Omar's dog—prone to car sickness—barfed all over the back seat, while Tayeb drove fast and swerving as if he still were in Cairo. Omar felt utterly humiliated when Tayeb would show up at Robert E. Lee to pick him up in a junky little car that smelled of dog vomit. With Omar's friends in the car, his A-rab cousin would deliver lectures on everything from liberating Balestine (why couldn't Arabs learn how to say "P"?) to how Taco Bell was superior to Burger King because Mexican food was derived via Andalusia from Arabic cuisine. Refried beans, Tayeb would explain, were descended from *ful*—fava beans—and tortillas from flat Arabic bread.

Omar just couldn't stand how his cousin delighted in how much more of an adult he was than anyone else his age. He would show this most readily to Omar, who was literally a captive audience, like when Tayeb told him about his experiences with women. He had tried to educate Omar about how to seduce women and what to do should Omar ever find himself alone with one, even instructing Omar how to stroke a woman's hair gently.

Omar hadn't even kissed a girl yet, and his prospects then were looking dim. Tayeb's alleged popularity with the opposite sex frustrated Omar, who blamed his limited success on being Arab and how different it made him from everyone else.

But then in his junior year government class, Omar had discovered that according to a test of political leaning, he was a liberal, even though he had been describing himself as a Republican all these years, because everyone in Tyler was. He also got into alternative music. So he had decided "the heck with it," he would be different, but on his own terms. He embraced what he thought it meant to be a liberal: he taped to his binder a Levi's ad picturing a Soviet girl wearing a fur cap with a red star with the caption "She Loves Levi's, Lenin, and Led Zeppelin," wore fashions unlike anyone else in Tyler, and shaped his hair to emulate the Cure's lead singer. After all, making himself deliberately ugly was different from *being* ugly.

And finally he had found a group of friends whom he loved dearly. They were all a little bit funky and different, and they had fun together. But Omar still wanted out of Tyler and did not want to screw it all up now.

On Wednesday, Omar and his parents went to Robert E. Lee to meet with Mr. Hall. Before they finished the perfunctory greetings, Omar's parents started apologizing profusely. "It's not like Omar," they assured Mr. Hall. "We are so sorry," and Omar could see that they really did blame themselves.

"Mr. and Mrs. Da-Johnny," Mr. Hall began, "I wanna tell you that Oh-mar is one of the top students in our senior class. We are very happy to have him here, and his behavior has been exemplary. I would hate something like this to ruin a promising career."

Everyone was a bit reassured.

"And yet," Mr. Hall continued, "I think you will agree this sort of thing can't go unpunished."

Now they were all a bit worried.

"What can we do?" they asked.

"Oh-mar." Mr. Hall turned to him to share his verdict. "I have arranged for a guy to speak at the Rotary Club tomorrow, a physician who had sunk to an all-time low because of his drinking and drug addiction. And he has written a self-help book with Christ's help."

Omar was not sure where this was going.

Mr. Hall continued, "I want you to meet this guy who overcame his addiction through the salvation of our Lord the Lamb Jesus Christ, and I think that you should go with him to hear him speak at the Rotary luncheon tomorrow and then spend some time with him alone.

"I've decided to bring him to school tomorrow afternoon to speak at the 'Say No to Drugs' assembly that you have helped organize in part, and I want you to introduce him. I'm going to hold you on probation for what you've done; and if I hear anything that lets me think you're experimenting anymore, your punishment will reflect both incidents. Best thing for now is to learn and listen."

Oh thank God, Omar was relieved. He would not be expelled.

Omar's parents also seemed quite relieved. The Dajanis were not born-again Christians, but they were not about to jeopardize Omar's seemingly light sentence with that detail. It was Tyler, and after all, *they* were the different ones, so they were willing to be accommodating, especially in these circumstances.

The Dajanis were also not particularly religious. Omar's father, Mahmoud, was Muslim, and his mother, Ninon, was the daughter of a French woman who was Catholic and a Syrian man who was Alawi. She considered herself a Muslim, but would every once in a while slip into churches when they were empty, light a candle, and pray to the Virgin Mary. And no one in Tyler had ever bothered them, though a sweet classmate of Omar's—a Southern Baptist girl who sat in the back of French class with him—had been trying to convert him with brochures ever since she had asked him, "Are your parents Islams?"

Omar had corrected her, then "No, they are Moslems."

She had admitted she was worried about Omar and wanted him to find Christ. He had managed to gently brush her off back then, but the next day, after the meeting with Mr. Hall, he happily went to his intervention-instead-of-expulsion. Before hearing the saved doctor speak at the Rotary Club, Omar spent an hour with the tall and tanned man, listening to him talk about what he had gone through.

"I thought I was all powerful, Oh-mar. I was prescribing drugs, taking cocaine in my office, and I was having crazy sex with nurses," the doctor confided. "Only later did I realize I was nothing, just a sinner, and only then could I overcome the drinking and the drugging."

Omar had not known "drugging" was a word. He thought the doctor was essentially cheesy, and nothing like himself, but the threat of expulsion scared him straight.

A few weeks later, Omar was visiting his friend Stephanie. Her mother came up to him and took him aside. Referring to the town gossip, she said, keeping her voice down, "Oh-mar, I just wanted to tell you that rumors are spreading about you. They say you were caught smoking pot."

Omar felt a flush of embarrassment burning at his cheeks.

Stephanie's mom continued, emphasizing that she knew "there was just no way that Knee-none and Ma-mood's son would do anything of the kind."

Omar arrived at Northwestern University in the fall of 1987 with three major goals: 1) becoming a confident, cool, urban intellectual—a person with culture, wit, and interesting liberal friends from places like New York; 2) falling deeply in love with a beautiful and sophisticated girl; and 3) becoming a liberal political advocate.

Nearing the end of the fall quarter, he hadn't had so much luck yet on the girlfriend, nor with becoming a liberal political advocate, mostly because he still wasn't really sure what that meant, though over the summer he had attended a demonstration in Washington, D.C., against nuclear weapons and actor Martin Sheen had been there too!

But on the friends front, he couldn't have been happier. At the center of his new group were Jen and Lissy. They were from Philadelphia and

Cleveland, respectively, which for Omar were closer to New York than Tyler was ever going to be, and he was completely charmed by them.

Jen told hysterical stories about her grandparents Rudy and Adele that made Omar cry from laughing while Lissy told them about her warring parents and how her sarcastic mother needled her father. At the core of their stories, of who they were, was a self-deprecating yet wholehearted embrace of their being Jewish—idiosyncrasies and all. The girls talked about what being Jewish meant, and subsequently the group would discuss ethnicity. They were curious and asked people, "Where is *your* family from?"

Omar had never had such conversations back in East Texas; in Tyler, there was "black," "white," and "Mexican." There was no category for him. At Robert E. Lee High School, the black kids were bused in and were never in the gifted classes to which Omar was assigned, and there were barely any Hispanic kids in his school. Everyone around Omar was white, so he just tried to fit in with them. But the whites in Tyler were blond and had straight hair, unless it was permed, and they had names like Tiffany, Mandy, and Jason unless they were Oh-mar or the Indian girl in his grade, Indu. In Tyler, Omar had no notion that there were different ways to be white.

The world of curly-haired Jen and Lissy, on the other hand, could accommodate other categories. To see white people possessing the warmth he associated with Arabs, behaving with foibles, having grandparents who also bought smelly foods, did crazy things, and seemed "not so American" in the Tyler sense of the word, was really familiar to Omar. And yet, they were so exotic.

There was something a bit thrilling in being around the people—Jews—whom modern history had made Arabs' "Other" and whom Omar vaguely understood to have been part of his family's own tragic history. He had some understanding that Palestinians had been displaced by Jews. He knew that his father's family—who had centuries-old roots in Jaffa—had been forced to flee by fishing boat to Syria in April 1948, subsequently losing their lands and home with the founding of Israel. So meeting Jewish Americans was charged for Omar. It was electric in part because there was a taboo in it, but mostly because Omar didn't expect the connection to feel so powerful, to feel bonded to these friends on so many levels.

For Omar, it didn't seem that his being Arab was an issue or constrained their friendships. While everyone in the group identified as

Democrats, the group was not particularly political. The fact that they were each connected to peoples who had been locked in conflict for the last century was just fodder for jokes, like when Omar first met his roommate. Kent, who was also Jewish, had been raised in Indiana and knew much more about basketball than about Judaism or Israel. Together, they decided to decorate their door in the colors of the Arab-Israeli conflict and jokingly named parts of their dorm room the Gaza Towel Rack and the West Closet. It was their shtick, and they used it when they introduced themselves to everyone the first few weeks of school.

So Omar was caught off guard when, in December after returning home to Tyler for winter break, Palestine intruded on his life, and he found himself actually paying attention. On December 8, 1987, an Israeli army tank transporter ran into a group of Palestinians in the Gaza Strip, killing four and injuring seven.

The thirty-mile-long, six-mile-wide strip where 650,000 Palestinians were packed, many in impoverished refugee camps where sewage passed through open troughs in the street, was a powder keg ready to be lit. Since the initial four deaths, the Palestinians had been demonstrating against the Israeli Occupation daily, and each day a few more were being killed.

At home, Omar watched the daily violence with his father. The last time Omar had seen his father this engrossed by the events over there had been when he had sat tensely in front of the TV watching coverage of Israel's invasion of Lebanon.

Omar now was taken by the images that he saw. Young kids were throwing rocks at armed Israeli soldiers—with only the strength of an arm or aided by a slingshot—taunting the soldiers to "Kill us all! Come and kill us all or get out!"

The soldiers often answered with real or rubber bullets, and Omar was struck by the sound of gunfire ricocheting off the stone edifices that were Palestinian homes, schools, churches, mosques, and offices.

When he returned to campus for the winter quarter, he continued to follow the events, most closely in the *Daily Northwestern*, the school paper. He found himself getting more and more angry. The paper ran AP wire stories from the region on a daily basis, and in addition, staff reporters covered a protest of Palestinians at the Israeli consulate in Chicago. A staff photo showed the image of a little boy on the shoulders of a teenager, flashing a peace or victory sign and brandishing a toy gun. Four days later, the *Daily* published a letter from a fellow student, the president of the Northwestern Israel Public Affairs Committee (NIPAC). In it, Jonathan Barrish wrote:

> The picture that you published in the *Daily* on Friday, Jan. 8, is an excellent illustration of the problem Israel faces in solving the Palestinian issue. The picture showed a child attending a rally who was making the victory sign with one hand, and holding a toy gun in the other. Until the attitude of violence on the part of the Palestinians (as exemplified by the toy gun) is replaced by one of peace, there will never be a solution to this vexing problem.

Omar read the letter and thought, how manipulative! To seize on a little kid and his toy gun when it was Palestinian kids being shot at! He sat down and immediately penned a letter, hoping it would at least get published.

The letter ran the following day.

Omar had directed his letter toward both the staff of the *Daily* and the NIPAC president. In it he wrote:

> As an American of Palestinian origin, I am both appalled and offended by the bias with which your newspaper has dealt with the Palestinian issue.
>
> Throughout this last week, items have appeared highlighting Arab rioting and stone-throwing. However, only once, and then in passing, did you mention the reason for this rioting. Is it not significant that Israel is actively and forcibly deporting a great number of Palestinian people from the only home they have ever known? How many Americans, faced with a similar situation, would not react in much the same manner? This issue surpasses, or should surpass, national or ethnic loyalties; this is a matter of human rights.
>
> Next I would like to address Mr. Barrish's contention of a Palestinian "attitude of violence." His ludicrous basis for this assertion is a toy gun in the hand of a young boy. How many men on

this campus or, for that matter, in this country can honestly say that they never possessed or played with a toy gun in their youth? Conversely, the headline "Violence no route to peace" should be a message to the Israeli army, which has just recently murdered more than 25 Palestinians. I have a difficult time believing that an 8-year-old boy or a 65-year-old man poses any sort of threat to one of the most powerful militaries in the world.

The United States government, as part of the United Nations, for the first time has condemned Israel for this inexcusable violence. It is beyond my comprehension how both the *Daily* and Mr. Barrish can so easily overlook it.

In January 1988, Omar finally lost his virginity to the prettiest girl in his dorm, realizing his goal of having sex before his eighteenth birthday.

Then shortly after his letter was published, Jonathan Barrish called Omar.

The fighting between Palestinians and Israelis had made its way further onto the Letters pages of the *Daily*. Some of the letters were addressed specifically to Omar, and during a service at the Hillel Center, a rabbi expressed concern about anti-Semitism on campus, naming Omar Dajani as an example.

Omar had been unprepared for the reaction.

Barrish had written an entire editorial in the *Daily* asserting that, being familiar with the Israeli political and social system, he knew that Israel had the resolve to put an end to the pointless bloodshed and hatred for peace. What was needed, he had written, was an Arab leader willing to follow Sadat's example. According to Barrish, "History has shown us that when an Arab leader makes peace with Israel, she is more than willing to meet them halfway. The way I see it, the ball is now squarely in the Arab and Palestinian court, but unfortunately for humanity, the score has been deuce for a long, long time." And then ten days later, the *Daily* had published another one of his letters to the editor about the situation.

Over the phone, Barrish told Omar he had read his letter and wanted to challenge him to a debate on the Israeli-Palestinian conflict.

One on one. No press.

Omar thought the bit about "no press" was funny—who would want to cover a debate between two college students?—but agreed to the duel.

As soon as he hung up the phone, he freaked out; he had basically exhausted his full knowledge of the situation in his letter and had not really relied on any scholarship but rather on emotion and the sort of rhetorical tactics he had learned in debate club. If he were to actually face this guy and not look or sound like an idiot, he needed to know way more about the story of Palestine.

Unlike other Arab-American or Arab families that Omar had encountered, his was not particularly obsessed with politics nor were they always talking about how much better "over there" was than "over here."

His father had dreamed of coming to America even before being forced to leave Palestine. His desire grew stronger while he was in Syria, where he had landed after Palestine. There he had been denied access to the best opportunities because he was Palestinian and not Syrian. In America, he had been able to put himself through college working at a hospital in Chicago and had always believed that anything was possible in this country if one worked hard. Omar's father once told him he had walked by a jazz club while visiting New York City, just after he had arrived in the States, and he had stopped and listened from outside. In that music, modern and exciting to his ears, he felt all the potential of this new country. And peering in at the elegant people—Americans—seated around tables covered with white tablecloths, he looked forward to being one of them.

When Omar's mother arrived and joined her husband, she came to love the country immediately. In Chicago, they had a diverse group of friends, Americans and newly arrived immigrants. She always laughed telling her children that she had crossed the Atlantic in first class aboard an Italian ocean liner with forty pairs of shoes to come live in a tiny basement apartment for two years that were the best years of her life.

In addition, Omar's mother was utterly distrustful of the Arab world after having gotten stuck for two years in Syria when she visited with her mother in Latakya with two of her American-born children. The Syrians had confiscated their passports and insisted they were "Palestinians." Omar's mother had left the States pregnant with twins, and when the stress had caused her to go into labor early, both babies had died as a result of the lack of optimal medical care in the small Syrian coastal town.

Yes, Omar's parents loved America and believed their children's future was here. They worried about Omar compromising himself by getting too wrapped up in the Palestinian cause. His father had explicitly told him, "If you want to contribute, become successful in America as an American, then you can try to make a difference in Palestine."

Notwithstanding his parents' concerns, Omar did not want to make an ass of himself at the debate. He reached out to his father's old school-mate from Jaffa, Professor Ibrahim Abu-Lughod, chair of the political science department at Northwestern. The professor lent him a few books and explained to Omar the difference between cities and lands lost in 1948—like Jaffa, where his father came from—and lands occupied in 1967 after the June War.

Omar read and read and read. He became increasingly incensed, thinking to himself, this can't be real. Why hadn't he known all this before?

His father had told him only the smallest part of the story—his family's part—of leaving Jaffa in 1948 on a fishing boat, thinking they would ride out the fighting in safety. They had thought they were coming back; they had no idea they would be forced to leave it all behind. His family had set out for Lebanon but landed in Syria because her shores were sandier, settling on the coast in Latakya. There he had met and fallen in love with his wife. Now Omar understood the greater course of events to which his father's history belonged.

Finally, Omar felt prepared to do battle. Then, the debate was can-celed. The NIPAC president had contracted mononucleosis.

But Omar's interest had already been piqued, and he continued to read about the past and follow the present on TV, in *Newsweek*, and in the *Daily*.

He found the Palestinian protesters to be brave and decent. These were not the gunmen and hijackers who had for so long personified the Palestinian cause. They were teenage boys and girls, professors and stu-dents, strong men and women. Omar felt thrilled and proud to be con-nected to them and felt a sense of movement; after years when it seemed that Palestine was a lost cause, suddenly there was something imperative about it. Something had to be done to stop the Israelis, now that the real-ity of their occupation had been revealed.

During his spring quarter, Omar watched a special episode of ABC's *Nightline*, broadcast from the Holy Land and featuring four Israelis and four Palestinians. Like many Americans, Omar was introduced for the first time to Hanan Ashrawi, a Palestinian woman and professor from Bir Zeit University in the West Bank. He thought she was amazing, and he was thrilled that she—and not some "terrorist"—was being presented as the face and voice of Palestine. He thought that this was someone with whom he would be thrilled to be associated. Omar felt so hopeful—the story was getting out!

At the dining hall with his friends, Omar chatted excitedly about what he was learning. They had never talked about it all—being Arab, being Jewish, both implicated in events half a globe away—in a serious fashion, and Omar sensed some discomfort. The conversations once prompted Jen, who had family in Israel, to comment, "Oh, but that's political, let's not talk about that," as if Omar had broken an unspoken rule that they wouldn't invite topics that would divide them as friends. Since they had different views, it was better just not to talk about them.

Toward the end of spring quarter, at the age of eighteen, Omar decided to travel to the Middle East for the summer. He had not been since he was eight years old, and he hadn't been particularly interested until now. His friends were superexcited for him, and his parents were happy that he would be connecting with his family overseas.

He was also looking forward to having an adventure and expected he would have to rough it; he remembered being a kid in Syria and grossed out by not being able to flush toilet paper down the drain and having to put it in the wastebasket instead. But that would be more than made up for with seeing the pyramids and other remnants of the ancient world that existed across the Middle East.

To prepare for the trip, Omar bought several books and practiced his father's elaborate system for avoiding pickpockets. It involved putting his money in a handkerchief and safety pinning it to the inside of his front pocket. He also went shopping with his girlfriend Mary to buy clothes for his trip. They decided to hit Banana Republic because, as Omar and Mary reasoned, the store would have appropriate attire for a safari, or a trek through the bush, or his trip to Egypt and Jordan.

They combed the racks and pulled aside khaki pants to buy. And they found the exact kind of shirts that they had come to the store seeking. One was the color of rust and another of a blue breathable material—perfect for an Arab summer—each with the label's characteristic gentlemanly adventurer epaulets buttoned at the slope of the shoulders.

From the plane circling above Cairo, Egypt looked to be color of pulverized red bricks. As soon as Omar walked off the plane, he smelled burning wood. Waiting for him in the airport was his cousin Basma, Tayeb's sister. Their father, Omar's uncle Ahmad Sidqi, had sent his car and driver to bring Omar back to the apartment building where Omar's uncle and grandmother lived.

Omar was amazed when he noticed that the car had diplomatic plates. He knew his uncle was a member of the executive committee of the PLO, but he hadn't thought of him as a diplomat, though now it made sense. Omar realized that, here, the PLO was regarded differently than in America, where the umbrella organization of all the different Palestinian political parties was associated only with Arafat, who was utterly despised. Here, as the representatives of a people, of a nation, the PLO deserved and had legitimacy, and someone was a diplomat, not a terrorist, for being affiliated with its leadership.

The driver, Abdelrahman, a Saidi from the south of Egypt, was positively horrified that Omar—the nephew of Ahmad Sidqi!—spoke no Arabic.

But no one spoke Arabic in Tyler, Texas. Omar's parents only occasionally spoke it to each other, a decision they had made after his mother—newly arrived from Syria speaking Arabic and French, but not English—bought fifteen cans of tuna fish on sale at the grocery store. When she proudly showed them to her husband, he asked when they had acquired a cat, looking over the tuna-flavored cat food. They had agreed from then on to speak only English so she could learn the language. So Omar knew very little Arabic.

Abdelrahman drove the way Tayeb did, speeding through the crowded streets of Cairo to Heliopolis or *Masr il-Gidida*, New Egypt, a well-to-do neighborhood in the Egyptian capital.

Omar had last seen his grandparents in 1983, when they had come to visit; since then, his grandfather had died, during Omar's senior year. When the news of his death had arrived in Tyler, Omar had petulantly demanded to be able to play tennis and not have to stay inside—he didn't really know these people living across the world anyway. His mother had chastised him then, "Be considerate of your father's feelings."

Now when his grandmother saw him, she hugged and kissed him and immediately pulled him to the dining table to eat the meal she had prepared. She was a tough woman who ran a strict household. She had been illiterate into her forties, when she had her husband teach her how to read so she could read the Koran; through the force of her will all her children today had graduate degrees. But she spoke no English, so she and Omar used food as their dialogue. She would say, "*Ahlan! Ahlan-wa-sahlan,*" welcome, welcome, and Omar would respond with what he had learned was the correct response, "*Ahlan fiki.*" Then they would stare at each other and she would say again, "*Ahlan! Ahlan!*" and Omar would again repeat his line. Then she would ask him in Arabic if he were hungry. He would nod, and then with relief she would start laying out food and smile, beaming, as he ate.

She spent the next four weeks feeding him.

His cousin Mehdi took charge of his social program—he taught Omar how to ride horses, and they galloped around the pyramids at Giza at sunset. Mehdi introduced him to friends who had houses on the Nile, and all together they spent afternoons on the riverbank for long picnics. Behind their grandmother's back, Mehdi would take him to KFC and Chili's for a break from her labored dishes like *sayyadiyyah* and *ma'lubeh.* He was surprised how cool his cousins were; both Mehdi and Basma had been student body president at the American University of Cairo. They took road trips outside of Cairo together, made jokes, and teased one another; Omar loved shocking them with alternative songs like Berlin's "Sex."

On his own, Omar spent hours wandering in Cairo with his guidebook. He was fascinated by the loud, crowded, layered city. He meandered through the labyrinthine alleys and bazaars of the Hussein district, the medieval city, learning its Fatimid and Mamluk history and comparing their architecture. He loved the ornamentation of the buildings of the Mamluks, the slave soldiers who had come to rule Egypt and Syria. The craftsmen of that era had chiseled the stone with unimaginable skill, rendering it to look as delicate as lace. He particularly adored the Sultan Hassan Mosque, which had been built in the fourteenth century. The massive walls that surrounded the *sahn*, a mosque's courtyard, hid modern Cairo from sight, and for a moment it felt like being in another time. He could see how the mosque's beautiful, silent simplicity underneath the open sky could move a heart toward the heavens.

He loved the shopping and bought the girls back at school silver necklaces and bracelets. He even began to hear beauty in the ever-present music that he had hated before. He began to appreciate Um Kalthoum—the original Arabic diva who always sang in her oversized dark glasses, waving her handkerchief as she sang to the entire Arab world for over fifty years. When he was younger and drove on family vacations to Florida, he would protest so when his father wanted to play her tapes in the car—Omar wanted Duran Duran. As a compromise, his father would play one of Omar's songs and then one of his. The problem was, a Duran Duran song was four minutes long, while Um Kalthoum would go easily for an hour singing the same song.

Abdelrahman would drop Omar off and pick him up, shouting as he drove the Arabic names for things and pointing to them. Omar learned to answer with a smile Abdelrahman's daily "*Izzayyak?*"—How are you?—with a very practiced and very Egyptian "*Miya Miya!*"—100 percent!

Egypt was nothing like the desert fantasy he had expected when he bought his safari gear from Banana Republic. But it was nonetheless seductive, with its crowds awake and out late at night; Omar found a whole region of late night people like himself. He loved the sweetness of the people—the way men touched each other unself-consciously, the endless little endearments like "*ya habibi*," "*ya hilu*," and "*inta bitnawwirna*"—oh my love, oh handsome, you light us up—that peppered the most casual of speech, and the hospitality, particularly among the poorest of the poor, who spared nothing to make him feel welcome.

What he loved best were the long walks he took with his uncle, arm-in-arm around the Merryland park beneath the apartment building where they lived. Unlike the conventional wisdom he had learned in Tyler, where one never talked about religion, politics, or sex, his uncle spoke as if they were all wrapped up in one. He was handsome—tall and slender with brilliant white hair. He was also a scholar and gentle, thoughtful, and interesting. He knew all the heads of the Arab states intimately and was much more involved in the Palestinian struggle than Omar's father had been. He also had met with many European leaders, including Pope John Paul, and Omar's mother kept a picture of their meeting on her vanity in Tyler.

With Arabic speakers, his uncle spoke only in *Fusha*, the classical Arabic of the Koran, and he spoke it to everyone from heads of states to shopkeepers to drivers. His Arabic was famous, and Omar finally understood who Tayeb had been trying to emulate.

Omar learned from his uncle about his family's history—they had been judges, landowners, officials, and *qadis* in the religious courts in Jaffa. He had known that his father's family, his family, had gone back centuries to Jaffa—he had looked through the book *Before Their Diaspora*, and had found the old pictures to be beautiful—but now his curiosity was aroused. His father had always lamented that when they left in the fishing boat they hadn't even brought the photographs, and now Omar found himself grieving for them as well.

Omar's uncle had broken with Arafat in 1984 and had never been a member of Fatah, Arafat's party. Speaking to him completely shifted Omar's understanding of the Palestinian movement, and the people involved in it. Instead of associating it with Arafat—who seemed to Omar as thoroughly unwholesome a face for the Palestinians as a person could imagine—he now thought of his uncle and his humanism.

From Egypt, Mehdi and Omar traveled to Jordan and stayed with relatives there. They were joined by family that came from the West Bank. Omar found it amazing to meet someone from his own family still living in Palestine! Even as he began to follow the events in the Occupied Territories, in his imagination Palestine had been almost fictional, with no form. He felt an incredible sense of family—they had come from all over the Diaspora, but they were all Palestinians, they all still knew who they were. He listened with anger as his cousin from the West Bank told him about life under the Occupation and how the Israeli soldiers—just kids themselves—treated Palestinians in their interactions.

Together they traveled to Petra—the ancient rose-red capital of the Nabataeans–and the Dead Sea. As they approached the lowest point on Earth, Omar noticed all the signs about security zones, and then before he knew it, he saw Jerusalem's twinkling lights in the distance. Oh my God, he thought, there it is. There is the land of Palestine.

Northwestern seemed so far away, and Tyler even farther. But he couldn't wait to tell Jen and Lissy and the others about it all. He had sent postcards to all of them and had bought gifts for each one. But most of all, he could barely wait to share with them when they all returned to Northwestern for the new fall quarter how great and idiosyncratic *his* world and *his* culture were as well.

The first Palestinian uprising, or Intifada, frequently made the American news. With little context provided, the images seemed another example of Arab irrationality and violence, tendencies exhibited even by the adolescent and teenage Palestinians participating daily in the demonstrations against Israeli Occupation.

At the same time, the children of the Arab immigrants who came to the United States in the late 1960s and 1970s were coming of age and, like their parents, were also watching the same images coming from the Middle East.

Some reacted by detaching themselves from the region, becoming "closet Arabs," opting for less-offending monikers to account for their difference, like Phoenician, Coptic, or Arabian, or passing for other ethnicities, like Italian, Greek, Puerto Rican, or African American. Others saw bravery in the youths' actions and decided it was time to embrace their identity as a means to reclaim it.

The different generations—parents and children—had to navigate the right balance of Arab and American ways in their lives. For some this was more difficult than for others. The most extreme example and one that horrified Arab Americans was that of Palestina "Tina" Isa, an Arab-American teenager murdered by her parents on November 6, 1989, in St. Louis, Missouri. They claimed to have killed their daughter, an honors student, because her American ways had dishonored their family.

But with the Intifada, members of many generations saw an opening to begin to offer a counternarrative from a Palestinian perspective, as the Intifada forced the world to pay attention to the actual residents

of the West Bank and Gaza Strip as opposed to the PLO leadership liv-
ing in exile. Arab-American groups organized trips for Americans to
the region.

The uprising in the territories also forced the United States and
Israel to seek ways to have diplomatic relations with the PLO. In Stock-
holm in November 1988, Yasser Arafat met with five American Jewish
leaders, with the full knowledge and support of both the American and
the Swedish governments. The meeting was aimed at finding a formula
that would enable the United States to begin dialogue with the PLO
and for the PLO to meet U.S. conditions for such a dialogue. Two days
of talks produced a statement that recognized Israel, called for a two-
state solution of Israel and Palestine, called for negotiations under the
auspices of an international conference based on U.N. resolutions 242
and 338, and rejected terrorism as a tool of either non-state or state
actors.

Indeed, other long-standing conflicts seemed to be coming to a close
in many places. In May 1989, the Red Army began withdrawing from
Afghanistan after eight years of fighting, and Iran and Iraq accepted a
cease-fire in July. In February 1990, Nelson Mandela was released from
prison in South Africa, after twenty-seven years behind bars, while in
October the Lebanese Civil War finally ended.

On July 25, 1990, Saddam Hussein met with the U.S. ambassador
to Iraq. He complained that Kuwait was slip-streaming oil from Iraqi
oil fields. The U.S. ambassador made vague references to the United
States "not taking sides" in intra-Arab disputes, and Saddam Hussein
invaded Kuwait on August 2, 1990. Kuwait fell quickly to the Iraqis, but
the Kuwaiti royal family established a government-in-exile in Saudi
Arabia, while hundreds of thousands of Kuwaitis fled to several Gulf
countries.

In these years, 57,547 Arabs came to America in the hopes of find-
ing home.

PHOTO ILLUSTRATION ALIA MALEK

Under Suspicion

D ays after the bombs first fell on Baghdad on January 16, 1991, Farah Nabulsi stood at her freshman locker in Laketown High School mentally rehearsing the steps her jazz dance instructor was choreographing to Janet Jackson's "Escapade." Every day, she tolerated the six hours of the school day until she went to Stephanie's School of Dance and thought that if she just lived from dance class to dance class, she might survive Laketown High—the only high school in Laketown—until graduation. Her mother escaped the small midwestern town every year when she traveled back to Jordan for the summer, taking Farah and her sisters with her. But her mother's getaway was a forced march that Farah hated, a trade of one prison for another. Farah found the temperatures in her mother's native country suffocating, and because of the

149

hungry stares of men on the street, she could not wear shorts and short sleeves.

The absences from America each summer cost Farah long-lasting friendships at school. Her disappearances from June to August led her classmates to forget she had just been there from September through May, and they would ask her on her return from Jordan: Does your family there have camels or cars?

Farah's mother would try to mend the hurt by explaining that she felt like a tree that had been removed by its roots and replanted where it could never grow. She felt alive only in Jordan, and only there did Farah ever see her mother laugh.

Even though Farah blew out her long, black, curly hair straight, opted for cafeteria food over her mother's cumin-scented leftovers, and starved herself to lose her Arab curves, when the bombardment of Baghdad began, she could not help but care. Her father's fixation on the nightly news finally seemed relevant to her. She would have asked him so many more questions, but her older sister, Sawsan, was always by his side these days, and their conversations appeared impenetrable to her—Farah simply did not know as much as Sawsan did about politics.

Farah reached into her locker to change books for class. Her classmate Laci approached her, flanked by two other girls. Farah had felt a natural kinship to Laci when they were younger. In a sea of white, blonde-haired, blue-eyed girls, Laci was a buoy, her Thai features unmistakable. But after Laci had pinned her down on the floor of the bus at the beginning of fourth grade when Farah had returned two weeks late from Jordan, Farah felt any kindness from her was tenuous.

Laci's white mother let her do all the things that Farah's mother forbade, like attend slumber parties and stay out late. But Farah had her father's white skin and hazel eyes, and Laci always seemed determined to prove that Farah's difference should be the more offending one. With Farah's locker door barely separating them, Laci hissed, with her hands on her hips, "My brother might die in Iraq because of you."

Farah could not find or form any words, and wondered if she should apologize. Though she was surrounded by many from her freshman class, no one else said anything either. Farah did not speak for the rest of the day and avoided Laci in the cafeteria, in the halls, at the lockers. She did not even tell her parents what had happened. Farah wondered, could she dance away the three and a half more years in Laketown?

Every day of the war became the same. Her sister Sawsan would ride with friends to school, Farah would take the bus, and the entire family became Laketown's personal Iraqi enemy. One morning, on Farah's way out the front door, rushing through the foyer with the marble floor which gave way to the living room with its Victorian-style furniture, she saw an aluminum baseball bat propped against the wall behind the door. When she asked her mother where it had come from, her mother told her it was a gift from one of her father's patients.

February 9, 1991, was supposed to be a brief respite from the nightly vigil Issam Nabulsi had been holding in front of his television ever since the United States had begun bombing Baghdad. His thoughts were never far from family left behind sixteen years ago in lands caught in between those countries that fired Scud missiles and those that responded with the Patriot kind.

Saturday would actually be a forced day of rest because it was his wife Zayneb's birthday. They planned to drive that night to Bloomington, Indiana—what he considered the kitchen of the country—to celebrate with dinner before joining the girls back at home for cake. Issam was already looking forward to what he knew he would order: he was a prime rib kind of man.

He woke up early enough to have his coffee, check on his patients at St. John's and County Hospitals, and still be home by noon. He stopped at his mailbox on the street in front of his house, the only house not flying an American flag. The flags had gone up overnight as soon as the United States began dropping bombs less than a month before on Baghdad. In the kitchen, he sorted the mail, instantly recognizing junk mail and bills. He stopped at a plain white envelope with no return address made out to "Dr. and Mrs. Nabulsi." Issam thought it was likely a letter from a patient. He opened the letter and read it, turning it over in his hands, and thought, "Do I need a gun?"

Issam handed it to Zayneb and thought about the words written out in cursive: *We know what to do with you Saddam-lovers.* Zayneb began to cry.

Issam always said racism brought him to Laketown. He had been heavily recruited by a hospital in a larger town when he was still just a résumé. But when the hospital realized the hot new physician out of Madison, Wisconsin, was not a "real" American—though Issam considered himself the biggest Badgers fan east of the Mississippi—the offer and the recruiter evaporated.

When he and Zayneb visited Laketown, a town of less than 10,000 on little more than four square miles, they thought it was quaint. Issam liked the lake, even though it was man-made, a remnant of the days when the state used an intricate system of canals to move people and goods. In desperate need of a pediatrician, the town made him a generous offer, and the Nabulsi family made the move.

Had it been a mistake to come to Laketown? he thought now. The only different faces were the handful of other "foreign" doctors also serving this factory town, a population that American-born doctors had long shunned. What other accommodations should he make? He had learned to smile each time an American mispronounced his first name and consoled all of them with this offering: "You can just call me Sam," as if it were his fault for being different.

The menacing letter had not been the first; he had received at least another ten between the house and his office, but this one was the first that made him fear for his family's safety. There had also been the not-so-opaque threats "to leave town" lobbed at his family in the "Letters to the Editor" section of the *Laketown News* every few days. And his secretaries and patients kept him in the loop about the rumors making their way around Laketown: his wife was snatching yellow ribbons from houses and his son was fighting in Baghdad against the Americans. What could Issam say? He was *"Abu al-Banat,"* the father of girls, and had five daughters, each one an unfulfilled hope for a coveted son.

These rumors cost him several patients, up to one hundred for all he knew, who preferred to take their children to a general practitioner rather than an Arab pediatrician. Issam had held on to the idea that this would pass and rationalized it benevolently; after all, Americans were living in fear that Saddam would use chemical weapons and there were predictions that up to 50,000 American soldiers could die.

For the first time, on his wife's birthday, he considered leaving Lake-town. But where would he go? To where he had been born? Though his parents still lived on their farm in the West Bank, it was now under Israeli occupation. He would not let his daughters live as second-class citizens because they were born Christians instead of Jews. One of the Arab coun-tries? Never: the rulers were antidemocratic dictators.

The best option was to move somewhere else in the States, and this time he would tell people they were from Poland or Romania. But what about Zayneb's skin color? They could say she was Mexican and if immi-gration bothered them, she was already a citizen. As he thought of any potential harm coming to his daughters, he realized dinner in Indiana was too great a risk. Going anywhere farther than a ten-minute distance from the children was impossible to consider. Dinner with Zayneb, a break from the war—the prime rib too!—would have to wait. They would stay in Laketown for dinner and would instruct the girls not to leave the house. Issam would not buy a gun.

But first, he went to Kmart and bought two baseball bats. One he kept under his bed and the other by the door.

Zayneb Nabulsi was the Arab bitch of Laketown who stole the yellow rib-bons off patriotic Americans' trees, lampposts, and mailboxes in the mid-dle of the night. Sixteen years ago, she had been just Zayneb Najaar of the Shmaysani neighborhood in Amman, and she never imagined she would live anywhere else.

But she learned to smile at the people of Laketown, and when her daughters told her mothers *were supposed to* bring cookies to their class-rooms on their birthdays, she bought dozens from supermarkets and sent them in Tupperware. And though she refused to open presents on Christ-mas morning wearing her pajamas the way they did in Laketown, prefer-ring the Arab tradition of opening gifts on Christmas Eve respectfully dressed, she did hang stockings on her mantle and filled them, much to her daughters' delights.

She did not tell the people of Laketown that even their supermarkets screamed at her that she did not belong, with their endless rows of shelves and products, selling cucumbers with milk with Tide with clothes. Each of these was an item bought from a separate store in Jordan, a separate relationship cultivated with a separate shop owner.

Only if they asked her "What was it like?" would she tell them that she missed how the breezes in Jordan were dry and comforting, not humid and stifling like in Laketown. Even if green were more fertile, she preferred the caramel color of Jordan's dusty desert land because it was home. She did not tell them in Laketown that she lived from summer to summer, when she could go to Jordan and wear a jacket on cool July nights.

When her mother called her from Jordan and asked her if there were any black people where she lived, she told her, "Just me, there's no one darker than me in Laketown, Mama."

In 1991, she did not tell her mother she was scared that their neighbors might kill them, that these Americans hated anything foreign, and looked at her with hatred and a look that asked: Who are you to have what you have? If they would have listened, she would have answered: Didn't my husband serve your community, hold your hands when your children were sick? Didn't he heal your children and not ours in Palestine and Jordan? Didn't we give you our dreams?

She did not tell her mother that now others, immigrants like her, and even those born here, were coming home across America to find their houses burned and their shops attacked. She did not tell her of the rumors of the camp in Louisiana where they would put them all. And she told only God that she hoped all this might be the push it took to convince her husband to finally take her home.

When her friends told her she was the Arab bitch who stole the yellow ribbons, as if she stole with them their lives, she laughed at the absurdity. What else could she do? Her daughters were here, and they were all now part of America.

By the night of February 12, 1991, Sawsan Nabulsi, age eighteen, had a will that was no longer her own. She sat by her parents in their living room, and no matter where she moved or how she fidgeted, her eyes remained fixed on the television a few feet in front of her, though the true horizon was Iraq. Baghdad's early morning was eight time zones away, and she watched in disbelieving horror as rescuers and weeping families dug charred bodies—many decapitated and limbless, many clearly children—from what Iraqis claimed was a bomb shelter and which the Americans had taken out with precision-guided smart weapons.

Sawsan thought, if this is what the American press is showing, how bad must it really be?

Her daily ritual had been fixed once the bombs began pounding Baghdad. Her life as a senior at Laketown High School was bookended by evenings in front of CNN, a nightly communion with the Iraqis. Their nights became her days and their days her nights, and so she never slept. The war was all she could think about, and her thoughts became a series of calculations: How crowded is that area of Baghdad? How many people can live in that kind of building? How much warning time do they have before their homes, neighborhoods, relatives become collateral damage? How many could make it to the bomb shelter? Who would be left behind? Who would be incinerated? How many tonight?

Her reaction surprised her. Ever since the eighth grade, she had been sneaking out of the house to share a can of Milwaukee's Best or stealing her parents' ouzo out of the liquor cabinet and refilling the bottle with water after drinking it down with her friends. She had thwarted her mother's many efforts to teach her how to read and write Arabic, and whenever her mother complained or criticized the United States—"Yil'an abu 'l-balad," Curse the father of this country—Sawsan would immediately defend America.

Even though Sawsan loved the summer trips to Jordan where she finally had a *teta*, a grandmother, she never left America without throwing a tantrum for being taken away from her life. And though she would never let her mother know, Sawsan secretly understood what her mother meant when she compared herself to an uprooted tree that could never grow.

Now, experts emerged everywhere in Laketown, regurgitating with conviction truths about Iraq, Kuwait, and the Palestinians and possessed of a moral clarity that absolved them of any remorse. Such a luxury was denied to Sawsan; she was cursed with too much knowledge. She knew that Iraqis looked like her *teta*, aunts, uncles, and cousins in Jordan, and that they all just wanted to get by. Every conversation outside her house, from the classroom to the cafeteria, became about correcting every misconception or mistruth from Iraq to Palestine, from liberation to occupation. But propaganda was as rampant as the yellow ribbons she saw everywhere, which to her had become a symbol endorsing the wanton death of innocent people. She wanted those troops to come home and to stop killing.

While Sawsan knew there were other voices of dissent in Laketown, they did not have Arabic names or speak with Arabic accents. They did not get the stares in public that followed them around town. Just recently, when she had gone with her sisters to Wendy's for takeout, the other patrons stopped eating their burgers and fries and stopped sipping their Frosties at the sight of the five Arab girls. They just stared at the girls until they ordered and left.

Watching the headless mothers and faceless daughters on TV now, Sawsan felt tears streaming down her face, and the fist that had formed in her stomach in January punched at her from the inside. Her parents sat calmly beside her; war was not so new, from the Palestinian dispossession to the civil war in Jordan. They had already spent so much empathy during the Lebanese wars and the Iran and Iraq war. Her mother, upset that Sawsan was so upset, was of no comfort. Only her father could console her, telling her, "Don't let this get to you. You're strong. You can handle this."

Both parents suggested she stay home from school the next day. Sawsan tried to sleep, losing track of when she was dreaming and when she was watching the TV in her bedroom. In the dark, whether it was the TV screen or the screen against the insides of her eyelids, she saw the same images.

That morning, dressed in her sweats, unable to contemplate breakfast, she consumed more CNN and read the *Christian Science Monitor* and the *Washington Post*. Before noon, the school called to check on Sawsan. In all the years of Nabulsi children going to school, no one had ever done that.

Sawsan's mother came to the couch where her daughter was sitting. The school was worried about Sawsan because that morning the assistant principal and her social studies teacher had spent two hours with the Secret Service, her mother explained. The agency had been tipped off by a parent of a student in her study hall that Sawsan had threatened to kill President Bush. The agents refused to disclose who made the call, but they insisted on being granted access to Sawsan. Her principal refused, and the agents, realizing the threat was baseless, told the school officials, "You run into this once in a while, especially when people get emotional about people of Arab descent."

When Sawsan's father returned home, he told her, "These hillbillies are going to do what they're going to do. Don't worry about it."

On March 3, 1991, American and Iraqi military leaders met on the battlefield to discuss the terms of cease-fire. The next day, a boy came up to Sawsan and asked her, "It's over now, are you happy?" She thought about it; in fact, she had felt instantly better. A ground war would have been twice as bloody for both sides.

Suddenly, everyone in Laketown remembered Issam did not have a son, only daughters.

A year later, the local florist confided to Zayneb that during the war other clients had threatened to boycott the shop if she kept selling flowers to the Arab bitch.

And Farah, who had started to speak Arabic at home, swept the talent portion of the local beauty pageant with her dancing, winning the entire competition on her way out of Laketown.

The First Gulf War and its aftermath had several effects on the Middle East. Iraq was effectively neutralized as a regional power. The attempted overthrow of Saddam Hussein by Shia and Kurds was brutally repressed, and the sanctions put in place since the summer of 1990 severely restricted the medicines and food available to Iraqis. Many Iraqis left their country; in the years between 1991 and 1995, 11,080 immigrated to the United States.

Because of its participation in the international coalition that fought Iraq, the United States acquiesced to Syrian dominance of Lebanon as it emerged from fifteen years of war. The south of Lebanon remained occupied by the Israeli army, and while the other Lebanese militias disarmed, Hezbollah in the south did not. But despite the end of the war, Lebanese immigration numbers remained consistent.

Also at the end of the Gulf War, the international context for negotiating peace in the Middle East changed dramatically. Iraq's defeat by a coalition of European and Arab countries allayed Israel's fears of future Iraqi attacks. Because of its support for Iraq in the war, the PLO was isolated by several Middle Eastern countries. Saudi Arabia and Kuwait cut off aid to the PLO, and other Middle Eastern states expelled Palestinian workers. Meanwhile, the accelerating disintegration of the Soviet Union reduced Cold War tensions that previously had complicated Middle East peacemaking efforts. In fact, the United States and the USSR together pursued an Arab-Israeli peace process, under the auspices of the Madrid Conference, which convened on October 30, 1991. It was attended by its two sponsors as well as the governments of Israel, Egypt, Jordan, Lebanon, Syria, a joint Jordanian-Palestinian delegation, and representatives of the European Community.

The goals of the conference were to launch bilateral peace talks between Israel and bordering Arab states, multilateral talks on key regional issues like refugees, and talks between Israelis and non-PLO Palestinians on five-year interim self-rule, to be followed by talks on permanent status issues.

Israel decided, however, that for peace to occur it needed to engage in direct talks with the PLO. Thus the Oslo negotiations were set in motion in January 1993. In August 1993, the Israeli and Palestinian chief negotiators initialed a deal, and on September 13, 1993, President Clinton subsequently hosted a formal signing ceremony at which Israel's Prime Minister Yitzhak Rabin and PLO Chairman Yasser Arafat shook hands on the White House lawn. Shortly after, in July 1994, Jordan and Israel also signed a peace treaty, ending a forty-six-year official state of war.

The Oslo Accords were a pivotal milestone in Israeli-Palestinian relations, aimed at propelling the peace process forward and providing for the expansion of Palestinian self-rule throughout most of the West Bank. The PLO recognized the existence of the State of Israel and Israel recognized the PLO as the legitimate representative of the Palestinian people. Israel committed itself to withdrawing from parts of the Gaza Strip and the West Bank and acknowledged the Palestinian right to self-government in those territories under a Palestinian authority. During a five-year interim period, a permanent peace settlement would be negotiated.

This time was seen by Arab Americans active in foreign policy issues as a breakthrough, when they were called upon to actualize their inherent potential as a bridge between the United States and the Arab world. It also looked to Arab Americans that maybe the conflict that they felt was responsible for their conditional status in America was drawing to an end. Indeed, Yasser Arafat would become a frequent fixture over the next few years at the Clinton White House. Soon, the evening news might focus on another part of the world; in fact, attention was turning to the disintegration of Yugoslavia, the crisis in Somalia, and the Rwandan atrocities. Arab Americans finally watched the news without feeling implicated by it every day.

However, new threats to American hegemony were emerging, namely the rise of Islamic fundamentalism. Indeed, religiosity was on the increase in the region, and immigrants coming from the Arab and Muslim world in this time were increasingly less secular. The new Amreeka was less homogeneous than it had ever been.

But notably, a long-passed member of the old Arab-American community was recognized on Memorial Day weekend of 1991. President Bush, members of the community, and several prominent American writers gathered to dedicate a national monument on federal park land to Khalil Gibran, the Lebanese American who told other Lebanese and Syrian Americans in 1926: "Be proud of being American, but also proud that your fathers and mothers came from a land upon which God laid His gracious hand and raised His messengers."

A total of 121,721 new Arabs arrived with the hopes of becoming American.

Then on Friday, February 26, 1993, a massive explosion at the World Trade Center—in which six persons were killed and more than 1,000 injured—announced the arrival of fundamentalist terror on American soil, which was new for America, but hardly new for the Middle East.

PHOTO COURTESY PRIVATE COLLECTION OF RABIH ABUSAHAN

Coming Out

"God hates fags."

On October 17, 1993, Rabih AbuSahan panicked at the sound of the chanting crowd. He had parked off campus at Wichita State University in Kansas and far away from Ahlberg Hall, where a gay rights activist would be speaking. He didn't want anyone who could recognize him to realize he was attending the lecture, and he had not counted on protesters. Though there were only some twenty of them—including children—they were disproportionately loud as they confronted anyone who walked near them. They guarded the main entrance with placards that didn't equivocate:

FAGS = AIDS

HATE IS A BIBLE VALUE

SODOMITES ROT IN HELL

Rabih began to turn around. He was afraid that if he hesitated they would know he was not just a casual passerby. Even though the protesters did not seem to notice him, he could not risk being mistaken for a homosexual. He was convinced being perceived to be gay would jeopardize his immigration status, and he wasn't even gay. Not really gay.

Before he moved to Kansas just that summer from Waterloo, Iowa, he had lived with Tom only because Tom had pushed him into that situation. Rabih had always wanted a child, and living with Tom let Rabih parent Tom's infant son during those three years. If anything, Rabih told himself, he was bisexual, though he resented being boxed in by any labels. Besides, with Tom being HIV positive and Rabih terrified of contracting the disease, they never had sex.

"God hates fags."

Rabih wasn't ready for this; he had no idea how to answer their assaults, even though they were the same taunts he had aimed at himself for the last three years. He agreed, God probably did hate fags. Rabih hadn't found anything yet in the Koran that said otherwise, or that would assuage the guilt he felt for having the feelings, cravings, and sex that plagued him. And as someone who had bachelor's degrees in both pharmacy and biology, with a minor in chemistry, Rabih was convinced that what he was doing *was* scientifically wrong—what was the point of non-reproductive sex?

He decided to walk back toward his car and go back to where he lived an hour away in south-central Kansas, in Hutchinson, a town of barely 40,000. He simply wasn't ready. Rabih did not have the argument built to answer these hecklers.

Yet as he turned to leave, he thought about what waited inside the building and past its venomous moat. Inside, he might learn not just the arguments to forgive himself, but he might even learn that he wasn't such an aberration after all. Inside, he might find a community to which he could belong, a community that was more than just bars and sex.

Rabih decided he would circle the hall; there had to be another way in. He walked away from the building's front entrance toward the side nearest him. Rabih was relieved to see two doors. He approached the one nearest to him and yanked. It did not move. He went on to the next one and pulled but found it locked also. What should he do?

He calmed himself down and walked around to the back of the building, looking for an entrance. But there was none, just a solid wall of unforgiving bricks.

Continuing around to the other side of the building, he spotted two more doors. One would have to be open. It would make no sense for all the doors to be locked. He took hold of the knob on the first door; it did not yield. He neared the second, thinking "This is it." He tugged at the handle. The metal refused to give way.

Rabih would have to go *through* the line of protesters if he wanted to attend the talk. No, he had no choice but to go back to Hutchinson— remote, isolating, lonely Hutchinson. He had to admit, there was a part of him that did want to get physically closer to the picketers and hear what they had to say, with the hopes they would be able to utter something about his deviance that would convince him with conclusiveness, elusive conclusiveness, that he had to abandon his ways. But walking through the front door would mean exposure. He would be exposed not just to the protesters but also to those he was living in secret from, hiding from. Those who he thought were watching him. Those whom he had convinced himself were the U.S. government. In his deepest paranoia, he even feared sometimes that they had cameras in his home and could see with whom he was sleeping, even see when he was whacking off. They would never let him become a citizen if they could make a case that he was gay.*

And yet, there was the possibility he might find some version of home inside the lecture hall. Could he ever be more than just an outsider? Ever since he had arrived in Iowa from Lebanon in 1985, when he was eighteen, he had been an outsider—from the foods he liked to the language he thought in to the dark hair that covered his limbs and chest in this land of flaxen and bald-bodied Midwesterners. His sexual desires

---

*Until 1990, homosexuals were banned from immigrating to the United States because they were considered immoral. President Bush signed the 1990 Immigration Act which removed the ban. However, this information was not disseminated by means that would necessarily have reached all gay immigrants, particularly those closeted and living in small towns.

further cast him out from the heterosexual norm, and the places he found in the States where his sexuality was accepted—from the adult bookstores where he cruised for the first time in Iowa to the gay nightlife scene available in cities—still left him empty and wanting more.

The bars were not for Rabih—he did not drink and not because he was a particularly devout Muslim; rather, he wanted clarity of mind. And he didn't have the stomach for the danger involved in finding anonymous sex in public places. Soon after moving to Kansas, he had gone riding at night through Carey Park, cruising for sex, only to be followed by a gang of men in a car that shone a flashlight in his face and called him queer. The incident had convinced him he needed to seek out another side of the gay world, what Rabih thought of as an intellectual side that focused on politics and human rights.

Ever since moving to Kansas just a few months before, to force a breakup with Tom, he had set out to nurture this intellectual side in all ways, taking classes at Wichita State in philosophy and poetry. He convinced one of his professors to give him access to the just-developing Internet, and there Rabih sought out information on what additional gay scenes existed. Online, he read about today's talk at Ahlberg Hall. Scott Nakagawa, head of the National Gay and Lesbian Task Force's "Fight the Right" project, had traveled to the university from Portland, Oregon, to deliver a lecture on gay rights. Rabih had been looking for a place where he could be himself, and when he learned of Nakagawa's appearance, he believed he might have stumbled on a community that could make him feel he was normal and that he belonged.

But the vociferous protesters outside were members of the Westboro Baptist Church in Topeka, a chilling presence in Kansas. From his pulpit at the church he had founded, the Reverend Fred Phelps, a disbarred lawyer and unsuccessful gubernatorial candidate, condemned homosexuality, preaching that God hated homosexuals. Phelps's infamy spread far beyond the back rows of the faux Tudor house where he delivered his sermons, however, when in 1991 he began picketing the funerals of Kansas men who had died of AIDS. His followers shouted that their loved ones deserved to die as mourners said their final farewells.

Rabih had also heard that Phelps faxed the workplaces of HIV-positive men who worked in health-care fields, warning that they would contaminate the blood supply. Whether or not this was true, and even though Rabih was not HIV positive, he worked as a hospital pharmacist and was terrified of anyone there thinking he was gay.

Rabih was convinced he had no choice; he had to return to his car and get away from this place, and get away fast. As casually as possible he stepped away from the locked side entrance and began to walk toward the front of the building, intending to continue to his car, coming within fifteen feet of the protesters.

As he did, he listened more closely.

"Fuck you, you fucking fags!" they yelled at anyone coming in or out of the building, regardless if they were just passing through. They had focused their attentions on the newspaper photographer, calling him "fag" repeatedly.

Rabih was shocked at how vulgar they were. There was nothing religious about "fuck you." Rabih heard nothing as to why God hated fags, nor was he struck by any religious insight; they were just bashing people. Rabih had already called himself all these names, there was nothing new here.

There was nothing intellectual in their arguments, no moral high ground, Rabih thought to himself. He was reminded of the militia men he'd seen growing up in his native Lebanon, hiding behind their Kalashnikov assault rifles. Rabih's father had taught him that the power of those men was derived solely from their guns. The power of Phelps's followers was more in Rabih's head, he realized, than in reality. Rabih could go to his car and be defeated by all these vulgar and obscene people who seemed incapable of making a real argument. Or he could find *his* normal. If he could just get to the staircase and up to the main door behind them, he would make it.

He looked straight ahead, avoiding all eye contact with the Phelps people—who had closed in on the photographer—and approached the main entrance. He thought of himself being like an antelope, sneaking past a pack of lions devouring a zebra. He slid by, holding his breath as he approached the door, pulled it open, and made it inside.

The auditorium was a small space with steeply sloped rows of seats. As Rabih began to descend, allowing gravity to speed him forward, he stopped suddenly as he spotted video cameras poised at the ready in a pit at the center of the room in front of the stage. Should he leave?

No, not after having come this far. Rabih looked around; maybe he could find a seat as far out of the lenses' range as possible. He chose a seat in the back and to the extreme right, up against the wall. He made sure to leave the "gay seat"—the seat straight men leave in between themselves in movie theaters so no one would think they were gay—between him and the man already seated in that row.

There were almost 150 people at the lecture; they were young and old, gay and straight, male and female. Rabih waited with the anticipation that something great might soon happen.

As Nakagawa took the stage, Rabih was comforted to see another gay man who was also a member of a racial minority. Nakagawa spoke for more than an hour, telling the audience that though religious conservatives were relatively small in numbers, they posed a large threat to freedom. He said that the influence of the Religious Right had exceeded their relatively small membership of fifteen million supporters because of organizational savvy and "stealth" candidates who would win office without stating their true agenda.

Rabih listened intently, taking notes. Whenever a video camera pointed his way, he used his notebook to hide his face, so there would be no proof he had been there.

"Be clear that, as you're confronting this movement of the Religious Right wing, that you're confronting a movement that's part of a permanent counterinsurgency in the United States," Nakagawa warned. "A permanent counterinsurgency to democratic values and the hope for the establishment of a true gender-equal and multiracial democracy in the United States."

Nakagawa told the audience that despite the efforts of the Religious Right, he remained hopeful that the movement's anti-gay campaign could be defeated if activists convinced the public that the rights of all groups were threatened when gays' rights were attacked.

Rabih felt his eyes were being opened and that he could finally identify an enemy—no longer was it biology or religion—but *these* people that were making him "not normal." They had a face, finally.

After the talk Rabih lingered, waiting for the safety of the herd to leave the building. A man seated several rows in front of Rabih approached him and introduced himself as Rob. He was a community activist in Wichita and invited Rabih to join him and friends to continue the conversation over some midafternoon pancakes. Outside, Phelps's people had already moved on.

Later that night, back in Hutchinson, Rabih reflected on the afternoon as he got into bed. He turned off the lights and slid under the covers. Before he could drift into slumber, he kicked off the sheets, turned the room's lights back on, and whacked off.

On June 26, 1994, wearing a T-shirt that declared in bold red letters "LEBANESE," Rabih marched up Manhattan's First Avenue with the Nebraska, Kansas, and Iowa contingent at the International March on the United Nations to Affirm the Human Rights of Lesbian and Gay People. People from all over the country and world had come to commemorate the twenty-fifth anniversary of the Stonewall Riots, considered by many to be the beginning of the gay rights movement in the United States.

On June 27, 1969, New York City police had carried out one of their regular raids on a gay bar, the Stonewall Inn, in Greenwich Village. They often harassed the customers and arrested transvestites. That night the patrons fought back, hurling beer cans, bricks, and anything else in reach at the police, who responded by beating many of the protesters and arresting dozens of others. The standoff escalated to five days of rioting by hundreds of people.

Rabih had agreed to go to the Stonewall 25 commemoration only because the World Cup was going on at the same time; otherwise, how would he explain to his coworkers, friends, and family that he was going to New York City the same weekend a major gay rights event was taking place there? The march on the UN was going to make the news—even if in Kansas, just for the novelty of the mile-long Rainbow flag that was going to be unfurled at the event. Rabih didn't want anyone to put two and two together, even though he was dying to be a part of what he considered such an important civil rights event. The World Cup and his love of soccer gave him plausible deniability.

Rob was on the committee organizing the road trip from Kansas to Stonewall 25. He assured Rabih that there were so many people coming to the event that no one would single out Rabih in New York City. The Reverend Phelps, who announced he would also be attending what he called "a threat to the moral fabric of our society," would be on *their* turf and unable to bully Rabih or anyone else for that matter.

Rob even convinced Rabih that no one would bother to watch him when there would be thousands of gay people on the streets that weekend. Rob had been coaching Rabih ever since they had met at the Nakagawa talk, gradually helping bring Rabih out of his furtive existence in Hutchinson. But living in the open did not come easy for Rabih. By the time Rabih met Rob, he had already spent most of his life hiding.

On January 10, 1985, with the situation in Lebanon spiraling out of control, Rabih's parents had packed him off to Iowa State University in the United States, hoping to keep him from the war's sights and from the fate that awaited many Lebanese young men. Those who did not go voluntarily to fight in any of the sectarian militias were otherwise conscripted—some into the ranks of those who sought comfort in alcohol and drugs or worse, others to serve as cadaver representatives of the "wrong" sect, in a tit for tat that in 1985 alone claimed too many lives.

When Rabih's parents told him during his first, brief visit in 1987 how they had hidden his brother from Shiite militia men who had come through their apartment building in West Beirut looking to round up Sunni boys in April of 1985, he knew he had been spared. With only seconds' warning that day, his parents had unfolded the sofa bed in the living room and crumpled Rabih's brother underneath the sofa's bowels. They then sat on top of him, drinking coffee as casually as they could muster, inviting their child's would-be killers to join them when they knocked on their door and demanded if they had any sons.

A scholarship from the Hariri Foundation to attend Iowa State University had kept Rabih safe from war, and he had traveled with eleven other scholarship boys from Lebanon to the Hawkeye State. The night he arrived in Ames on a bus from Des Moines, he found gigantic parking lots—he had never seen a space of paved asphalt as vast as that in his first Kmart—and skies that were tinged blue at night, instead of the yellows and reds that glowed in the bleeding Beirut sky.

When they reached the dorms that first night in Iowa, the boys were greeted by a Lebanese woman named Lina. She had huge breasts and the boys took turns flexing their flirtation. In the diner where they ate that night, they talked in Arabic about the cute girls coming and going and made crude sexual jokes. Rabih felt his cheeks burn in embarrassment. What if Lina or these American girls were their sisters? He figured he never laughed at these jokes or looked at girls because he was just too polite.

Not until five years later, while his girlfriend from college was away in Europe for the summer, did Rabih begin to investigate what he had started to feel and what he had been hiding from—his attraction to men.

He had just graduated and taken a job in Waterloo to stay near his girlfriend, who would not graduate for another year. There, he began visiting an adult bookstore. Under the guise of research for a paper—one he had already written the semester before on AIDS for his class on sexual diseases—he interviewed men, but only if they made eye contact and initiated a conversation with him. Rabih asked them,

"How do you know you are gay?"

"When did you realize you were gay?"

"When did you come out to others?"

"Do your parents know?"

"How does it feel to kiss another man?"

He never let on—or so he thought—that he desperately wanted that feeling himself.

When his girlfriend returned, they broke up. Then Rabih met Tom. Once Tom tested positive—the prerequisite test Rabih had insisted on before they became sexually involved—Rabih would lie in bed, huddled as far away as possible from Tom's skin, hiding from the disease, afraid AIDS would drip onto him from the dewy beads of sweat that glistened along Tom's naked, muscular back. At last, Rabih plotted how he would steal away while Tom was at work, how he would move to wherever the headhunter he was secretly working with was able to place him.

After three years of his asexual monogamy with Tom, Rabih finally got to Kansas, where the first available job appeared. He was determined to have sex, but instead of running the risk of anyone in Kansas learning of his desires, he kept them hidden, driving ten hours each way to Minneapolis every other weekend to meet men. He was afraid to go south, because he had always heard that the most intolerant Americans lived there. Kansas City was too close to where he lived his professional life, and Des Moines was impossible because his adoptive host family lived there.

In Minnesota, he continued to hide from those watching him. Rather than sleep in hotels, which would leave a record of his stay, Rabih pitched a tent on camping grounds, far away from other campers' view, and when he met prospective lovers in the city's bars or bookstores, they would follow him there.

By meeting Rob, Rabih discovered a community that he took steps toward joining, peeling back the protective isolation and loneliness in which he had encased himself.

Almost ten years his senior, Rob had reconciled his homosexuality with his parents and their intensely religious Presbyterian grounding. He was a community activist, involved in many civil rights causes, and could easily talk about homosexuality from a political and justice perspective. He offered Rabih the comfort and safety of a group to go out with; Rabih even traveled with Rob and his friends to Dallas, Denver, and Oklahoma City, the town Rob referred to as having the "highest sluts per capita." The conventional wisdom, Rabih learned, was that if you couldn't get laid in Oklahoma City, you were never going to get laid, period.

Rob had also started a local chapter of a national group, Men of All Colors Together, and soon after inviting Rabih to join, he changed the local name to "Men of All Colors and Cultures Together."

At one of the group's potluck dinners, Rabih voiced how hard it was for him to be what he called a double minority—marginalized from the mainstream because of both his sexuality and his ethnicity.

A black man answered, "Tell me about it."

For Rabih it was as if someone had suddenly turned on the lights in a dark room where all along Rabih thought he had been alone, revealing instead that he was in fact surrounded by many others. Rabih might still be on the outside of the majority of people in America, but he was standing there with a group to which he belonged.

During these exchanges, Rabih heard critical discussions of race and the minority experience in America, conversations he had not had with anyone in his mostly white world of Iowa and Kansas. He attended a lecture by Tony Brown and heard the phrase "Black is beautiful."

The notion that black could be beautiful was revolutionary for Rabih; in Lebanon being dark—which Rabih was—carried a stigma. All around him—TV, the neighbors, his classmates, gigantic billboards—everyone

idolized and idealized blond men and women, considered the oppo-
sites of Arabs. His parents, their friends, everyone in their social milieu
would say "`Arab jarab," which meant "Mangy Arab." The well-to-do in
Rabih's family spoke French, and they all laughed at the Syrians for teaching school subjects in Arabic. At Rabih's school, science and math were
taught in French.

Similarly, Rabih understood that being Muslim was the most Arab
and therefore most backward of all. At his grade school, he was taught by
nuns, who seemed impressed with their own benevolence for staying in
West Beirut through the war and teaching mostly Muslim children, after
many Christian students had fled with their parents to East Beirut.

But unlike how, in Lebanon, socioeconomic class or a French education could mitigate being dark, Arab, and Muslim, in the Midwest, no one
cared that Rabih was well versed in the works of Baudelaire, Voltaire, and
Molière. In the Midwest, Rabih was undeniably inferior, a dynamic only
compounded by America's own homegrown prejudices.

In Iowa, the other Lebanese scholarship boys had told the Americans
they were French to account for their difference; Rabih instead worked to
control his Arabic accent in English. He stopped stressing the "g" of words
ending in "ing." Eventually, he learned to drop the letter entirely, greeting Americans with "What's happenin'?" He also practiced pronouncing
"th" properly, instead of substituting a "z"—"the," not "za," and "they,"
not "zay." He wore baseball hats and stayed clean shaven; with a beard,
his college classmates told him he looked like a terrorist. They also complained about his name and its complicated guttural stop at the end of
"Ra-bee." As a remedy, his first roommate at Iowa suggested, "Let's call
you something else."

Rabih asked him, "What name should I have?"

"You don't look like a 'Rob,' " Larry responded, "so let's go with Rick."

The name stuck until Rabih's next roommate declared "Rick" didn't
fit, and Rabih then became "Robby."

Rabih had initially expected such accommodations—Americans couldn't pronounce his name anyway. But then he read *Robinson
Crusoe* and didn't much like the part where Crusoe declared to the Indian
whose life he had saved that "his name was to be Friday," never making
an attempt to learn his real name though they spent the rest of their lives

together. It reminded him of Kunta Kinte's renaming to "Toby" in the movie *Roots* that he had seen years before in Lebanon. Rabih felt that these seemingly minor changes inevitably lead to a lack of pride and a loss of identity. He decided this Rick and Robby business would not work.

Rabih marveled at how the African-American men he was meeting through Rob were not ashamed to be a minority and how they were openly proud of their race even in a culture where, as far as Rabih could tell, the majority mocked them, called them names, marginalized them, and did not particularly like them.

As a consequence, Rabih decided he would no longer speak Arabic in hushed tones when in public because he was worried about offending others with his native tongue. He began to wear a *kaffiyyah* as a scarf. If his mother could have seen him she would have thrown a fit, chastising him for wearing anything Palestinian.

With gay black men, Rabih also finally found an audience to voice his struggle to reconcile what seemed to be a forfeiture of his masculinity because of his sexual orientation. Rabih never understood the men who dressed in drag. He already felt that being gay was a betrayal of what a man—especially an Arab man—should be. He felt black men also understood and recognized the importance of being masculine, strong, and macho.

And though now at the march on the UN in New York City drag queens were a part of the festivities, Rabih didn't care. Here there was inclusiveness. He felt high, euphoric. Everything was falling into place, and Rabih felt part of something greater than himself, something that could easily drown out the hate of Phelps, the violence of the militia men, and the fear of being who he was.

He looked around at the groundswell on the streets of Manhattan. He recognized another Lebanese man in the California delegation behind him. He had met him the day before walking through the West Village toward the Hudson River. Rabih had heard men singing a song by the Egyptian diva Um Kalthoum. He had followed the voices to a group of Lebanese, Syrian, Palestinian, and Kuwaiti gay men. Rabih never knew there were so many!

As the Nebraska, Kansas, Iowa, and California groups turned the corner into the UN plaza, they came upon the flags of the world's nations floating in the air. Rabih immediately saw the green cedar tree symbol of

Lebanon in its flag. The words "*Kulluna lil-watan lil-`ula lil-`alam*" began to dance across his lips. He then heard himself singing them out loud, the words to the Lebanese national anthem, and another voice from behind him joined:

> *We are all for our nation, for our emblem and glory!*
> *Our valor and our writings are the envy of the ages.*
> *Our mountains and our valleys, they bring forth stalwart men.*
> *And to Perfection all our efforts we devote.*
> *We are all for our Nation, for our emblem and glory!*

On the morning of Wednesday, April 19, 1995, Rabih believed his boogeyman, the war—that animal that had reduced his family to near poverty and seen him exiled to the lonely cornfields of Iowa—had tracked him down in Kansas and after ten years had caught up with him at last.

As always on his day off, he reveled in the laziness of the morning. He slept in, made eggs for breakfast, and brewed tea before sitting down to read the *Wichita Eagle* newspaper. He turned his stereo to 90.1, Radio Kansas, the local NPR affiliate. Rabih regularly listened to NPR because it was one of the few sources for international news that gave him more than just snippets and sound bites. The station played only classical music during the day, and though Rabih didn't particularly care for it, the symphonies and concerts kept him company.

At 10:00 A.M. the station broke from music programming as it did every hour for the NPR news brief. Rabih put the paper down to listen. Today the lead story was not international; it was only miles away. A blast had just occurred in Oklahoma City.

Rabih quickly turned on his TV to CNN. The footage being shown alternated between a shaky handheld camera on the street and one from a helicopter hovering above the victim building. Half of it looked as if it had been sliced away in a dissection. Walls were completely gone and what had not crashed to the ground stories below was left hinged between the structure that once was and the open air that had replaced it. The bottom two floors were pancaked into stacked debris, releasing a black cloud of dust that wafted with the smoke into the blue skies above.

Glass was blown out of windows for several blocks and trees were ripped from the ground and torn apart. The glass shards had traveled far, shredding passersby' clothes and skin. People lay on the ground; some staggered around bloodied; others were being carried away on stretchers.

Anchors and correspondents spoke of reports of more bombs. One commented, "This looks like it's a video from Beirut or something."

Rabih couldn't believe this kind of a disaster was happening so close by, in a place only 250 miles away. And the way it looked, the way it felt, was, in fact, so much like Lebanon.

Rabih had never associated bombings with something that could happen here, that could reach him here, here in America. The 1993 World Trade Center bombing had seemed so distant when it happened, even though he had called his parents in Lebanon then to assure them he was unharmed. He made many such calls with every potentially fatal occurrence that would happen in the United States and that might make the news in Lebanon, whether it was a snowstorm in Maine, a hurricane in Florida, or an earthquake in California. His parents had no idea how big "over there" was.

Rabih had barely gotten used to the Midwest's open spaces. When he first arrived from Beirut's poisoned womb, he always felt vulnerable. American homes seemed so flimsy—they weren't built to withstand a bomb, a grenade, or a spray of gunfire; a bullet could so easily go through this wall and out that wall. In Beirut, people lived in concrete apartment buildings flanked by other similar towers of cement. The closer the building next door, the safer one would feel. In Kansas now, Rabih was again painfully aware how far away the neighboring structures—a hospital to the south, small single-family homes to the north, and a cornfield to the west—stood from his building, a mere two-story complex.

And back was the foreboding feeling that he had brought with him from Lebanon and that was in the recesses of his mind every day in his early years in the States—that *fi shi baddu ysir*—something was going to happen. In Lebanon, they had all grown accustomed to the reality that every day something was out there. They didn't know it yet, but it was happening out there, and it was going to affect them somehow. In Lebanon, they listened to the radio each morning, tuning in to the different partisan stations hoping to piece together where the fighting, sniping, or bombing would impede going to school or work or church or mosque or market—much like how in the Midwest, Rabih saw people obsessing over weather reports so they could dress accordingly. But in Lebanon, Rabih had become used to the futility of planning. So during college, when in January his classmates would ask him his plans for spring break, or when Americans would ask him at Easter what his plans were for the Fourth of July and Thanksgiving, Rabih would answer with a startled "I can't think that far ahead."

With time, Rabih found that the days in the Midwest had a sameness, stability, and predictability that facilitated long-term planning, and he began to adapt. But there were moments when he was disappointed after a while when nothing different ever happened.

Now Rabih perched on the edge of his couch, his face close to the TV, watching the same footage over and over and hoping for any information or details he may have missed the first, second, and third times.

A federal building was possibly the target because the FBI operation against the Branch Davidian compound in Waco, Texas, had been run by the FBI in Oklahoma City. And today happened to be the two-year anniversary of that attack that had claimed the lives of several women and children. But there had been no claim of responsibility yet from anyone.

Soon it became clear people might be trapped, and Rabih obsessed over those he imagined were stuck in their cubicles, pleading for help, though no one could hear them. He wanted to go to Oklahoma City and assist in any way he could. In Lebanon, whenever something similar happened, the men would immediately gather and help—whether it was looking for people in the rubble or donating blood or transporting survivors to hospitals.

Now Oklahoma hospitals were calling for any local certified medical personnel to contact them or to just show up immediately. Rabih had the regular reflexive reaction, "I can help," but he also thought, "Not only can I help, I'm qualified. I can give medicine and counsel and CPR."

But as Rabih continued to watch more CNN, he realized helping would not be possible. One hour into his TV viewing, at 11 o'clock that morning, former congressman David McCurdy was being interviewed by a CNN anchor. Her first question to him was, "Mr. McCurdy, what can you tell us about your experience with this explosion today?"

McCurdy answered, "Well, my first reaction when I heard of the explosion was that there could be a very real connection to some of the Islamic fundamentalist groups that have, actually, been operating out of Oklahoma City. They've had recent meetings—even a convention—where terrorists from the Middle East that were connected directly to Hamas and Hezbollah participated. Now, it's too early to tell, even though one station in Oklahoma City is reporting that Nation of Islam was taking credit. There are others who think it may be linked to the Branch Davidian episode. But I think it's obvious that this is a terrorist attack."

Rabih was shocked. The CNN anchor asked McCurdy how he knew about such meetings occurring in Oklahoma City. McCurdy cited a recent documentary entitled *Jihad in America*, a film made by journalist-turned-terrorism expert Stephen Emerson. McCurdy said that the documentary had footage of "major conventions" and meetings taking place in Oklahoma City, in Norman, Oklahoma, in Kansas City, in Texas, and throughout the Midwest.

The interview was soon followed by news that the Justice Department was treating the blast as a terrorist act, that other sources were saying that law enforcement had found links to terrorism in Oklahoma City, and that a possible connection to Islamic terrorist groups was being explored. By the afternoon, CNN was reporting that three "Middle Eastern–looking" men were seen driving away from the building in a brown pickup truck and the FBI needed help finding them.

Rabih's mother had chastised him when she saw the beard he had grown, a thin one-inch border that traveled his jaw line and ended in a goatee. "Why do you have this Hezbollah beard?" she shrieked when she last saw him in Beirut.

"Mom," he had told her, "this is an intellectual beard," something he had cultivated once he had moved to Kansas, hoping to embark on what he thought of as his intellectual phase. After ten years in America, as different as he felt, Rabih thought his exterior, wrapped up in parkas and baseball caps, blended in, so much so that sometimes his own reflection surprised him when he caught it unexpectedly in the reflective surfaces of buildings on the street.

How could Rabih now go to the site of the blast and help in Oklahoma City, which would be full of government people with guns and dogs, chasing after Middle Eastern–looking men? He imagined that they would say to him, "What are you doing here? Spying? Seeing your handiwork?"

In fact, how was Rabih going to leave his house now that the entire nation was hunting Middle Eastern men?

If only he could get to Wichita. He knew people there, other Arab people—if anyone were to attack him, they could help. There was only one other Arab in Hutchinson, the Lebanese Druze owner of the Taco Bell. He had always been nice to Rabih, giving him free Pepsis. But even though they would greet each other while Rabih waited for his regular Taco Supreme, they were hardly friends.

Rabih wished he could go to Wichita, but he needed gas, and what would he do when he stopped to get some? What would *they* do? If anyone spotted his Middle Eastern–looking face, paying for gas or groceries, they might wait for him outside, ambush him, and beat him. Even though to some, Rabih looked intimidating with his 6'1" frame, 200-plus pounds, and dark complexion, he had never been in a fight his entire life. He had used his masculinity only to seduce other men.

Rabih phoned his friend Bassam. Ritualistically, people in Lebanon would get on the phone when something happened. They would share their accounts, whom they personally knew near the location, who they thought did it, and what they thought would happen next.

Bassam, a graduate student at Indiana University, told him how in the classroom, a professor had angrily discussed what had just happened in Oklahoma City while staring straight at Bassam. He told Rabih that during the hostage crisis in Iran in 1979, people who weren't Iranian but looked Middle Eastern to their assailants were targeted by backlash. Similar things had happened in other times and places, but things had passed, Bassam told Rabih, as a way to analyze the situation instead of panicking. But Bassam agreed that if an Arab had done this, they would be in deep shit.

After the Stonewall 25 events in New York City last year, Rabih had continued to participate in gay activism; he was even involved in this year's planning committees for the upcoming June Wichita Pride Parade. Now, he felt betrayed by America's freedoms.

He reprimanded himself for trusting the culture and the system; he had been cautiously and partially coming out, getting involved in the gay cause, though still too afraid to engage in any Arab causes. He had put out there incriminating information about himself—that he was gay and Arab—and now it could be used against him. Now that Arabs were no longer welcome, the fact he was gay only endangered him further—he was sure the two facts together would get him deported.

The freedom he let himself indulge in would no longer be relevant with this bombing, in a time of war. If the U.S. government were to haul him away now, who would stand up for him?

When Rabih first moved to Kansas, all the signs had boded well. The number of the building he moved into was 1701, the number of the *Enterprise*, the starship in *Star Trek*. The one-bedroom apartment was also just one block away from the hospital where he would be working. As had become his ritual ever since college, to make a place a home he planted the Mediterranean plants he grew up with from the seeds his father always sent to him with other Lebanese traveling to the Midwest. There were jasmine, gardenias, marjoram, and *yasmin franjiyyeh*, foreign or French jasmine. It looked like the white jasmine that hung from trellises all over Lebanon but was instead magenta with a pink dot where the petals connected or white with a crimson speckle for a core, which is why in Lebanon they called it *Abu Nu'ta*, father of drops. Here its name was periwinkle, and in his pharmacy studies Rabih learned it was the source for vinca, used in chemotherapy.

But then, the plants all died—the apartment faced northeast and Mediterranean plants thrived on sun—and now Rabih felt trapped by the beige wall-to-wall carpeting and white walls of his *Star Trek*–anointed apartment in Kansas.

Rabih called Rob in Wichita, nearly hysterical. "Can I come over?" Rabih asked him.

"Why?" Rob responded.

Rabih told Rob of the coming violence against Arabs in America, rippling out from the epicenter of Oklahoma City, about to engulf the entire country and even more imminently reach Rabih in Kansas.

Rob seemed unmoved. He asked Rabih exactly what he imagined would happen. Rabih told him of the mobs he envisioned that would get angrier and angrier and how if they got too angry, they would lynch Arabs like they did black people.

"You're exaggerating, you're worrying too much," Rob said.

Rabih insisted. What would he do about going in to work? Even though he needed groceries now, he could survive on takeout. But he would have to leave the house to go to work tomorrow. The future was approaching fast.

Rob talked Rabih through his fears. He made Rabih categorize people into who would hurt him and who would not. While Rabih had to concede his coworkers would not likely hurt him, he was adamant a risk remained with those who might see him driving or in line at the grocery store or filling up at the gas station. Rabih explained that any ignorant nineteen-year-old white kid with his buddies could see him, ambush him, and beat him up.

Rob granted that could be a possibility, but added, "In three or four days this will die down and blow over."

Rabih next called Ted in New York City, a Jewish man he had been dating since they had met at Stonewall. Rabih again tried to share his anxiety, but Ted also pooh-poohed it. "You're in a different state, hours away from Oklahoma City!" he rebuked Rabih.

Rabih turned back to CNN, which was more than eager to indulge him in a regurgitation of the same unchanging information. CNN reiterated the comparisons to the 1993 World Trade Center bombing, reported that Defense Secretary William Perry indicated he thought the tragedy was linked to Iran and terrorist groups, and repeated the FBI calls to find three Middle Eastern men.

Rabih considered calling in sick for the next morning and waited for more information.

From phone calls with Bassam and through the Listserv for gay Arabs in the United States to which they both belonged, Rabih learned that mosques, Arab-American shop owners, and community centers were receiving death threats and finding their property vandalized. Talk radio hosts were calling the suspects "heathen savages" and asking listeners what should be done with the "ragheads" and "towelheads." Online chat rooms issued calls to go "kick some Arab ass." Arab Americans asked if they should keep their children home from school the next day.

CNN paraded experts dismissing any connection to Waco and speculating it was likely Islamic terrorists. None declared it more vociferously than Stephen Emerson, the creator of the documentary *Jihad in America*, whom Rabih came to think of as the "Arab-hater extraordinaire." After the World Trade Center bombing, Emerson had confidently declared the Serbian Liberation Front was to blame. Now he made the case it was Islamic militants at work in Oklahoma City during a repeated clip in which he said, "The trademark of this bombing is clearly in the same manner that the bombers who did the World Trade Center, the Buenos Aires Jewish Center last year, as well as the numerous bombings in the Middle East over the past decade. A truck bomb, lots of explosives, basically a low-tech type of technology designed to kill as many people as possible. This is not the same type of bomb that has been traditionally used by other terrorist groups in the United States other than the Islamic militant ones. And for that reason, I believe there's a strong indication that ultimately it's going to go in that direction."

Rabih called in sick the next morning. He spent the entire day again watching CNN. Early in the morning, the network reported that a blue Blazer believed to have been used by those who carried out the bombing had been found overnight in Oklahoma City. It had been rented out of Dallas. A spokesperson from the Texas Department of Public Safety informed CNN that his agency had received an FBI all-points bulletin for the vehicle, but that it had been canceled once the car was recovered. He did, though, give details about the suspects that had been included in the APB: "They believe they were en route to Laredo or Nuevo Laredo, Mexico, to board a plane and depart to an unknown destination. We did receive a description on the subjects—two male subjects, Middle Eastern subjects, approximately six feet tall, between 25 and 28 years of age. Second subject was between 35 and 38. They both had black beards."

At a press conference later that morning with the FBI, journalists asked about reports that there was an APB out in Kansas for three Middle Eastern suspects. The FBI would not confirm.

In the evening, Attorney General Janet Reno confirmed that two suspects had been identified, white men who were believed to have rented a vehicle that had been used in the bombing. A third man was being escorted back from London as a possible witness. A reporter also questioned Reno as to whether the Defense Department had lent the Justice Department Arabic speakers for investigation of the Arab community.

"I don't think you should distinguish one community," Reno responded. "I think we are following every single lead that we can, regardless of community."

At the end of the press conference, CNN reported that the truck used in the bombing had been rented in Junction City, Kansas, 100 miles from Rabih in Hutchinson.

An hour later, CNN was staking out Dulles Airport in northern Virginia in anticipation of the return of the man being escorted back from London. The camera panned to show a line of official vehicles with police who would pick up the man straight from the runway once the airplane arrived. "The man," the correspondent said, "was ultimately destined for Amman, Jordan."

Also on Thursday in Oklahoma City, a woman named for the dawn in Arabic—Sahar—an Iraqi refugee who had fled Saddam Hussein's persecution of Shiites after the Gulf War, huddled with her toddler daughter and son in her bathroom. An unknown group of people threw stones at her home, banged on doors, and broke windows. Six-and-a-half months pregnant, Sahar suffered internal bleeding and gave birth to a dead baby boy, Salaam. His name meant Peace.

Rabih drew the shades, called in sick again, and spent the next five days at home.

On June 17, 1995, the man who carried the Rainbow flag wore nothing but heavy black boots, a black leather Speedo, and a silver-studded black harness that crisscrossed his naked chest.

After two years of only marches, the floats, bikes, horses, motorcycles, and decorated cars had returned to Wichita's Pride Parade. One of the Stonewall organizers had even brought a section of the mile-long flag from the previous year's march on the UN. It would be carried by some of the almost 300 people who had turned out to participate in Wichita.

At the gathering point, the organizers laid out markers and poster board for the revelers to make signs. Rabih stood there, debating what to write on his sign; slogans like "Equality Now" were way too daring. Anything that would have suggested homosexuality was normal seemed to Rabih to be too political, too counterculture; he couldn't afford to be associated with those messages lest he risk being found out and then deported. What the INS could do to Rabih was still—as before Oklahoma City—never far from his mind.

Just as the anti-Arab hysteria had passed when Timothy McVeigh and Terry Nichols were arrested, Rabih had also pushed the terror he felt for those five days out of his mind's memory. He had been relieved when the country learned it was white guys—guys who looked nothing like him— who had carried out the bombing. But he did move out of his apartment within a month of the bombing and relocated to Wichita, though he still drove an hour to and from work in Hutchinson every day.

Only when he and the guys returned to the Copa Cabana in Oklahoma City for the first time after the tragedy did Rabih remember again how it had felt.

He had gone to Oklahoma City with Rob and friends to do what they always did there—get drunk and get laid. Before the bombing, they used to go frequently, often once a month. But it had been months since their last trip. Like their other weekends, they had left on Friday evening after work, getting to the Copa Cabana in time to take a quick shower, don their best jeans, and visit the bars along the strip outside the city's downtown.

But on Saturday that weekend, they had made a trip to see the site of the city's sadness. The area was cordoned off and bore none of the bustle, people, or noise of a city center. As Rabih walked around, he was reminded of something he had once known intimately—an explosion never affected just the site of the blast. For nine blocks empty buildings stood staring out of glassless windowpanes. Ground that had held the roots of trees was barren. Lawns that were once perfectly manicured were overgrown, and grass had begun to grow out of the crevices between the blocks of asphalt. The way nature had already begun to reclaim a site of man's savagery reminded Rabih of his past, of Lebanon; yet to see it in this setting, an American city, made Rabih think of the post-apocalyptic future of movie scenes.

Directly across the street from the bomb's bull's-eye Rabih spied one tree that had survived the blast. It was tilted and half of it was clearly blown away, but it had survived. Rabih stood still. He wanted to clone this tree. He wanted to make it bonsai. He wanted to take it with him back to Kansas.

Now at the Pride Parade in Wichita, only an hour from where Rabih worked in Hutchinson, in plain view of journalists covering the event, and with hundreds of potential witnesses, he was debating what to write on his sign.

A group of four or five local hecklers had gathered, though they were not Phelps's people, but Rabih could not afford their discovering his identity and learning he worked in a hospital. If only he were a citizen, he thought. Once you get to be an American, you can't be kicked out of your job, your home, your country. He reached into his pocket and took out the teal blue bandanna he had brought with him. Other people at the parade were in all sorts of getups—leather, bike gear, drag. Rabih told himself that if they could accessorize, so could he!

As the parade got ready to start, Rabih hurriedly decided what to write. At the last minute, he was handed a black flag with an upside-down pink triangle to carry at the front of the parade, with the color guard. Now that his hands were no longer free, he secured the sign by folding its top edge into the waist of his shorts. As he took his place next to the man in leather and the man who had come from Stonewall, he tied the bandanna around the lower half of his face—a bandit in teal blue—and pulled his baseball cap down to the top of his sunglasses. No one would recognize him.

As he walked, the sign slapped against his thighs. Across the poster board, he had written in black marker, "Hi Mom."

Though the Oklahoma City bombing proved to be an act of home-grown terrorists, legislation passed in its aftermath focused on foreign terrorism. President Clinton signed into law the Anti-Terrorism and Effective Death Penalty Act (AEDPA) as well as the Illegal Immigration Reform and Immigrant Responsibility Act (IIRIRA). The former allowed for the use of in camera, ex parte presentation of classified evidence against non-citizens accused of being threats to national security, while the latter provided courts with greatly expanded authority to deny bond to non-citizens facing criminal charges or deportation.

The combination of secret evidence deportations and denial of bond was used almost exclusively against persons of Arab ethnicity and/or Muslim religious affiliation to detain them for long periods in jail without charge or the ability to mount any form of effective defense. The use of such evidence was challenged by Arab Americans in the courts, and even though the government frequently lost, with courts ruling that secret evidence incarcerations are a violation of Fifth Amendment due process rights, it nonetheless subsequently sought to keep detainees in jail as long as possible and avoid a definitive ruling on the matter while continuing to engage in the practice.

U.S. targets did come under attack in the following year. In 1996, a bomb exploded at the U.S. military complex near Dahran, Saudi Arabia, killing 19. On August 7, 1998, terrorists launched coordinated and devastating attacks on U.S. embassies in Kenya and Tanzania, killing 257 people and 11 people, respectively. The attacks were believed to have been committed by an Islamic terrorist network associated with

Osama bin Laden, a wealthy Saudi businessman said to be living in Afghanistan.

In response, utilizing cruise missiles, U.S. military forces delivered powerful surprise attacks against a number of sites in Afghanistan in an effort to destroy key bases used by those alleged to have been involved in the bombings. An attack was also made upon an alleged chemical weapons factory located in Khartoum, the capital of Sudan.

On October 12, 2000, another attack was carried out against a U.S. Navy ship in the Yemeni port of Aden. The USS Cole, a modern missile-armed destroyer, was crippled by an explosion that ripped a huge hole in its hull and left seventeen sailors dead and thirty-nine wounded.

These attacks signaled a new phenomenon, the privatization of terrorism, in which individuals such as bin Laden replaced government-sponsored terrorism groups.

The cast of characters in the Middle East was changing in other ways. Long-time leaders King Hussein of Jordan and Hafez al-Assad of Syria died, in 1999 and 2000, respectively. Al-Jazeera satellite TV launched in 1996 as an independent channel funded by the emir of Qatar. Though it was based in the emirate, it broadcast to much of the Arab world, tackling controversial issues and breaking state-run TV channels' monopoly on information.

While the war in Lebanon ended, Israel and Hezbollah continued to battle in the south of Lebanon. Finally in March 2000, the Israeli cabinet voted for the unilateral withdrawal of Israeli troops from southern Lebanon by July 2000; Hezbollah, however, refused to disarm. Another 16,054 Lebanese immigrated to the United States in these years.

Hopes for a lasting Israeli-Palestinian peace began to evaporate with the 1995 assassination of Israeli prime minister Yitzhak Rabin by a right-wing Israeli and had all but disappeared when Israel's prime minister Ehud Barak and PLO head Yasser Arafat met at Camp David in the summer of 2000 and failed to reach an agreement. These hopes were virtually eviscerated by late September 2000, after Likud leader Ariel Sharon visited the Noble Sanctuary (Temple Mount) in the company of 1,000 armed guards. In the context of the summer's tense negotiations over Jerusalem's holy places, and Sharon's well-known call for Israeli annexation of East Jerusalem, his decision provoked large Pales-

tinian protests in Jerusalem. Israeli soldiers killed six unarmed protesters. With these killings, the Second Intifada began.

In this time period, Arab Americans were becoming increasingly visible. With the albeit limited successes of Oslo, it became acceptable for Arab Americans to be in the political discourse. On college campuses, Arab Americans who had always been the only ones in their school found others, and suddenly speaking out about foreign policy was not as frightening as it had been. Similarly, more fully Americanized Arab Americans were finding themselves in numbers in other professions and organizing, for example, protests, conferences, film festivals, political campaigns, literary journals, and theater groups. At the same time, with Lebanon and Palestine potentially stable, more and more Arab Americans were able to return or visit the Arab world for the first time, strengthening their understanding of and connection to the region.

Some 133,690 Arabs still opted to come to America.

Courted

O nly when Maya Berry saw the Secret Service, the metal detector machines, and the line of people spilling out of the ballroom doors at the Grand Hyatt in Washington, D.C., on May 7, 1998, did she believe President Clinton was really coming. Not only would he be in attendance at that night's banquet of the Arab American National Leadership Conference, he was going to deliver the address. Maya just couldn't believe it.

Every two years, during the presidential and midterm elections, Maya's employer, the Arab American Institute (AAI)—an organization that promoted Arab-American participation in U.S. campaigns and elections in addition to lobbying for their interests in Washington, D.C.—brought community activists to the capital. Here, they would brief them on the issues and on how to move forward during the election cycle.

The institute had been cofounded in 1985 by James Zogby, a long-time Democratic Party activist whose family had originally come from Lebanon, and Republican George Salem, a D.C. lawyer who had served as solicitor of labor under President Reagan and whose parents had come from Ramallah to Florida.

In the past, AAI had invited sitting presidents to headline the banquets, though in the end, their invitations would trickle down to a surrogate from a campaign or an administration. But by now, AAI could finally feel confident that at least a cabinet member would attend, and in the past Senators Dole, Daschle, and Specter—even Vice President Al Gore—had spoken at their events. But folks at the institute had little hope a president, a *sitting* president, would attend.

Maya mentally compared who would address their events with the star-studded lineup that would compete for face time at the annual Policy Conference of the American Israel Public Affairs Committee (AIPAC).

Of course, things were getting a bit better. Just that morning Maya, AAI's director of government relations, had escorted attendees—mainly small business owners, lawyers, activists, and representatives of professional associations—to several sessions on Capitol Hill. Republican and Democratic senators and representatives had met with them to talk about Iraq, Lebanon, and the peace process. Several of them, including Senator Spencer Abraham and Representatives Nick Rahall, John Baldacci, Ray LaHood, and John E. Sununu, were themselves Arab Americans. They had also received a briefing on Arab-American and legislative priorities.

But not long ago and never very far from Maya's mind, candidates and politicians shunned any association with the community for fear of jeopardizing a candidacy or a political career. It was a surefire way to alienate the important Jewish and pro-Israeli constituencies.

Just a few years ago—most recently in the Dukakis campaign—Arab-American money and endorsements were routinely rejected by people seeking elected office. As far as Maya was concerned, if you couldn't give money in the American political system, you might as well give up the right to vote.

But things *were* changing, and Maya thanked Oslo and the peace process for that.

With Palestinians and Israelis negotiating their coexistence together, it no longer seemed necessary for politicians to have to choose to support either Jewish *or* Arab-American voters. Politicians had not generally chosen Arab Americans. That paradigm had been fueled by the idea that the two groups were diametrically opposed because of their differing views on the rights of Palestinians. But Oslo had changed the American political world in which Maya moved from Jewish *or* Arab Americans to pro–peace *or* anti–peace process people. Once that became the dividing line, Jewish and Arab Americans were found together on both fronts. Clinton favored the Jewish and Arab Americans who were for this peace, a peace on which he was staking a claim for his legacy. As such, Jewish peace groups became more a part of Maya's work than other national Arab-American organizations, like the Anti-Discrimination Committee (ADC).

While by no means did Arab-American groups have the same power or effect over U.S. foreign policy in Palestine and Israel, the Clinton administration seemed to recognize that they needed the community on board to make Oslo work. This was a drastic change. For years, Arafat's twin status as representative of the Palestinian cause and pariah in mainstream American discussions of the conflict had stigmatized Arab Americans who supported the Palestinians in a myriad of ways. But now, Arafat was coming in and out of the White House with impressive frequency, and "Palestine" and "Palestinian"—and by extension "Arab American"— seemed not to be the dirty words they once were.

This same shift emboldened Arab Americans in schools, on campuses, and in activist circles. Civil rights groups now seemed able to accommodate both Jewish and Arab-American participation. Individual Arab Americans found they were no longer necessarily the only ones at school or at work or in the neighborhood and that they had allies in other ethnic groups. Arab and Arab-American professors were on university faculties, and curious Americans had made their way to the Occupied Territories with greater frequency and had seen and heard for themselves the Palestinian reality and narrative.

Maya had also experienced firsthand how they had found room in the Clinton administration, which had begun to treat Arab Americans with the same mechanism they used to organize and liaison with other community groups. Arab Americans were able to weigh in on the other issues that also affected them, such as health care, immigration, and education policy.

And now the president of the United States was coming, really coming! And Maya could really believe it.

As soon as AAI received confirmation that the president himself would definitely be attending—about thirty-six hours before the event—they got the word out to the Arab-American community. The event sold out in no time. Phones continued to ring at AAI headquarters long after there were no more tickets to sell. People pleaded that they *had* to get tickets so their children could come to such an historic event.

Outside the Independence Ballroom, where the president would be speaking, people filed through the metal detectors and had their bags inspected gleefully. Victory, it felt like victory, for a community that had been so unsuccessful in the great American political game. The room was packed, well over capacity, with standing room only. In addition to Arab Americans who were active in community organizations or in politics, there were several others not particularly involved in either but who wanted to be there the day a U.S. president came to speak to *them*. Even Prince Bandar, the Saudi ambassador to the United States, was there.

Maya knew many of the attendees through her work at AAI. She had come to the institute from Michigan, where she had been the emergency food and shelter coordinator and then teen health director at the Arab Community Center for Economic and Social Services (ACCESS). But her interest in politics had started much earlier; in her family, they still told how Maya, as a six-year-old, would take her baby sister's bottle and curl up with the newspaper. She had been obsessed with the news from a young age because she believed it held the key to understanding why she and her family had left Lebanon abruptly in 1976, as the civil war, barely a year old, appeared to be only just beginning.

Even after she had settled into their new life in the eastern section of Dearborn—then a neighborhood of Italian and Polish Americans and few other Arabs—she felt as if she still had one foot "over there." Her parents were schizophrenic in their feelings about America and Lebanon. They had come to Michigan thinking they would just ride out the war, then return to Beirut, renting out their house to another family but never selling it. And yet her mother would often say that "once you drink the water of America, you cannot leave." Every summer there would be uproar over whether or not the girls could wear shorts. But when her youngest sister was elected class president, homecoming parade floats were built in their yard.

Maya had felt the difference between the two places was clear—in Lebanon, people were fatalistic. In the United States, they were optimistic. Her parents made it clear to them that there was no other place in the world like America. Here were freedoms, here were rights, here was a constitution.

That clear, comforting difference, however, dissipated for Maya after the massacres of Palestinians by the Phalangists in the refugee camps at Sabra and Shatila in 1982. Grappling with the horror of it, she had made a collage of images of the mass murder from *Time* magazine. She had been particularly struck by a photo of a woman killed and lying dead on the side of an alley in one of the camps. Something about the Palestinian had reminded Maya of her own mother—the dead woman's dress, her short and stout body, her chubby feet. Maya saw the United States as having played a role in this bloodletting because of its support of Israel. At age fourteen, Maya could not understand: we helped do this? We—Americans—are not the murky stuff, Maya thought then. *Our* sense of right and wrong is clear. After the murder of at least 800 Palestinians in Lebanon, by Lebanese Phalangists whose way was lit by flares shot up into the nighttime sky by Israelis who had invaded Lebanon with American arms, Maya understood that the murky was here too.

Her horror and disappointment over Sabra and Shatila were still with her when two years later she was sworn in as a citizen in Detroit's Cobo Hall in a ceremony attended by 1,547 other new citizens and presided over by President Ronald Reagan. She had been barely able to see the president, though she could see Sam Donaldson's bushy eyebrows just fine. Though she had been so excited to see the journalist whom she watched all the time on TV, she refused to take any pictures in protest, when taking photos was something she loved. In those days, she spent hours in her brother's makeshift darkroom developing rolls of film shot of all the inconsequential things in her life.

In this way, Maya had told Reagan that she was not totally cool with him. She did, nonetheless, think that it was freaking-incredibly-cool that the first person to address her as a "fellow American" on the day she became an American was the president of the United States. And she still had the flag given to her that day.

While a student at the University of Michigan, Dearborn, she had become involved with the college Democrats, working on voter registration drives on campus. It was also at the university that she had begun to hang out with other Arab-American students; in addition to Lebanese Americans from other parts of the country, she met Syrian, Palestinian, and Egyptian Americans. In elementary school, it had been just Maya and a kid named Abdel, who somehow became "Charlie." And then at Fordson High School, where Arab Americans—specifically other Lebanese Shiites—were actually the majority of the student body, Maya had shunned them. They trash-talked about other students in Arabic, and thought anything Lebanese—restaurants, bakeries even—was superior to anything else.

But she had never thought to merge the two areas of her activism— Democratic Party work and Arab-American work. Only when she volunteered to get out the vote in the Arab-American neighborhoods did she encounter the world of community organizing. She was soon hired at ACCESS and thrown into the labyrinth of community services, from emergency shelter to teen health issues.

It was for ACCESS that she had traveled to Washington, D.C., to discuss the community's health needs at a very small meeting with Hillary Clinton, organized by Jesse Jackson. She had been to the nation's capital only once before, when she had insisted her father bring her as a high school senior trip. At the meeting in the West Wing, Maya felt that the first lady had genuinely listened to her as she spoke about the precarious position of medically underserved communities that were not a federally designated minority, like Arab Americans. Maya felt she was in her element. So when the offer came to move to Washington to work full time with AAI, she seized it.

Her family—her parents, five siblings and their families—were all in Dearborn, and they had not wanted her to go. But just as they had accepted her marriage to Darrel—a white guy!—they had come to accept this too.

The move to D.C. had brought her into a whole new world. At AAI she worked less with the community and more with the power brokers who were based in Washington. She lobbied Congress and the White House on issues that mattered to the community, which included the profiling of Arab Americans at airports, the use of secret evidence against Arab Americans in deportation hearings, and the treatment of Arab Americans in Israel.

While her access to those in power was quite free, access did not mean influence. Maya met regularly with all the right people, but on some issues she never made an ounce of progress.

Tonight all that was at the back of her mind. Tonight, she felt like a kid at Christmas. All around her, people were trading smiles of pride and anticipation.

As was standard procedure with the president, the room was on lockdown. Once President Clinton arrived, no one in the ballroom was either coming or going. Maya stood against a wall facing the stage on the left. AAI staff had been frantically running around seeing to every last detail and giving up seats to assuage those indignant that the event was oversold. Now—seated, standing—they all waited for the president.

When Clinton entered, the crowd went mad. They were on their feet clapping, whistling, and cheering. When Maya saw the president, she still couldn't believe he was there. And boy, was he tall.

As the crowd finally took their seats, AAI's president, James Zogby, welcomed Clinton, saying, "Mr. President, some of the applause you hear makes it clear that this is an audience that truly loves you, but also there's a little bit of love here for Hillary Clinton." Zogby was referring to the first lady's comments advocating for a Palestinian state just days before. The White House, however, had had to back away from her statement amid condemnation from some Jewish groups.

Maya listened to Zogby briefly invoke the more-than-a-century-old history of Arab Americans and the community's values—a respect for tradition, commitment to family, and free enterprise. He also raised the community concerns of the "painful practice of airport profiling," a desire for the Palestinian people to "live free and secure in a state of their own," and a need to end the "unbearable suffering endured by especially the children of Iraq."

President Clinton embraced Zogby as he rose to take the podium.

"I understand that I am the first sitting president to address an Arab-American conference," he said to loud applause. "I'm honored to be the first president," he continued, "but I'm surprised, frankly, and also a little disappointed, because the Arab-American community has made an enormous contribution to this country with basic values that made us great: love of family and belief in hard work and personal responsibility, and a passionate devotion to education, which I hope we will see engulf every single ethnic group in America today."

President Clinton talked about how his good childhood friend was an Arab American who had come to Arkansas after being orphaned and who grew up to be the valedictorian of their high school class and later became a physician in Pennsylvania. His attitudes about Arab Americans, Clinton said, were first formed by that friendship. He wished more Americans could be exposed to different types of peoples, and thus be freed from their prejudices.

"I know it is true that Arab Americans still feel the sting of being stereotyped in false ways," the president said. "I have done what I could to warn against that. The saddest encounter, I suppose, was when we went through the heartbreaking experience of Oklahoma City, and many people were quick to rush to judgment. And I remember that terrible day when I urged the American people not to do that."

While Maya had encountered people at the Department of Justice whom she didn't feel were on the right side of issues—particularly on secret evidence and airport profiling—she felt confident that President Clinton's feelings were genuine, and that he truly did understand her pain.

The president talked for nearly thirty minutes about the importance of diversity, spreading the prosperity the nation was enjoying to all Americans, strengthening the education system, and achieving peace in places of the world that had not known it for years.

"We are now also, as all of you know, working very hard to regain the momentum for peace in the Middle East," he said to applause. "The last year has been so frustrating for the people of the Middle East, so frustrating for the peace-loving people in the Palestinian areas and in Israel, that it's easy to forget how far we have come in the last few years."

President Clinton affirmed his commitment to finding a solution and to getting the stalled process moving again, and he asked for the community's support.

"I ask you to remain resolute and to remain passionate, but always to be large," he said. "Do not give away the best part of your own lives. Do not give away the best part of your hopes. We will prevail. Thank you, and God bless you."

As President Clinton finished his remarks, the crowd rose to its feet again in a deafening applause. And as he came down off the stage set up in the front of the ballroom, people rushed to fill the area that had been roped off as a receiving line.

Then from a table near the front, Maya saw Abdulrahman Alamoudi, head of the American Muslim Council, mount his chair in his dress shoes, suit, and tie, cup his hands around his mouth, and start shouting.

Maya leaned forward to hear what he was saying.

"Mr. President," the tall man shouted. "Mr. President, what about secret evidence?"

Maya felt immediately deflated. Why now, she thought, the one time they were being treated like every other community? The issue of secret evidence was important, but this was hardly the way to effect change. Those that saw Alamoudi either ignored him or motioned to him to shut up and get down off his chair.

Secret evidence was a major political issue for the community, but Maya could not believe Alamoudi had just done that. Tonight, of all nights. She worried that his stunt would taint the news coverage of the event and the community. But she—and it seemed most people around her—just wanted to celebrate this moment, this one moment when they weren't losing. The community was so used to never getting anything, but tonight they got something—it was an historic moment—and they didn't care that the peace process was in the toilet, or that Janet Reno was not budging on secret evidence, or that their political power did not rival other ethnic groups. People were so happy that no one was in the mood to challenge the president in that undignified way.

If the president heard him, he gave no indication of it.

Alamoudi remained on the chair for another moment before climbing back down.

————————

When Khaled Saffuri called Randa Fahmy Hudome in May 2000 and asked her if she wanted to attend a meeting of Arab- and Muslim-American leaders with Texas governor and presumptive GOP nominee George W. Bush, Randa said, "Of course, yes!"

She had liked Governor Bush as soon as she saw a TV interview in which he declared that if he didn't win the presidency, he was more than happy to go back to his life in Texas. She had been invited because of her position as counselor to Republican Spencer Abraham, the only serving Arab-American senator; his state, Michigan, had a large Arab-American population.

It had been a long, dry eight years since the Republicans had been turned out of the White House, and in Randa's opinion, Bill Clinton had soiled the office, not only by having an affair with an intern, but by doing it in the Oval Office—in the people's house. She wanted—wanted badly—back in for the party that she had always loved ever since she was a child and that she felt was hers.

Her interest in politics had begun when her father invited her to watch Nixon's resignation on TV with him. "Come and witness history," he had beckoned her in the summer of 1974. They had sat side by side on their living room couch and watched Nixon deliver the words that ended his presidency. She had continued to follow the saga with her father, and in years to come they would share the same couch as they watched the political parties' conventions every four years. She loved the crazy hats, the fights on the floor, and the fiery speeches. Randa had even unfastened the radio attached to her red, white, and blue bike from Sears with its red, white, and blue tassels and brought it into bed with her to listen to election returns under her covers, before she was even twelve years old. In the morning over breakfast, she and her father would discuss who won, who lost, and the margins.

Randa shared politics with her father the way other children and their fathers shared sports, and they had their team, the GOP. Her father was a lifelong Republican—at least as long as he had been an American.

Both of her parents had come to New York from faraway places in 1957 and 1958—her mother from Iran and her father from Egypt—to study education at Columbia University. There, they had fallen in love and decided to stay in America. Her father was Sunni and her mother Bahá'í, and they had married in a civil ceremony on the university's campus, with no family in attendance. Their fellow international students from China to Nigeria to Turkey had witnessed the nuptials instead.

Randa's parents had started from nothing in America—a land where they thought anything was possible—and had eventually landed in Dallas, Pennsylvania, a small town outside of Wilkes-Barre. Each left family, friends, and country behind, moving to a place the locals called "Back Mountain," a place where they were the only foreigners.

Wilkes-Barre had become a city because of its coal mines, and its miners had made the unions quite a force in the Susquehanna River Valley town. It was, therefore, a Democratic town. More affluent Dallas, on the other hand, was Republican territory.

To Randa's parents, Democrats seemed to believe the government should help a person make it while they instead believed in making it on their own. After all, if *they* could make it in America, then so should those who had had the good fortune to be born here! And given where they both came from, they didn't think the government could ever be all that helpful anyway.

Naturally, then, when her father ran for the Dallas School Board in 1979, he ran as a Republican. Randa had been in charge of his successful campaign while she was still a junior at Dallas Public High. She had gone door to door campaigning for him, handed out buttons at fairs, and on Election Day she stood outside the polls politicking. So when her Strutters squad needed new uniforms and pom-poms, she went straight to him, and he made it happen.

She had proudly worn the outfit—white skirt, white turtleneck with a blue "D," white knee-high patent leather boots, and powder blue beret atop her feathered dark hair—when she was chosen to escort Ronald Reagan during his campaign stop in Wilkes-Barre in 1980. Randa adored the charismatic California governor and found warmth in his booming voice when he greeted her.

Yes, Randa was eager to see her party back in power; she knew 2000 was the year and Governor Bush was the man. She also believed that the Muslim and Arab Americans who had raised money and helped get Spence

Abraham elected to the Senate and who were present in sizable numbers in states like California, Michigan, Pennsylvania, and Ohio could be part of a Republican victory in November.

Grover Norquist, the conservative activist for tax reform, had already begun to target Muslim Americans as a constituency ripe for the picking by the GOP. Muslim Americans spanned racial and ethnic lines—most American Muslims in fact were African Americans, longtime Democrats. But Norquist was interested in those Muslim Americans who had come from countries in the developing world. Within their ranks there were many who were religious, or socially conservative, or small business owners, who would therefore naturally find the GOP appealing.

Those groups tended to organize politically along national origin and racial lines, but new national organizations had begun to emerge in the last decade. Norquist had tapped Khaled to head the Islamic Institute in 1997, to facilitate the political participation of economically conservative Muslim Americans.

Randa had gotten to know the Arab- and Muslim-American constituency only as an adult. Though her parents were both from the Middle East, and though as a family they had spent every summer vacationing in Lebanon, Egypt, and Iran, she hadn't known or been part of any Arab-, Iranian-, or Muslim-American community. In Wilkes-Barre, there was only the Christian Syrian and Lebanese people that had settled there, in Allentown, and in Bethlehem since the 1890s and had assimilated generations ago. Of course Randa's parents knew them, and on Saturdays her family would travel to downtown Wilkes-Barre, to a Lebanese grocery, where the smells of spices, coffee, and olives reminded Randa of the world she visited in the summers.

She did not speak Farsi or Arabic, her parents' native tongues, and she was raised with the message from them that she and her siblings were Americans. They celebrated Christmas—after all, Jesus was a prophet in the Koran—hunted eggs at Easter, and dressed in costumes for Halloween. Her father's job as a professor at the local college placed them in professional social circles, and many of his friends were his Jewish colleagues. Her parents did not rant about the United States vis-à-vis the Middle East, though during the 1967 and 1973 Middle East wars, her father often disappeared into his bedroom, where he kept his bulky shortwave radio. He tuned it to the BBC and hunched over it, listening with his ear pressed right against the speaker. Randa had learned then that the American media could not tell them fully everything that happened over there.

Professionally, Randa had come to know a cross section of people moving in both Arab and Arab-American circles only after an epiphany had convinced her to quit her job at the law firm of Willkie Farr & Gallagher. As she dressed for work one morning in 1991, she watched on TV as Secretary of State James Baker talked about the new peace discussions between the Palestinians and the Israelis in Madrid.

With Baker had been a husky-voiced Palestinian woman named Hanan Ashrawi, identified as the Palestinian spokesperson. Randa was blown away. Ashrawi was eloquent, and she talked about Palestinian rights in a way Randa had never heard expressed before. It was unusual to see and hear a woman articulate the situation of the Palestinians with a poetic command of the English language, instead of some man with a big mustache who looked like what a "terrorist" supposedly looked like.

Randa had stood dumbstruck; how cool would it be, she had thought, to work with someone like Ashrawi toward something as important as peace in the Middle East? She felt she could and should play a part. A year later and after two years of practice, she left her job at the firm. She took a salary cut and was hired by the National Association of Arab Americans (NAAA), a lobbying group for U.S. foreign policies toward the Middle East.

At NAAA, Randa learned the ropes herself with little guidance. Soon enough, she was escorting Ashrawi for visits on Capitol Hill, and eventually she accompanied Arafat himself, once the Oslo Agreement legitimized the once-hated Palestinian leader. Her work introduced her to groups like the Arab-American Anti-Discrimination Committee (ADC) and the Arab American Institute (AAI). But she had her fullest immersion in Arab America only after Spence Abraham convinced her to give up her life in D.C., move to Michigan for a year, and get him elected to the Senate.

Lobbying on the hill, she realized that she was playing David to AIPAC's Goliath. She was convinced that in order to inject some logic and justice into congressional policies toward the Middle East, it was necessary that more Arab Americans get elected to Congress. In Michigan, she confronted the traditionally Democratic Arab-American establishment and made it clear that *they* needed to support Spence even though he was a Republican because once he took office, she warned prominent activists, "I will have a very very long memory."

Now she was eager to work not only to get Spence reelected this year, but also to help put the Texas governor in the White House.

To that end, Randa flew to Austin the day of the meeting. The governor's Greek Revival–style white mansion impressed Randa with its old regality. The mansion sat on an entire city block in the Texas capital; across its front porch, five columns stood tall guarding the entrance.

Inside, the group was shown to the double parlors, painted in bright yellow and resplendent with nineteenth-century American art and furniture. Randa spotted Karl Rove, Governor Bush's chief strategist, and introduced herself, because Rove knew her husband, Michael Hudome, a Republican political consultant who had worked on John McCain's campaign that winter.

Randa already knew everyone who had gathered for the meeting. She and AAI's George Salem had been invited as representatives of the Arab-American community, and the rest came from different Muslim-American organizations.

Khaled had worked at the ADC and with Randa at the NAAA, but he had come to believe that Arab Americans were not monolithic enough to organize easily. He believed that Muslim Americans—excluding African-American Muslims—fell into line much easier, and they listened to their imams, whereas Arab Americans did not listen to their generally self-appointed leaders. Khaled believed Muslim-American votes would be easier to deliver as a bloc, and that would translate into access to any administration they helped put in power.

When the governor arrived, they all stood. Randa immediately thought he was as good looking and charming as he was on television.

Governor Bush sat by Khaled, who started the meeting thanking everyone for traveling to Austin and thanking the governor for meeting with them. He told the governor that they were excited to work toward electing him the next president of the United States, but that they wanted to raise some concerns and receive some assurances before they returned to their communities and told them to vote for Bush. Khaled then turned the floor over to the preselected persons who would raise the issues they had all already agreed on discussing.

Khaled had learned from his days lobbying on behalf of Arab issues that there was little hope for success on foreign policy issues, particularly Palestine. So he asked Muslim-American leaders to think about what they wanted from their government domestically. They responded with a craving for a validation of their existence—they wanted candidates to visit mosques; they wanted Muslim Americans represented in campaigns and administrations; they wanted the words "Muslims" and "mosques" to be added to the oft-invoked lists of American faiths—Christianity, Judaism—and American places of worship—churches and synagogues.

They also wanted the practice of secret evidence to stop. And because Jerusalem was a city holy to Islam, Khaled agreed that it could be raised independent of the Palestinian quagmire.

One by one, the representatives went through the issues. Governor Bush expressed surprise that Jerusalem had any importance in Islam but seemed receptive to the desire for inclusion. When the issue of secret evidence was raised, Randa could see that the governor was having trouble following. The issues were already complicated, and now they were being presented with much passion, but little coherence.

Randa had seen this happen before. Often those who represented and spoke for the community were politically green men who lacked savvy and understanding of the political process. She decided to chime in.

"Governor," she said, after introducing herself as a lawyer to Senator Abraham of Michigan. "This is an issue your attorney general will have to deal with. It's the government's use of classified evidence—allowed under the 1996 Anti-Terrorism and Effective Death Penalty Act—against noncitizens and used to deport them on grounds of terrorism."

Governor Bush nodded his head and looked at her amused.

The meeting came to an end, but Governor Bush remained with his visitors as they took pictures together and individually with him. Someone presented him a gift of a Koran.

As they mingled casually, someone else raised the issue of ending the sanctions against Iraq.

Bush responded, "That's funny, I just met with a bunch of Iraqis who want us to invade Iraq and get rid of Saddam."

On August 16, 2000, the night vice presidential nominee Joseph Lieberman was to address the Democratic Convention, Maya stood on the floor with the Michigan delegation, much more excited about Hadassah Lieberman than she was about Joe. The senator's wife in many ways was very different from Maya. Yet, there was something about her that appealed to Maya. She had a different name, she was the daughter of parents who had survived a war and emigrated from afar, and now she was half of a history-making partnership that spoke to the diversity and opportunity of America.

Lieberman himself, however, had not been a terribly welcome choice among parts of the Democratic Party. African Americans questioned his commitment to affirmative action. Maya found his membership and leadership of the centrist Democratic Leadership Committee problematic, and she never felt comfortable with Lieberman's talk of religion. Faith, for Maya, was a private matter.

And his positions on foreign policy issues—Lieberman supported the sanctions against Iraq and had pushed to move the American Embassy from Tel Aviv, Israel's recognized capital, to disputed Jerusalem—were also troubling to Maya. Moreover, those positions were going to make him a tough sell to the Arab-American community, and Maya was already having a tough time convincing them to get behind Gore.

The vice president had a reputation for being an AIPAC baby because most of Gore's prior career had been as a U.S. senator, thus the organization had been lobbying him much longer than, say, a governor. He was regarded as incapable of being the honest broker needed in the Palestinian-Israeli conflict, especially now that the July negotiations at Camp David between Israeli prime minister Ehud Barak and Palestinian leader Arafat had failed. Many in the community feared that with Lieberman as Gore's potential vice president, no fair deal would be had. Such voices argued that because Lieberman was an Orthodox Jew, his bias to Israel ran much deeper than that of other politicians whose commitment lay in political expedience, and his bias could not be moved.

But things weren't that simple, though Maya didn't think nuances would be enough to disavow the gut reaction many in the community had. Just earlier that day at the AAI-sponsored issue forum held at the Westin Bonaventure Hotel in downtown Los Angeles, a discussion of how the Arab-American community should view Lieberman had ensued.

Maya's boss, Jim Zogby, had told the delegates and press who had come to hear the panel about 1984, when then–Democratic presidential nominee Walter Mondale had returned Arab-American financial contributions to his campaign, and about 1988, when then–Democratic presidential nominee Michael Dukakis had rejected Arab-Americans' endorsement. Neither nominee wanted the taint of association with Arab Americans to ruin his chances of winning.

Maya had not been at those conventions. But she remembered the 1992 convention, the first time she was a delegate and when she got a taste of Arab-Americans' less-than-desired presence firsthand. With other Arab-American delegates, she had moved about Madison Square Garden in New York City with a huge green banner that said "Palestine Statehood Now." The banner matched the green stickers that they had been handing out with the same message.

Convention personnel had followed them around, and Maya could hear them on their walkie-talkies relaying their coordinates.

Later, a woman from the National Education Association and another Michigan delegate had refused to shake Maya's hand after staring at the green Palestine sticker on Maya's shirt. Maya was taken aback—within a state's delegation a feeling of camaraderie dominated, in spite of variations in policy preference. Yet despite being allies on so many other major issues, this difference amounted to too much of a deviation.

The overall reaction—that somehow Maya was not allowed to talk about the issue—made her want to talk about it even more.

But at that 1992 convention, Maya learned a sobering lesson in how unwelcome their presence really was. Michael Ifshin, general counsel for Clinton's campaign and former general counsel at AIPAC and a member of its executive committee, had told Zogby clearly, "You have no place in this party. Go to the Republicans."

The Arab-American delegates had refused to be told in which party they could participate. Trying to give them some practical advice, another Democratic insider had told them, "Go get your cousins to let you in," referring to the Jewish Dems.

Maya had been shocked when she [had] heard [those] words. She hadn't realized she needed her cousins to give her access to her own party.

In the end, though, it had actually been Lieberman himself who got them in. Zogby had visited Lieberman at his Senate office shortly after the 1992 convention to complain about the Arab-American community's exclusion from the Clinton-Gore Campaign for fear of alienating the Jewish vote.

Zogby told those at the issue forum that Lieberman had said in reaction, "I'm an Orthodox Jew, and I want Arab Americans involved in this campaign. It's wrong, and I'm not going to stand for it."

A few days later, Zogby had received a call from Clinton adviser George Stephanopoulos inviting Arab Americans to meet with the campaign at its headquarters in Little Rock.

And in those eight years under Clinton, the White House Office of Public Liaison had made Arab Americans a regular part of its outreach. This had translated into a place for them in the National Democratic Ethnic Coordinating Council (NDECC) with the Democratic Party. A sign of this progress for Maya was that in 1996, the party itself made *Arab Americans for Clinton Gore* paraphernalia.

Now, at the 2000 convention, the number of Arab-American delegates was the highest ever—fifty-five had come from all over the country. The night before, Arab Americans had thrown a hugely successful party— "Meet Us at the Casbah"—complete with dance performances and Arabic food, and set at the Moroccan-inspired Figeroa Hotel.

And just last month, in July, Lieberman had cosponsored a resolution with Michigan senator Spencer Abraham in support of religious tolerance toward Islam.

The resolution condemned anti-Muslim intolerance and discrimination, recognized the contributions of American Muslims, and pledged to uphold a level of political discourse that would not involve making a scapegoat of Islam or drawing political conclusions on the basis of religious doctrine.

Of course, Maya and Arab Americans still had issues with the Democratic Party; again the platform at the convention reflected the same highlighting of Israel as a special U.S. ally, reducing the rest of the Arab world to Israel's "neighbors" and advocating for the moving of the U.S. Embassy to Jerusalem. But a discouraging platform on Palestine was nothing new, and it was the same with the Republicans.

But this ticket didn't need any more handicaps; convincing Arab Americans to vote for Gore was already going to be an uphill struggle. Gore was simply not as charismatic as President Clinton—who managed to be loved by Jewish and Arab Americans alike, and who had an at-ease manner that seemed to elude "Al the android." And Gore seemed confused as to how he could simultaneously claim credit for the successes of the Clinton administration without being tainted by Clinton's scandals.

Yet even if Maya thought the choice of Senator Lieberman was strange and horrible, she was committed to supporting this Democratic ticket. The access Arab Americans had gained under President Clinton's administration had its own momentum, and should Gore win, which was likely, they could expect to start placing folks throughout the administration.

Maya also felt that given that she was Arab and Muslim, her objections to Lieberman would be reduced simply to anti-Semitism, that the Arabs could not vote for a Jew, and that was a narrative she was not about to fuel.

But for now, tonight, Maya was excited about Hadassah and excited something different from the norm had become a part of their shared mainstream.

Georgia congressman and civil rights leader John Lewis took the stage to introduce the Liebermans. He spoke about the senator's commitment to civil rights—a clear attempt to assure wary African-American voters. He extolled the diversity of the attendees at the convention. "We are Black, White, Brown, Yellow, Protestant, Catholic, Muslim, and Jewish. We are young, old, straight, and gay."

He then welcomed Hadassah to the stage.

On cue, the delegates, Maya included, raised above their heads the official blue signs with "Hadassah" spelled out in white script. Hadassah herself appeared, dressed in a baby-blue suit, and took her place under the gigantic "America 2000" suspended behind her.

Delegates chanted her name.

She seemed positively amazed to be there. "Wow," she said, "thank you!"

After the cheering, the chanting, and the applauding calmed down, Hadassah shared with the audience a few thoughts about her "Joey."

"Family, faith, neighborhood, congregation, and community are the guideposts of his life," she told them. "Some folks have said my husband is just a regular Joe. He is that, and he's much more."

And then she introduced the man she called, "my husband, my best friend, and the love of my life, Joe Lieberman."

The main event finally began as the senator made his entrance to the victorious theme music from *Chariots of Fire*. By then the "Hadassah" signs had been dropped to the floor and those that said "Lieberman" had been passed from the back of the delegation forward above delegates' heads.

These long column-like red signs, which had "Lieberman" written vertically in white script, would not do for Maya.

She instead squatted to the floor below her and grabbed one of the night's earlier signs. From her purse, she took a black marker and flipped the sign over. "Arab Americans for Joe Lieberman," she wrote.

Maya stood back up, raised the small piece of poster board above her head, forced a smile, and played ball. She felt it was important to make this statement, that she and her community were not anti-Semitic. If she had had her pick of picks, it would never have been Lieberman. But it was a done deal, and Maya felt this ticket was much better for the country than the would-be cowboy and his chaperone of a VP pick.

Throughout the night, the flash of what seemed like hundreds of camera bulbs went off in her face.

After the way things went with Condoleezza Rice on October 4, 2000, the Bush campaign warned Randa that she had better control her community or forget getting a meeting with their nominee the next day.

Before Dr. Rice's appearance at a town hall–style forum in Dearborn, Randa had tried to dissuade her from speaking about Iraq. Randa had explained that the audience would include many Iraqi Americans. For them, the sanctions regime had been a slow death for loved family members and country left behind. She told Dr. Rice that the anger they felt was readily accessible, and so to tread carefully.

Dr. Rice had responded that she had been the provost at Stanford and knew how to handle tough groups.

Despite Randa's best efforts, an audience member had eventually spoken out of turn, shouting out a question on Iraq. Dr. Rice had answered with an aggressive position on Saddam Hussein, setting off an angry reaction from the crowd.

But Randa still knew in her heart this was the ticket. She was convinced that Governor Bush understood the community and their issues, and that they would have access to and input on his policies once he was president. So Randa would see to it that tomorrow's event with the nominee himself ran more smoothly.

A state that was traditionally Democratic, Michigan was in play in this year's election, and the conventional wisdom was that whoever wanted to win would have to win Michigan—blue-collar, union stronghold Michigan. But there were over 350,000 Arab Americans in Wayne, Macomb, and Oakland counties. Randa had already organized and mobilized them before to help elect Spence, a Republican, to the Senate in 1994, which was why she had been tapped by Michigan governor John Engler, a Republican, to organize tomorrow's event. She believed the Arab- and Muslim-American communities could be the key to sealing the deal in Michigan.

The Democrats had made it easier by picking Senator Lieberman, who didn't help mitigate Al Gore's reputation as the "Champion of Israel." No doubt the Democrats recognized this, which was why they had dispatched Joe and Hadassah to Dearborn immediately after the Democratic Convention to meet with the community. Randa herself liked the senator; she had worked with Lieberman to pass the Senate resolution on Islam.

But Randa was sure that after meeting the charismatic governor tomorrow, the community's hearts would be won. She just had to see to it that it happened; she knew the campaign was serious about potentially canceling.

The event with Governor Bush would be much different from the one with Dr. Rice. Tomorrow, only a small group of preselected invitees would be allowed to attend, and Randa would decide who would ask questions during the time allotted for Q&A. And she would make sure the attendees knew exactly how to behave. She would have one hour alone with them before the nominee arrived, and she intended to read them the riot act.

The next morning Randa was at the Hyatt Regency Dearborn early.

Those who had been invited arrived on time, under the threat that they would not be allowed in otherwise. And everyone in Dearborn knew that Randa kept her word; after all, they had gotten to know each other in the six years since Spence had been elected to serve them in the Senate.

The invitee list was kept to around twenty people, and Randa made sure that all faiths and nationalities were represented. She had chosen the group of mostly men because they were the leadership of the community. They were also a bipartisan group. Once they were all seated by their name cards around the hollow rectangle table, Randa addressed them.

"Here's the deal," she told them, speaking so everyone was sure to understand she was not messing around. "Governor Engler and Governor Bush are coming. Governor Engler will speak. I will speak. Governor Bush will speak. And then I will open it to questions."

She continued, "I will call on people to ask questions. No one will speak out of order. No one will be impolite. And no one will speak to the press."

One of the men turned to his neighbor and said within earshot of Randa, "I've never been spoken to by a woman like that in my life!"

But then Governors Engler and Bush arrived, and everyone rose, seeming a little starstruck—a presidential nominee was meeting with *them!* Governor Bush went to each and every person, shook hands, and introduced himself. This was the genuine warmth the governor was so good at exuding and that Randa believed would put everyone she had just reprimanded at ease.

Randa welcomed Governor Bush and told him that they were happy to have him in Michigan, home to a large concentration of Arab and Muslim Americans. She credited Governor Engler with spearheading outreach to the community and credited the community with electing Senator Abraham.

Randa had prepared a briefing memo for Governor Bush but did not know if he had read it. Hoping to remind him of the issues important to the community, Randa outlined them in her opening remarks.

Then Randa revved up to what she hoped would be a nail in the Gore campaign's coffin.

She said, "Not only does Al Gore not tell the truth about inventing the Internet—but he does not tell the truth about profiling," pausing for effect before continuing, "in fact he invented it. It was the Gore Commis-

sion on Airport Profiling that recommended and launched the pilot program for profiling."

And just to be sure, "This is an issue that negatively affects our community."

Randa had done the research on airport profiling that summer and
had felt like she had hit the jackpot when she discovered that in 1996,
in the wake of the TWA 800 disaster, President Clinton had tasked *Gore*
with chairing the White House Commission on Aviation and Security.
It had been that commission that had adopted the so-called Computer
Assisted Passenger Screening (CAPS) system to weed out possible terrorists, even though there had been no evidence of terrorism in the TWA
800 case. Though officials denied it, it appeared that CAPS essentially recommended Arab ethnicity as the principal factor in identifying potential
terrorists.

Since then, she had seen to it that Gore's "role" was noted in all the
materials that went out on behalf of the campaign to the Arab- and
Muslim-American communities.

And on the issue of secret evidence, Randa explained to Governor
Bush and the audience, "As a result of recent legislation passed in the Senate and the House, the use of secret evidence—particularly in deportation
hearings for immigrants—is of great concern as well to our community.
Secret evidence can also be used to make accusations against suspected
terrorists; this is both a legal problem and a civil rights problem for our
community."

Governor Bush then addressed the group himself. He thanked them
for coming, asked for their support, and said he was eager to work with
them. He told the community he really wanted to get to know them and
deemed them very important. And he told them that he would look out
for their civil rights.

At the end of those remarks, he said that now he wanted to hear from
those in the community and their concerns.

Randa selected who would ask questions, and a frank discussion
ensued about Bush's potential foreign policy toward Lebanon, Iraq, and
Palestine. Secret evidence and airport profiling were again raised, as were
the needs of the community's many small business owners.

Throughout, the governor was casual and warm, just a regular guy.

Randa knew this would go far with those who had met him, and she hoped they would pass on a good word about Governor Bush to their families, friends, colleagues, and constituents.

On October 11, 2000, Maya feared that as long as Bush showed up and didn't drool, he would be declared the winner of tonight's debate, as he had after the first one.

Maya was also specifically worried about the Arab-American vote in Michigan. The Republican nominee had already met with community members there one week ago. The next day, Mike Berry, a prominent Arab-American Democrat in Michigan, had publicly endorsed Bush, saying that "after 50 years of professional and political experience, yesterday I was introduced to the most sincere and credible candidate for the presidency that I have ever met."

He had added, "I'm still a Democrat, but this year Governor George W. Bush has my full support and my vote, and I look forward to watching him lead our country."

Both Arab-American Democrats and Republicans had been boasting within their respective parties that their voters were present in big numbers in key states like Ohio, Pennsylvania, and Michigan—Michigan especially was said to be in play this year. And both were interested in showing the community's strength in a bloc vote. Maya knew that Randa Fahmy Hudome from Spencer Abraham's office was already working the GOP hard to get them to pay attention to the same constituency Maya was seeking to deliver for Vice President Gore.

In these closing days of the campaign, Maya was back in Michigan frequently. She was organizing Gore's upcoming meeting with Arab Americans in Dearborn for that Friday, October 13, just two days away. Tonight, she was watching the second debate between Bush and Gore in her parents' basement in their little brick house in East Dearborn.

During the last debate, the pundits had seemed obsessed with Gore's sighs and strange breathing. Maya was less concerned with those aspects of Gore's performance tonight, and more with how stiff he seemed so far. Again. She was already worried; even on TV, Bush seemed so much more casual and normal compared to robot Gore.

On screen, moderator Jim Lehrer turned to Vice President Gore and asked him, "Would you support or sign, as president, a federal law banning racial profiling by police and other authorities at all levels of government?"

Gore answered, "Yes, I would."

"I think that racial profiling is a serious problem," Gore continued. "I think we've now got so many examples around the country that we really have to find ways to end this. Imagine what it is like for someone to be singled out unfairly, unjustly, and feel the unfair force of law simply because of race or ethnicity. Now, that runs counter to what the United States of America is all about at our core. And it's not an easy problem to solve. But if I am entrusted with the presidency, it will be the first civil rights act of the twenty-first century."

Maya perked up. She appreciated Gore's adding "ethnicity," which made it inclusive of Arab Americans, who were in a racial limbo in general. It also gave Maya something to use with the community.

Governor Bush then responded that he too could not imagine what it was like to be stopped and harassed because of race. "That's just flat wrong, and that's not what America is all about. And so we ought to do everything we can to end racial profiling," he said. He added that he didn't, however, want to federalize local police forces—except in egregious cases—because he was a believer in local control of governments. "I do think we need to find out where racial profiling occurs and do something about it and say to the local folks, get it done. And if you can't, there will be a federal consequence," Bush told the audience at Wake Forest University in North Carolina and at home.

"And that could be a federal law?" Jim Lehrer clarified.

"Yeah," Bush answered.

Lehrer asked the vice president if he agreed.

Gore answered that he did, and that one of the solutions lay in better training of police officers. Gore noted that racial profiling was part of the greater issue of race in America. Gore invoked the murder of James Byrd, who was singled out because of his race in Texas, as a way to argue for the passing of a hate crimes law.

"I think these crimes are different. I think they're different because they're based on prejudice and hatred, which gives rise to crimes that have

not just a single victim, but they're intended to stigmatize and dehuman-
ize a whole group of people," Gore concluded.

Lehrer turned to Bush. "You have a different view of that."

"No, I don't, really," the governor shot back.

"On hate crime laws?" Lehrer asked, taken aback.

"No," said Bush again. "We've got one in Texas. And guess what? The
three men who murdered James Byrd, guess what's going to happen to
them? They're going to be put to death. A jury found them guilty. It's going
to be hard to punish them any worse after they get put to death. And it's
the right cause. It's the right decision."

Maya was incredulous. To hear the Texas governor talk about civil
rights issues as if he had a track record of either caring about getting new
laws in place to protect people or actually even enforcing existing laws
was remarkable.

Bush continued, confidently. "Secondly, there is other forms of racial
profiling that goes on in America. Arab Americans are racially profiled in
what is called secret evidence. People are stopped, and we have to do something about that. My friend, Senator Spencer Abraham of Michigan, is
pushing a law to make sure that Arab Americans are treated with respect."

"What did he just say?!" Maya screamed at the television. *Holy shit,
he just said Arab Americans while 37.5 million watched and heard!* In the
blink of an eye, Arab Americans were no longer an existentialist conun-
drum. Yes, they existed, other people finally knew it, and yes, apparently
their vote counted.

The tree had fallen and people heard the noise it made!

Bush was still talking. "So racial profiling isn't just an issue at local
police forces. It's an issue throughout our society. And as we become
a diverse society, we're going to have to deal with it more and more. I
believe, though—I believe, as sure as I'm sitting here, that most Americans really care. They're tolerant people. They're good, tolerant people.
It's the very few that create most of the crises, and we just have to find
them and deal with them."

Quickly, Maya began to crash. Everyone else in Michigan—all Arab
and Muslim Americans across the country—had heard or would hear
about what Bush had just said too.

She called her best friend at AAI, her husband, and her boss.

"Did you just hear that?" they all asked each other in a mix of exuberance, disbelief, and worry. They tried to figure out what Bush had in fact said. He had not gotten the issues right—Arab Americans were profiled at airports and secret evidence was used to deport Arabs. But would that matter? Maya could not believe the Republicans had been smart enough to do what they had just done.

"There goes Michigan," her AAI friend said.

All Maya could do now was hope that at Friday's meeting in Dearborn, Gore would make his case and make it well.

In the next days, the Democratic side of AAI worked to try to stem the community's embrace of Bush. AAI immediately sent a letter from D.C. to the Republican nominee thanking him for his historic comments at the debate and asking him to clarify what he meant, as a way to force Bush to commit to what he had said and prove that his words were more than just a gesture.

But then because of an emergency related to the attack on the U.S.S. *Cole,* docked in Yemen, Gore was forced to cancel his meeting with Arab Americans in Dearborn. He instead met with Jim Zogby, American Arab Chamber of Commerce President Ahmed Chebbani, and William Swor at the White House.

The next day, however, Gore made it to Michigan, and Maya saw the vice president at a union rally, attended by many Arab Americans, all sporting T-shirts or signs with AAI's "Yala Vote" slogan. During the rally, Gore told the crowd, "I strongly support the step in the right direction that's been made by John Conyers and David Bonior in the current version of a bill that bans the use of Secret Evidence," referring to Michigan's congressmen. "We have to stop that practice in the United States."

Maya felt good. Unlike his opponent, these were not mere empty words, but a real commitment. AAI would make sure to follow up that Monday with a press release playing up Gore's comments.

But then, before they had a chance to capitalize on Gore's substantial commitment, the Arab American Political Action Committee (AAPAC) endorsed Bush. AAPAC was a Michigan-based organization that had started in 1998 and that was keen on proving—particularly to AAI—that *it* spoke for and could deliver the community in Michigan. Its bipartisan members were local political activists.

In its endorsement, AAPAC acknowledged that there was little difference between Bush and Gore vis-à-vis foreign policy. But its membership was clearly swayed by the difference in how much attention the candidates had paid to them. They believed the fact that Bush mentioned them and their issues—albeit imperfectly—at a nationally televised debate only days after meeting with them was proof positive of the access they would have to his administration. They were also impressed that, unlike past presidential candidates, Bush had pursued and welcomed their endorsement.

How misguided, Maya thought; the AAPAC folks really had little sense of the bigger picture.

In that week's *The Arab American News*, a bilingual Dearborn paper published by an AAPAC member and Bush supporter, the article on AAPAC's endorsement cited, in addition, a portion of a letter from Bush to AAPAC asking for their support. The Republican nominee had written:

"I am a uniter, not a divider. I will work every day to unite all Americans around common goals—regardless of background, religion, or place of origin. I will fight discrimination wherever it happens—and on this subject I know that Arab Americans have special concerns. The present administration has pursued policies that, in practice, have adversely affected your community. My administration will act with more fairness. . . . Under the Clinton-Gore administration, Arab-American air travelers have experienced harassment and delay simply because of their ethnic heritage. Such uses of passenger profiling are a violation of Constitutional rights and must be stopped."

Randa got wind at 2:30 P.M. on October 19 that the Michigan Arab American and Chaldean Leadership Council was holding an AAI-organized meeting that evening at 6 P.M. in Michigan. They were to decide on a so-called community endorsement of a slate of candidates, which they would announce at a press conference the same evening. Well, what the hell had the AAPAC endorsement been, then? Randa suspected that AAI head and Democrat Jim Zogby was trying to orchestrate an endorsement for Gore.

Those who had been working to deliver Arab- and Muslim-American votes to the Republicans had come too far to let this happen.

The Gore campaign had been forced to react to what Randa and the others were doing. And as far as Randa was concerned, they weren't reacting particularly well.

That morning Gore had faxed a letter to tonight's attendees asking for their endorsement, but he had still not even met with the community. He had canceled his meeting in Dearborn and had not yet rescheduled. His announcement at a union rally in Michigan of a repeal of secret evidence seemed like much too little too late.

While Randa thought the meeting with Governor Bush on the fifth had been immensely successful, the tide had definitively changed on October 11, with the governor's spectacular performance at the second debate. That evening Randa had been at a fundraiser in Wisconsin for Spence's reelection campaign hosted by the Arab-American chairman of Wisconsin Energy, Richard Abdoo. She had rushed back to her hotel room to watch the debate. When she heard Governor Bush parrot a jumbled version of her own words back at her, with the specific mention of Spence, she fell to her knees in shock.

The next morning over breakfast, she and Abdoo could not stop talking about it. Even the non-Arab Americans who had attended the fundraiser and still had no idea what Bush was talking about were very impressed that Spence had been mentioned by name!

Then AAPAC came out with their endorsement, and the *Wall Street Journal* wrote an article titled "Gore's Arab American Problem." Randa had prodded the journalist just the day before with a memo tying secret evidence and airport profiling to Gore.

No way were the AAI Democrats going to undermine them now!

Randa looked at the invitation list for the meeting that George Salem had faxed over to her. She identified whom she believed to be Bush, Gore, and Nader supporters. She split up the list with a colleague and called all those she was sure were GOP supporters. She told each one that AAI was staging a cooked meeting, to get to that night's meeting at the Ramada, and to make sure there was no Arab-American endorsement of Gore.

Only at 4:30 P.M. did she accidentally call a Gore supporter who told her, "Bush? Bush? I would never support that crook!"

But Randa just kept calling the names on her list and hoped that the gentleman would not tip off too many Gore supporters as to what she was doing.

On October 29, 2000, Democratic nominee and Vice President Al Gore was finally meeting with a group of Arab-American Democrats in Dearborn at the Hyatt Regency, a meeting Maya had helped organize.

The Republicans and local Bush supporters had been very effective in controlling Gore's message. They had successfully hung airport profiling around his neck and blamed him for all the ills of Clinton's foreign policy without crediting him for any of its successes. His choice of Lieberman as a running mate had convinced many that his bias toward Israel would be unchecked. And to their credit, the Republicans had successfully reached out to the community and made them feel as if Bush really cared about them and would continue to listen to them if elected president.

None of this could have been more disastrously obvious than at the endorsement meeting of the Arab American and Chaldean Leadership Council of Michigan, just ten days before. The day of the meeting, Maya had received angry calls from people, telling her they had been called and told that AAI was trying to sneak in an endorsement for Gore and that they had to attend the meeting to stop it. Maya had explained to them that the meeting was for the community to endorse a slate of candidates—and that a vote would determine who was endorsed, at both local and national levels. She invited anyone who called her to attend the meeting. But many people—people not from the council—showed up ready to rumble.

During the heated three-hour meeting, Maya had never been more disgusted. Those were Chicago-style politics. Anytime Gore supporters spoke, they were heckled down. When Steve Yokich, the president of the United Auto Workers, spoke in support of Gore, his authenticity as an Arab American was challenged.

"Who are you to us? You don't speak Arabic," angry Bush supporters had yelled at the tough third-generation union member, whose grandparents had emigrated from Lebanon.

Maya had sensed a level of intimidation from the moment an aide to Republican governor Engler had shown up at the meeting. Maya and her AAI colleague had objected right away to the aide's presence, but no one had dared ask her to leave. Many of those in the room ran organizations or companies that depended on state contracts. Indeed, when Maya and the other staffer left the room when the actual vote was taken, Governor Engler's aide stayed, continuing to note who had said what and, Maya assumed, who had voted how.

At the end of that meeting, the attendees had endorsed Bush for president, citing his outreach to their community and their disappointment with Vice President Al Gore.

A few days later, on October 23, the American Muslim Political Coordinating Council Political Action Committee (AMPCC-PAC) had endorsed Bush at a press conference at the National Press Club. The umbrella group of several Muslim-American organizations cited appreciation of Bush's accessibility to them and his elevated concern about issues its community held dear—namely stopping the use of secret evidence against Arab and Muslim immigrants and the profiling of Arab Americans at airports.

The press had been feeding this idea that Arab and Muslim Americans were one and the same. Maya resented the lumping together of these two communities, and she resisted the idea of organizing on religious grounds. The way she saw it, it was Arab-Americans' ethnicity, not their religion, around which they should organize. Arab Americans—Christian and Muslim—had been excluded from full political participation because of the Palestinian issue and the perceived threat they posed to pro-Israeli hegemony in American politics. From a foreign policy perspective, Maya was most active on Arab-related issues—like Palestine, Lebanon, and Iraq—because they had a shared heritage and language. She didn't feel more connected to Pakistan or Bosnia because she was Muslim. Human rights abuses or injustice there concerned her, but they did just as easily in Guatemala, Burma, or South Africa. She didn't want to see the ethnic identity swallowed by what seemed like an artificial construct, especially one that excluded the vast majority of American Muslims—black Americans.

AAI's follow-up with Bush and what he meant exactly by his remarks at the debate had yielded nothing; the campaign never responded. Gore's substantial commitment on secret evidence failed to get any traction in

Michigan. Maya and other Arab-American Democratic organizers had been forced to be in a reactive mode, and they had already lost too much ground to Bush; they always seemed to be one step behind.

Maya hoped that today's meeting would at least allow Gore to convey to the community who he was; from a political perspective, the meeting *had* to happen. He could not skip Arab Americans, especially not while spending the day campaigning in Michigan as part of his last-minute push for the state and its eighteen electoral votes.

The meeting was going to take place in a small room at the Hyatt with a preselected group of Arab-American Democrats. Zogby flew in from D.C. to chair the meeting. Prior to Gore's arrival, they met to discuss who would raise what issues, so that they could collectively be as effective as possible.

Gore soon arrived and took a seat at the head of the table.

One prominent Arab-American Democrat pointed out to Gore that he'd given them nothing in public to fight with.

The vice president assured them that if elected, he would be "evenhanded" in his approach to American policy in the Middle East.

Naturally, the issues of secret evidence and airport profiling soon came up.

Gore responded that he had made his position clear on those issues and reiterated that he believed the use of secret evidence to be abhorrent to the Constitution.

Then one of the AAPAC Democrats who had voted against endorsing Bush approached the vice president, handing Gore an envelope that held a list of the names of all the southern Lebanese currently being held in Israeli prisons, and who AAPAC wanted released.

Gore respectfully received it, opened a Diet Coke, and leaned back in his chair. He let out a sigh, and clearly frustrated, snapped, "Did you hold my opponent to the same standard? Are these the same expectations you have of my opponent? What has he *guaranteed* you?"

Where the hell was this guy the whole campaign? Maya thought. Gore was pissed, and Maya loved it. The way he sat back in his chair, his response seemed so human, so unprogrammed, so un-robotic. And he was right, Maya thought, the community had been giving Bush a pass.

As far as the community was concerned, she thought the majority of Arab-American Democrats would vote for him, though the majority of

Arab-American voters would not. The meeting had happened too late to have a ripple effect. But, Maya comforted herself, Arab Americans were not the only constituency to win over in Michigan.

Maya wished Gore could have debated this way. Things would have been so different, and they might not be here fighting for Michigan. If only, she thought, America could have seen more of *this* guy.

But this meeting was quickly coming to an end. Gore still had a long day ahead of him in Michigan. He had to get to rallies in Warren, East Lansing, and Muskegon. But before all that, after this meeting with Michigan's Arab Americans, he had to get to an African-American church in Detroit to sing Gospel with churchgoers at Sunday services.

On the morning of June 28, 2001, President George W. Bush was scheduled to address the employees at the Department of Energy and launch his new energy plan. Randa was excited to be seeing him again. Though Spence had lost his Senate seat, she was thrilled that her guy had won the White House.

And Arab and Muslim Americans had voted for him. Seventy-two percent of Muslim Americans and 45 percent of Arab Americans had voted for Governor Bush (only 38 percent of Arab Americans had voted for Gore), even though both Bush and Spence had lost in Michigan. Each had garnered 47 percent of the vote there, with Spence losing by 67,259 votes and Bush by 194,621. But the president had then turned around and appointed Spence quite the consolation prize—a position in the new cabinet.

Spence had been sworn in on January 20, 2001, as secretary of energy, and he had taken Randa with him from the Senate. At the Department of Energy, Randa was in the Office of the Secretary and oversaw the Office of Policy and International Affairs.

But she had not forgotten the community. In the spring, she had accompanied a group of Armenian Americans to a meeting with the president. They had invited her along because she had always been accessible to them when she was in the Senate. Afterward, when the audience was able to shake hands with the president, he had surprised all of them, especially Randa, when he said, "Hi Randa! How are you? You're over at Energy with Spence, right? Are you keeping him in line?"

Randa had been so surprised—she didn't think the president would recognize her outside of the Arab-American context. "Yes, Mr. President, I'm very proud to be serving in your administration," she had responded.

After the meeting, Randa had started thinking that the Arab- and Muslim-American communities, which had supported the president during his run, should get a similar meeting with him. Seeing him again today at Energy had encouraged her to pursue it.

The president had gotten off to a good start with his speech. Trying to quiet down the loud applause after he took the stage, he joked, "Conserve your energy!" setting off laughter.

Turning to Spence, he said, "Mr. Secretary, I appreciate your leadership. He's a man of high energy and good wisdom. And I picked the right man to lead the Energy Department for the country."

President Bush also thanked the employees at Energy for their service, and then recognized the members of a Canadian-Mexican–United States energy task force in the audience, with whom Randa was standing. His speech stated his commitment to developing a comprehensive strategy for making the country more energy efficient.

Afterward, the president shook hands with members of the audience. When he saw Randa, he again said "Hi, Randa" and kissed her.

Jaws dropped around her—no one there knew her campaign history.

Randa thought to herself, given that he seemed to actually remember her, he would likely really get a kick out of seeing the community again.

Randa decided to reach out to an old acquaintance, Ken Mehlman, who had become deputy assistant to the president and director of White House political affairs. She asked to meet with him, and they set a time for July.

When Randa arrived for her meeting with Mehlman, Tim Goeglien, head of the Office of Public Liaison and essentially the president's guy on the Religious Right, was also present. Randa wondered why he would be at a meeting about Arab- and Muslim-American outreach.

Randa asked why the president had yet to meet with Arab and Muslim Americans. She also wanted to know why the person appointed to handle Muslim Americans at the White House, a young Pakistani-American lawyer, was working on an unpaid volunteer basis. Goeglien snapped at

Randa that it was an honor to be working for the president even if it wasn't for pay.

After some discussion, though, they thought that maybe the volunteer could be hired at Energy and then detailed back to the White House.

Mehlman meanwhile told her he would look into the possibility of a meeting with community members.

When Randa got back to Energy, she debriefed Spence right away. She vented to Spence—the community had supported then-governor Bush—they had helped put him in the White House. They had asked to be included. She thought they had finally arrived in Washington. They deserved a meeting. Was there something up?

"What do you want me to do?" Spence finally said.

Randa asked her longtime boss to back her up on this, because the community had really rallied for the president. She asked Spence to use his clout and request a meeting at the White House between leaders of the Arab- and Muslim-American communities and President Bush.

In the meantime, Randa got to work finding funding for the White House volunteer.

She also heard that one of AAI's brightest assets, Maya Berry, had just been hired by House Whip David Bonior of Michigan to be his legislative director. Randa respected and liked both of them; more important, the more Arab Americans they had on the Hill—in either party—the more they could get done on the issues they cared about.

Weeks later, Spence stuck his head in Randa's office. They had been granted a meeting with the president to discuss community matters. He told Randa to do a prep memo for him detailing all the issues in a format that could be passed on to the president if it were requested during the meeting.

Randa was exuberant.

The meeting had been set for 3:30 P.M. at the White House on Tuesday, September 11, 2001.

The attention shown to Arab Americans during the election led many to believe the community would enjoy both visibility and continued opportunities to be heard on policy matters. Because the first President Bush and his secretary of state, James Baker, had been perceived to be friendly to the Arab nations, some community members believed his son would be as well.

One of the first things President George W. Bush did when his administration came to power in January 2001 was to eliminate the State Department's special Middle East envoys. He was critical of Clinton's personal investment in the peace process.

In Israeli elections in February, Ariel Sharon was swept to power by an electorate that had overwhelmingly turned its back on the land-for-peace formulas of the 1990s and now favored a tougher approach to Israel's "Palestinian problem." The death toll soared as Sharon intensified existing policies such as assassinating Palestinian militants, air strikes, and incursions into Palestinian self-rule areas. Palestinian militants, meanwhile, stepped up suicide bomb attacks in Israeli cities. President Bush placed the blame on Arafat and maintained a hands-off approach markedly different from President Clinton's.

With renewed violence and uncertainty in the Middle East, 34,447 Arabs immigrated to the United States in 2001.

In March 2001, ignoring an international outcry, the Taliban rulers of Afghanistan destroyed two 2,000-year-old Buddhist statues in the cliffs above Bamian. That May, they ordered religious minorities to wear tags identifying themselves as non-Muslims and forced Hindu women to veil themselves the way Muslim Afghan women had already *been forced to. In July, the Taliban banned the use of the Internet, playing cards, computer discs, movies, satellite TV, musical instruments, and chessboards after declaring them against Islamic law. In August, they arrested Christian foreign-aid workers for proselytizing. Two were American citizens.*

© ALIA MALEK

Beginnings

O n the morning of September 11, 2001, Monsignor Ignace Sadek was where he always was on Tuesday mornings: in the rectory of Our Lady of Lebanon Maronite Cathedral in Brooklyn, New York. He was in his quiet office buried within the recesses of the church, preparing his homily for the midday mass.

Around 10:00 A.M., he decided to check on the young gardener tending to the grounds that surrounded Our Lady of Lebanon on its shaded block at the corner of Henry and Remsen Streets in Brooklyn Heights, separated from Manhattan by the East River. As he came out into the daylight, he noticed that the sky had changed—no longer was it the clear blue day that he remembered; instead, it had become clouded by debris.

In front of the church he bumped into a parishioner, a gentleman his age from Lebanon, who anxiously asked him in Arabic, "Did you not hear? Are you a stranger to Jerusalem?"

Ignace explained he had been at work in his office, away from the radio and television.

"Two airplanes have hit the Twin Towers, and they are falling down!" the parishioner exclaimed.

Ignace had been to the towers just two weeks before, when his friend, a bishop, had come to visit him. He often took visitors to the Twin Towers for their views, so high in the heavens that people below were rendered the size of ants. They had waited nearly two hours on line to ascend to the top.

Ignace began to shake.

What can I do? he asked himself. I am a priest, I have to do something!

His seventy-one-year-old legs began to move quickly, and he almost ran toward the Promenade, a scenic overlook on the East River with views of lower Manhattan and its skyline dominated by the Twin Towers. When Ignace arrived, he could not see a thing. He could not see whether the towers had truly fallen or whether they were hidden behind the curtain created by the wind chasing debris across the river.

As he stood on the edge of Brooklyn, the waters of the East River obscured but restless below him, the black suit he had worn since he was twenty and his own signature black beret which he had worn since he was twenty-five turned the color of the white collar he wore around his neck.

Ignace's calling to be a priest came when he was fourteen years old. He was a boarder at a grade school in Batroun, a coastal Lebanese town far from the village he had lived in with his parents until they both had died.

At fourteen, he had already realized that the typical Lebanese life of marriage and family was not for him. And he had always been attracted to the church, especially its music and the beautiful sound of the organ.

But it was the life of an aspiring young nun from France that set his destiny in stone.

Being an orphan, he had grown accustomed to being alone, and had come to believe, even as a young child, that he could count on no one.

In the summer of 1935, as a five-year-old, he had watched his mother die of what he later understood to be cancer. The evening she passed, Ignace had studied the priest as he delivered her last rites, praying over her as she lay dying. Ignace had watched her lose her life until she was extinguished. And then life had lost her. He had wept.

After his mother's death, Ignace slept next to his father in his bed.

Two years later, in the spring of 1937, when Ignace was seven, his father died of pneumonia.

What Ignace remembered of them later were just flashes: his mother talking, as she held him on her lap while she visited her mother in the village of Masrah; his father, lying on his belly, late at night, reading the Bible aloud by candlelight so that Ignace could hear.

He was raised by his grandmother in Zane, a village of 100 families, 700 meters above the Mediterranean Sea and in the embrace of the Kadisha Valley, which took its name from the Aramaic word for "Holy." Aramaic, the language in which Maronite rites were performed, was also the language of Christ. Kadisha Valley, a deep gorge carved by the river of the same name, had sheltered monastic communities for centuries.

After his parents' death, Ignace was sent away to a school run by Les Frères Maristes, an order dedicated to the education of young people. He returned to his grandmother only for holidays and the summer months.

At the school, Ignace felt lost; he knew no one and he had no one. Though several other students also boarded, they were not orphans like him. They all had parents.

It was already clear in Ignace's mind that he could not count on anyone except himself. So he threw himself into his studies and taught himself much more in his subjects than called for in the curriculum. But in the words of the French nun St. Thérèse, which he read in her native French and especially in her poem "Vivre d'Amour," he saw his path. The love he felt for God, and that he could feel God had for him, filled him.

From Batroun, he entered the seminary in Ghazir at age fifteen. During his studies, he traveled to Jerusalem. By day, he visited the sites where Jesus lived and died, and in the evening he listened to the singing of the nuns from the Orthodox convent at the slope of the Mount of Olives.

During the wars that ravaged Lebanon, he shepherded his parish in Kfour Kasrawn through the manmade storms. But finally, in 1988, he decided to

come to America rather than be dragged into the politics devouring Lebanon, which threatened to conscript him as well. He had always wanted to
see America, so he packed his books and arrived in Wilkes-Barre, Pennsylvania, at age fifty-five, speaking not one word of English.

Ignace was impressed by Americans; he found them to be sensitive,
human, and very faithful. He admired how the American people rushed
to respond to those in need—if a little baby crying from hunger were
put on TV, in no time that child would receive donations from across
the country. He also reveled in how the whole world was represented in
America's peoples. The mixture was what made the country so rich.

He cared for St. Anthony's Maronite Church in Wilkes-Barre, bringing several bouquets of fresh roses every Sunday so that the scent of their
perfume would adorn her. After ten years in Pennsylvania, he came to the
Cathedral of the Maronite Diocese in North America, Our Lady of Lebanon in Brooklyn Heights. He had been its priest for three years now.

Standing at the edge of the Promenade on September 11, 2001, Ignace
began to weep for all the souls he imagined were already lost and being
lost.

He silently mouthed the absolution in Arabic:

*May the Lord Jesus Christ forgive your faults, and by his authority I for-
give you from every bind of sin, in the name of the Father, the Son, and the
Holy Spirit.*

After all, he reasoned, souls did not depart their bodies immediately,
and his words would have enough time to find their mark.

After 1860, immigrants from modern-day Lebanon and Syria began arriving on America's shores. In the Old Country, these immigrants had been
ruled by the Ottoman Empire and came almost entirely from the minority faiths of Christianity and Judaism. Like many who immigrated to the
New World, they came seeking economic opportunities. When early in
the twentieth century, the Ottoman ban on conscripting Christians and
Jews was lifted to stem the external and internal threats to the empire's
existence, they left for freedom.

They entered America through Castle Garden, the immigrant-processing center in New York Harbor, until Ellis Island opened in 1892. The Syrian Jews—mostly from the cities of Damascus and Aleppo—settled along Broome and Allen Streets on Manhattan's Lower East Side, already home to Jews from Europe. Of the Syrian and Lebanese Christians who opted to stay in New York, many joined the huddled masses who decided to make only a short trip from the gateway castle and later isle at the tip of Manhattan to its Battery neighborhood on the Lower West Side. Like other immigrants from Poland, Greece, Ireland, and the Slovak lands, these Syrian and Lebanese settled where they first stepped foot, crowding into tenement buildings along streets nearly hidden in the shadows of the financial district and its great skyscrapers.

The tenements were brick-faced buildings harnessed with zigzagging fire escapes from which laundry was hung to dry. Their first floors were given over to commercial activity while residents lived on the higher floors. Most of the apartments had two or three rooms with a bathtub in the kitchen and a toilet in the hallway that was shared by other building residents. With the elevated train that ran along Greenwich Street, many rooms were dark, the sun blocked by the tracks, which were so close to some of the tenements that one could almost touch the wooden pathway. When the train passed, folks shouted to hear one another.

By the late-nineteenth century, there were so many Syrian and Lebanese immigrants that the area became known as "Little Syria." Washington Street was its main drag, and it served not only those immigrants who lived around it, but also those Syrians and Lebanese who worked as peddlers in every single state in the Union. The neighborhood also attracted those other New Yorkers craving the exotic, with its signs adorned in sinuous Syrian script and its stores and local peddlers selling Eastern trinkets and wares. *Harper's Weekly* ventured into Little Syria in 1895, its correspondent penning an article titled "The Foreign Element in New York." The *New York Times* reported from the colony in 1899 and 1903 in "New York's Syrian Quarter," and "Sights and Characters of New York's Little Syria," respectively. The subhead on the latter was: "A Quarter of the City Where Uniform Politeness Goes Hand in Hand with a Determination Not to Allow Total Conquest by the Spirit of Rush and Bustle."

The community soon founded several places of worship to serve the different Christian sects to which the Syrian and Lebanese immigrants belonged. In 1890, the Maronites founded St. Joseph's Maronite Church, one of the first Arab parishes in New York City and indeed in the entire United States. Its congregants prayed in a rented hall at 127 Washington Street. Within ten years, St. Joseph's parish moved into its own church at 81 Washington Street, until in 1910 it expanded several doors down into a newer church with a school for the children and a house for the pastor at 57–59 Washington Street.

Nearby, the Arabic-speaking Melkites (Greek Catholics) prayed from the basement of St. Peter's Roman Catholic Church on Barclay Street until they moved into their own church in 1916 at 103 Washington Street. In 1895, the Antiochian Orthodox followers also established their first American parish, worshipping from the second floor of a tenement at 77 Washington Street.

As Syrians and Lebanese began to reap the golden opportunities that had attracted them to America, some began in 1900 to move across the East River to Brooklyn. The South Ferry, which ran from South and Whitehall Streets in Manhattan near Little Syria, let off at the foot of Atlantic Avenue in Brooklyn. Again, staying where they arrived, the immigrants moved into houses in the neighborhood, and Atlantic Avenue soon became the main commercial artery of the new colony.

Churches and societies were organized. Another Maronite parish, Our Lady of Lebanon, was founded in 1903 at a house and grounds at 295–297 Hicks Street. Meanwhile, the Orthodox established a church at 301–303 Pacific Street in 1904, later moving in 1920 to 355 State Street. By 1907, Syrian Protestants were using the Second Unitarian Church at Clinton and Congress Streets for Sunday meetings, and by 1910, the Melkites were also praying in Brooklyn.

After the turn of the century, a growing nativist mood had spread across the country and legislative measures were taken to limit immigration; by 1924, the open doors had swung shut, and very few Syrians were arriving on American shores. But the community already in America and in New York specifically was flourishing on both sides of the East River.

A vibrant Arabic press published several Arabic language newspapers, even one, the *Syrian World*, in English. In 1929, an Arabic play was performed at the Brooklyn Academy of Music and by 1930 films from the

Middle East were regularly being shown there. Arabic music programs could be heard on the radio in the 1930s on Brooklyn station WBBC.

Then in 1946, Little Syria in Manhattan was slated for destruction; the City of New York claimed many of the mother colony's properties for the coming Brooklyn Battery Tunnel. St. Joseph's Maronite Church at 57–59 Washington Street was one of them. Its premises were vacated in 1947, and, with the rest of the neighborhood, it was razed to the ground to make room for the Manhattan entrance plaza of the tunnel. When the church came down, the parish took its cornerstone. St. Joseph's bought a building a few blocks away at 157 Cedar Street, remodeled it, and laid the old cornerstone from the Washington Street church at the base of the new, modest red-brick church at the corner of Cedar and West Streets. St. Joseph's church reopened its doors in 1949.

But the congregation of St. Joseph's Maronite Church was already dwindling; many Maronites, like the rest of Little Syria's people, had migrated across the East River to Brooklyn. Sunday services at St. Joseph's were virtually unattended, though Monday through Friday at noon, the church was full of Latin Catholics who worked in the area and who, on their lunch breaks, would light candles during midday mass. Recognizing the demographic changes, the Maronites sold the church to the Catholic Archdiocese of New York in 1969, on the condition that the Maronite Liturgy could always be celebrated at St. Joseph's.

The tiny remaining Maronite parish was absorbed by Our Lady of Lebanon across the river, which in 1944 had moved to a sanctuary on Remsen and Henry Streets that had been the Congregational Church of the Pilgrims. Our Lady of Lebanon replaced the stained glass windows that the Pilgrims had taken with them with windows created by a French artist as well as the Lebanese artist Saliba Douaihy. Douaihy also painted in the church a mural that depicted the mountains of Harissa in Lebanon and its large statue of the Virgin, arms outstretched, that was visible all the way from the coast below.

But mass would be celebrated at St. Joseph's for only a few more years. Construction of the World Trade Center had changed the face of downtown Manhattan, and its existence meant a growing need for services to support it as well as more office space to compete with it. St. Joseph's was demolished in 1984, a casualty of the ever-expanding development that the construction of the World Trade Center had generated in Lower Manhattan.

In Brooklyn, the Atlantic Avenue area remained a commercial center, but by 1970, most families had moved away, many relocating to Bay Ridge, farther south in Brooklyn. But with upheaval in the Middle East in the sixties, and U.S. immigration laws relaxing in 1965, other Arabic-speaking peoples, Yemenis and Palestinians, began arriving, revitalizing the old Arabic neighborhood around Atlantic Avenue. Mosques were founded, Islamic bookstores were created, and restaurants and groceries opened to serve new and old patrons alike.

Ignace shopped at Sahadis on Atlantic most frequently, buying the olives, cheeses, oil, and preserves that smelled and tasted like home, stopping to chat with those he knew.

In the airplanes, in the field in Pennsylvania, in the towers, Our Lady of Lebanon in Brooklyn lost eight souls on September 11, 2001. They were Robert Dirani, Catherine Gorayb, Peter Hashim, Mark Hindy, Walid Iskandar, Jude Moussa, Jude Safi, and Jacqueline Sayegh.

Ignace presided over no funerals for the eight that died because there were no bodies to be buried. Instead he said a memorial service for those whose families requested it.

Some of the victims were part of the larger community of the church; others, Ignace knew quite well personally.

He had baptized Catherine's infant daughter just two Sundays before. During the baptism, he had noticed that Catherine had cried through the entire ceremony. He had wondered why then, and after she died, he said to himself that she must have been touched by a prophecy that she would soon lose sight of her daughter.

Jude had been raised in the Brooklyn church. Though his mother was Druze, he was a dedicated and joyful member of the congregation, who always had a hug and a kiss to share.

And Jacqueline had contacted him Friday evening just before that horrible Tuesday, telling Ignace that she was engaged! She had asked him to prepare a copy of her baptismal certificate, which was required so that she could marry her fiancé in his church. She had told Ignace that she would come by on Monday morning to pick up the paper; when she didn't, he had told himself she would be by on Tuesday. Now, he didn't know what to do with the envelope, so he left it where it had been waiting for her, in the sacristy where the priests vest.

Just beyond the church's doors, all of America was reeling as well, and some New Yorkers sought scapegoats among themselves in Brooklyn. On the other side of Atlantic Avenue, the executive director of the Arab American Family Support Center had quickly yanked the group's name off the front door right after the attacks; she had bolted all the doors that led to her office, barricading herself inside with a legal pad and telephone. She fielded two sorts of calls—threats of violence from outside the community and desperate pleas for help from within.

At the Dawood Mosque on Atlantic Avenue, people spat and cursed at members. The Brooklyn Islamic Center was the target of a firebombing attempt. Someone hurled a Molotov cocktail at a mosque in Bensonhurst, while pork chops were flung over the back fence of the Al-Noor Muslim School in Sunset Park. In Park Slope, a motorist blocked the path of a cab driver, yelling "Get out of the car, Arab," pounding on the hood as he shouted, "You are going to die, you Muslim."

And a Bangladeshi mail sorter coming home to Brooklyn on the subway was knocked to the train floor and kicked and punched repeatedly by anonymous men.

New York police officers were soon standing sentry outside many of the city's mosques, and Atlantic Avenue and Steinway Street in Astoria—a Queens neighborhood also home to many Arab Americans—were both lined with police. A man stood outside a Steinway Street mosque holding a homemade placard that read "get out of our country."

Outside New York, the trauma played out similarly. A mosque in suburban Dallas had its windows shattered by gunshots; in San Francisco, a mosque found on its doorsteps a bag of what appeared to be blood; in Virginia, a vandal threw two bricks through the windows of an Islamic bookstore with threatening notes attached; and in Chicago, a mob of hundreds set upon a mosque shouting "Kill the Arabs," while an Assyrian church on the north side and an Arab community center on the south-west side were damaged by arson. Women reported having their head scarves yanked off or being spit at, businesses were vandalized, employees were suddenly fired or demoted, and children were bullied by classmates and teachers alike.

In some cases, individual Arab and Muslim Americans responded by taking off their *hijabs*, keeping the kids home from school, displaying the American flag everywhere, and changing their names to something a little less "foreign." Institutionally, every major Arab and Muslim organization immediately denounced the attacks; national leaders who had gathered in D.C. to prepare for a meeting with President Bush the afternoon of September 11 refocused their efforts on releasing such a statement the same day. Other Americans—neighbors, friends, colleagues, classmates, lovers—reached out in solidarity.

The federal government quickly released statements warning that any violence or discrimination against Arab or Muslim Americans or anyone perceived to be so were wrong, un-American, and unlawful. Within one week, nearly a thousand incidents of hate and bias were reported; several Sikhs—non-Arab and non-Muslim South Asians who wear turbans— were murdered or attacked. Investigations and prosecutions quickly followed.

But while one government hand had given, another was taking. Immediately following the attacks, over 1,200 resident aliens in the United States from Arab and Muslim countries who were not named or charged with crimes disappeared without notice to anyone into undisclosed detention centers.

Suggestions were made that camps be established for U.S. citizens from the Arab- and Muslim-American communities, while the denaturalization of naturalized citizens from these groups was also considered.

Arab and Muslim Americans and legal residents were pulled off planes in front of other passengers and subjected to interrogation; some were allowed to board eventually, many weren't. Polls in September found that a majority of Americans favored the profiling of Arabs, including those who were American citizens, and subjecting them to special security checks before boarding planes.

The attorney general—who earlier in the fall had attended a Ramadan *Iftar*—ordered the "voluntary" interviewing of 5,000 legal residents from Arab and Muslim countries and singled out for arrest another 5,000 Arab and Muslim immigrants who did not leave the country after being ordered deported, though they represented only a fraction of the 320,000 people of all backgrounds who violated deportation orders. The issuing of visas to people coming to America for business, school, and tourism ground to a halt.

Fearing that harm could come to his parishioners, Ignace decided to hang the American flag outside Our Lady of Lebanon. He also cautioned his flock not to speak Arabic audibly outside the safety of the church.

In early 2002, Ignace received a call from Bovis Lend Lease, the construction company that was clearing the World Trade Center site. They had been told by the chaplain of St. Peter's Catholic Church, near the foot of the towers, to contact him. Workers had come across something in the wreckage of stone and steel that might interest him.

As soon as Ignace fully grasped the meaning of the chaplain's words, he responded, "I'm leaving immediately!"

The destruction of the towers had unearthed the cornerstone of St. Joseph's Maronite Church, the original parish from whose rib Our Lady of Lebanon had been founded.

With the help of four men, Ignace transported the 400-pound cornerstone across the East River to his church in Brooklyn, making the same journey most of the inhabitants of Little Syria had made a hundred years before.

The bruised cornerstone was placed in the church's vestibule on a marble pedestal made by a parish member. A survivor of the attacks, its engraved testament reads for anyone to see: SANCTI JOSEPHI, ECCLESIA MARONITA, ROMANA CATHOLICA.

After the attacks of September 11, the United States declared war on terrorism. In addition to the men and women already on active duty, the government called 41,392 Reserve and National Guard members out of their civilian lives to serve in the country's armed forces. Securing the homeland would involve leaving U.S. borders, and on October 7, 2001, the United States began its military attack against Afghanistan, where the Taliban regime was playing host to al-Qaeda and its leader, Saudi-born Osama bin Laden.

The greater war on terror also had a concurrent domestic front. Of the 1,200 Muslim and Arab noncitizens arrested and detained within weeks of the 9/11 attacks, none were found to have any direct links with the terrorists or their actions. In addition, the Department of Justice summoned for voluntary interviews 5,000 noncitizen men in the United States on nonimmigrant visas from Arab and Muslim countries suspected of harboring terrorists. Only five people declined to be interviewed, and 104 letters were returned because of incorrect addresses. Although the interviews yielded no information relating to the terrorist attacks, Justice indicated soon afterward that it would be contacting another 3,000 young Arab men for more voluntary interviews. Major Arab and Muslim organizations, initially supportive of the government's efforts to combat terrorism, widely condemned the continued singling out of their communities and indicated they were no longer willing to cooperate with such tactics. To this changing America, another 31,362 Arabs immigrated in 2002.

Overseas, the Taliban were effectively ousted in three months, though Osama bin Laden eluded capture, and by the end of 2001, *there were only 2,500 U.S. service members on the ground in Afghanistan. Then, in January 2002, the world's attention spun around the globe to Cuba, as news began to emerge that the United States was detaining alleged Taliban fighters at Guantanamo Bay.*

Both these domestic policies and events around the world meant Americans were ever more aware of Arabs and especially Muslims and Islam. But this newfound visibility after September 11 meant not only scrutiny and suspicion on behalf of Americans toward Arabs and Muslims, but also newfound interest in and curiosity about things Middle Eastern. Thus Arab- and Muslim-American communities saw an opportunity to share their experiences and perspectives—which had often been excluded—on the culture, politics, history, and religion of the Arab and Muslim worlds. In many cases, community activists and advocates had been trying for years to elicit such interest from institutions that had closed their doors to Arabs in the past, and ironically, because of the al-Qaeda attacks, they finally found receptive audiences. Following an initial shrinking away after the attacks—many Arab- or Muslim-themed events, concerts, and lectures were canceled—groups refound their footing and organized or participated in a variety of, for example, campus teach-ins, public education efforts, and film and literary festivals. At the same time, Arab or Muslim characters were included in pop culture mediums, from the sophisticated—like Russell Simmons's Def Poetry Jam—*to the more common—like the family drama* 7th Heaven.

Arab Americans also became visible and vocal contingents in progressive movements, such as those focusing on civil rights and liberties. And of course, in the antiwar movement, which began to gain vigor as the United States set its sights on its next global target in the war on terrorism—Iraq. In February 2003, with nearly 10,000 troops already in Afghanistan, 90,000 U.S. troops were deployed to the Persian Gulf, and on March 20, 2003, the United States invaded Iraq.

© GINA CAVALLARO

Native Foreigner, Foreign Native

On the morning of March 12, 2003, Lance Corporal Abraham Al-Thaibani's wife pleaded with him to stay home a bit longer at the couple's basement apartment in Brooklyn. Esmihan's eyes had begun to tear, their jade tint deepening as they did now almost every morning when she began to barter for more time before he left her to report to the Marine compound in Garden City, Long Island. Her mood was always reflected in her eyes, and ever since she learned a few weeks before that he would soon be sent to Iraq for the coming war, they were clouded with fear.

"Don't go, don't go to this war," she told him as she did daily. "Run away to Canada, or say you're hurt," she urged in a barely contained whisper.

Just moments before, she had sat calmly beside him on their bed as he studied loose photos that they had not yet put into albums. He looked at the smiles on his and Esmihan's faces the day they had married in 1997,

243

squeezed in between their relatives and surrounded by little girls wearing white dresses almost as elaborate as the bride's. They had been so young—he a college freshman and Esmihan just out of high school, though they had fallen in love years before in middle school. Abraham remembered how bewildered he was that day but now, in comparison, those faraway times seemed so much easier.

"Why are you leaving early?" Esmihan asked him, though Abraham always gave himself some extra time so he would never be late.

"Hang out for one more hour," she implored, "or just be late."

But Abraham would not relent, especially not today. Leaving her this morning was already hard enough. Tonight he would not be coming back. Waiting at Garden City were the buses that would transport his reservist platoon to North Carolina. From there, they would be leaving for Iraq. He had not yet told Esmihan.

"Just a bit more?" she asked, making her final offer, though she already knew it was pointless.

Abraham kissed his wife good-bye and then held her closer and longer than usual. "I'll see you later," he said, smiling. In fact, he did not know if he would ever see or hold her again. He pushed the thought out of his mind.

He hated to lie to Esmihan, but whenever he imagined how she would react if she knew, he was convinced this way was better. Even though she had already cried this morning, as she did in bouts every day, at least this way, she might also laugh a little on the day he left.

He had been careful, meticulously careful, not to belie the ruse. He had quietly and gradually gathered the things he would be taking with him to Iraq in his locker in Garden City, and he had left the new Molly Pack he had been issued in a fellow Marine's car. He had gone to his parents' apartment above his own the night before, and even though he had wanted to somehow express to them not to worry about him in Iraq, he simply kissed them both good-night on the forehead, as if he were only going to sleep and not to war.

Abraham's four-year-old son Farid was thankfully too young to know any better. Abraham had spent the morning trying to make him laugh. He tickled him and told him how much he loved him. But as he tried to hug his little boy a little longer, Farid squirmed and pulled away. Abraham had been only twenty when Farid was born and was both working and attending college full time. From his home in Carroll Gardens in Brooklyn, he commuted to John Jay College on Manhattan's Upper West Side. After class, Abraham walked thirty blocks to his union job as an elevator operator, the same job his father had been working ever since he had emigrated from Yemen in 1968. Though his father had been a police officer in Qatar, he understood when he arrived in America that police jobs were for tall Irishmen, and he never pursued the work he loved. Abraham's daily shifts from 4 P.M. to midnight hardly put him in the mood for more family responsibility. Any spare time he could scrounge up, he preferred to spend with his friends shooting pool and hanging out, and so Farid had spent more time on his grandfather's lap than on Abraham's.

Abraham had realized his folly while separated from Farid and Esmihan during the year he had just completed at Camp Lejeune in North Carolina. He had spent the last months since January almost smothering Farid, even going to day care with him. Abraham had squeezed his 180-pound, 5'9" frame into the little toddler chairs and watched his son play with other children. At one point, Abraham had called out, "Farid, Farid," to get his attention.

Another child had snapped at Abraham, "Hey, his name is not Fahreed, his name is Frank."

"Oh, yeah?" Abraham had shot back. "Did you make him?" he asked, jokingly, though the cross-eyed boy drew back startled.

And yet, despite the constant time Abraham spent with Farid, the boy still mistook his grandfather for his father.

The morning he left for the war, Abraham held on to Farid until he scolded himself, enough! He tried to chase away thoughts that this might be the last time he held his son, and if it were, he prayed to God, Look after him, let him grow to be a good man. But Abraham didn't cut any deals with God for himself—he had not been a great Muslim and did not expect any favors. He would not be a hypocrite.

Ever since Gulf War I, when Abraham was twelve years old, he had committed himself to the idea that he would one day serve in the military. In 1991, he had walked the brownstone-lined side streets of First and Second Place on his way to P.S. 142, noticing that all the houses had yellow ribbons tied around the tree trunks out front. In his neighborhood in Brooklyn, it seemed to Abraham that every household either had an immediate member or a close relative fighting in the war. The yellow ribbons were badges of honor that were earned by a family in full for one son's sacrifice. But Abraham's parents had not tied a yellow ribbon to anything. No one in his family was in the military. Looking at those yellow ribbons flapping against the bark of the trees, Abraham had realized he didn't even *know* anybody in the service. He simply could not understand why *he* didn't have anybody.

But for the long months that the short 1991 Gulf War took place across the desert from his parents' native Yemen, Abraham arrived at P.S. 142 with his own fight to face. Ever since the war began, the kids—who had discovered he was not Hispanic but Arab—had taunted him, "We're going to kick your Arab ass." And Abraham had been suspended plenty of times for responding with blows. But as soon as Desert Storm and Americans' attentions fizzled, the boys quickly dropped their fists and forgot why they had been fighting.

Thus Abraham had enlisted in the Marines in 1998, while he was still in college. His parents had been proud, and he was ready to go to Afghanistan after the attacks on September 11, 2001, when paper fell from the sky—unrealized deals and dreams—and floated across the river to his street. The debris from the attack had coated the ground and the air in his neighborhood with white dust, which had made it impossible for Abraham to see more than a block ahead of him as he ran through the streets that morning looking for Esmihan. Outside the house, she always wore a *hijab*. Abraham had figured, within minutes of the attack, that the head scarf would make her an easy target for her fellow New Yorkers' rage and grief.

Now, here he was going to Iraq, though he did not think Iraq had ever attacked his country. Behind his back, others in the Yemeni- and Muslim-American communities whispered they hoped he and the other Arab-American soldiers would come back in body bags.

Then, while Abraham was still training in North Carolina in December, his teenage brother Ismael had declared his intention to enlist in the Marines.

Abraham had tried to talk him out of it, once it was clear there would be a war with Iraq. He did not want his little brother exposed to what

Abraham had tried to tell Esmihan was his own duty. He tried to scare Ismael, first with the goriness of war and death, and then with the lack of glory in urban, house-to-house warfare. When that failed, he made the same appeals that had not swayed his own self, about Iraqis looking like his and Ismael's parents.

Ismael had shot back, why should Abraham be the only special one in the military?

"Fine," Abraham yielded. "You're going to break your mother's heart," he told Ismael, his own heart already aching for his baby brother.

In the early sunrise hours of April 11, 2003, three weeks after the Americans had invaded Iraq, a Marine shouted out to Abraham and his partner in counterintelligence, "Something just happened on the bridge with Abe's platoon!" Abraham was already climbing into the passenger side of the desert-colored Humvee, ready to head out on a reconnaissance mission from the Iraqi college the Marines had transformed into their headquarters in Nasiriyah in southern Iraq. He scanned the radio and found the panicked play-by-play shouted by a reservist with his old platoon.

"Shots fired!"

"Civilians hit!"

"Civilians hurt!"

Abraham and his partner changed course and rushed to the bridge leading over the Saddam Canal, which had been commandeered by the Echo company of the 225th, Marine reservists from Pennsylvania, New Jersey, and New York. Abraham had trained and served with Echo 225 until arriving in Iraq, when he was attached to Marine counterintelligence because he spoke Arabic. As Abraham and his partner drove through the deserted streets of Nasiriyah, the screams continued over the radio. Abraham thought of his Marine brothers under fire and urged his partner to hurry.

As intelligence officers, Abraham and his partner needed to know of and head off any potential provocation to the Iraqi population. Injured civilians would surely undermine their efforts to win the hearts of Iraqis who had failed to see the Americans as liberators. Abraham knew Echo 225 had no translator with them at the bridge; the only Arabic they were equipped with were the words he had taught them back at Camp Lejeune, where they gathered before flying to Kuwait, before they were helicoptered to Nasiriyah with the mission to secure the Shiite city. And on top of it all, it was Abraham's platoon.

Abraham's partner pulled up to the northern entrance to the bridge, and Abraham braced himself for a big firefight.

"Oh, man, what happened?" Abraham shouted out as the Humvee slowed down at the coil of barbed wire guarding the bridge's entrance.

An older Marine whom Abraham recognized ran up to pull back the wire. "It's horrible, it's horrible," Matthew told Abraham, shaking his head. "It's little kids," he said in disbelief.

Abraham's partner maneuvered through the sandbag bunkers, speeding a hundred feet down the bridge, and parked the car close to the southern entrance checkpoint. Abraham jumped out and scanned the people lying in front of the bullet-riddled van, blood and broken glass all around them. The smell of gunpowder still hung in the air, and he could smell the heated steel of the guns that had just been fired. All he heard around him were the screaming and crying coming from the bodies lining the bridge.

He did a quick and incomplete accounting as he ran over: there was the driver, the only man in the group, lying shot on his side, screaming that he was going to die; he saw a little boy, wounded in the head; there was a woman wailing and bobbing back and forth; there was the doctor frantically tending to another injured woman; and then he saw the two casualties.

Lying side by side, wrapped in the khaki green liners from soldiers' ponchos, were two toddler-sized bodies; their blood had soaked through the plastic cocoons in which they had been carefully swathed. Someone told Abraham they were two baby girls. Abraham paused for only a second—he could save only those still living.

"Who's shot?" Abraham shouted out in Arabic, and as he did, he realized that the wailing woman held a lifeless little boy in her arms; he had been hidden by the folds of her black *abayah*. Oh my God, Abraham thought. "Is the baby all right?" he asked the woman again in Arabic, kneeling down to check the child.

She swatted Abraham away from her son, continuing to cry and howl until she realized that someone was finally speaking to her in Arabic. She took Abraham's hand. "What happened? Why did these people do this?" she asked him, gasping for air.

"We thought the war was over," she continued, her large black eyes drowning in her grief. "Why did you kill my babies?" She nodded to where her two daughters lay dead and bound in their camouflage wrapping. "*Akhadtuli nafasi,*" she screamed at him as she began to hyperventilate, bobbing in place, You took my breath.

The doctor came over to Abraham and told him that the woman had been shot in her lung. Abraham then saw blood seeping from underneath her. But her son was OK, the doctor assured Abraham. The boy had just passed out—maybe that was for the better—from all the shock. But they wouldn't be able to treat these wounds here on the bridge, the doctor told him; they had to get them to the Tallil Air Force base, twenty kilometers south of Nasiriyah. A cargo ambulance was already on the way.

Abraham wanted to know what had happened. Signs were posted hundreds of yards from the checkpoint warning Iraqis in Arabic that the bridge was open only to military traffic. For those who could not read, there were pictures that should have communicated the same message. And Abraham had made sure to teach everyone at least one word— "stop"—in Arabic.

"*W-a-q-f*" he had sounded out at Camp Lejeune for all the boys from Harrisburg, the ones who had shot at this van full of civilians.

The Marines manning the checkpoint told Abraham they had yelled out several times in English and Arabic for the van to *Waqf*! but it had run past the stop sign, past the barbed wire. And to the Marines, it seemed like they were speeding up. The soldiers finally opened fire on the nine civilians with M–16s and then the machine gun, with the doctors even shooting their Beretta 9mm handguns, because the van had continued to come at them. With the Marines blinded by the Iraqi sun rising in front of them, they could not see into the van. They could not see the babies.

This shooting would be classified as justified, Abraham realized.

Finally the ambulance arrived. The mother of the two dead daughters—already heavy without her newly added sorrow—would not budge. She begged Abraham to carry her son, but he let another Marine do it so that he would be able to help the woman. Her arms free, she threw dirt from the ground beside her into her face, beating her cheeks and crying, "I can't believe this happened, I can't believe you did this. We didn't need you to do this, Saddam never did this, he never took anyone's life in my family."

Abraham looked around. He was the only one on the bridge able to understand her. This is fucked up, he kept telling himself. But he could only imagine what he would do if he were in the same situation and his family were suddenly dead.

"*Yalla,*" he said to the woman in Arabic, let's go. "We need to get you medical attention," he explained. "We have to get you into that vehicle." He pointed to the cargo ambulance.

She was calm and quiet for a moment and reached for him to help her. He held her hand and hoisted her to her feet.

Suddenly, she began yelling again. "You should be ashamed of yourself, *inta `arabi,*" she said, you are Arab! "You are coming to an Arab country to kill Arabs?"

When she said that, Abraham thought, I have to deal with this too? He tried to stay thick skinned, but he was pissed off and shook up. Killing women and children, he thought, I didn't sign up for this.

They finished loading the civilians into the ambulance, including the bodies of the two baby girls. Abraham and his partner drove behind them in their Humvee to Tallil. They were both quiet as they drove through Nasiriyah's deserted streets. More than anything, Abraham felt sadness for the woman whose name he never thought to ask. He tossed out into this new world a silent prayer that there would be no more situations like this morning's sunrise.

He hoped someone was listening.

Abraham strolled along the riverbank underneath the crossing where the two baby girls had been killed a few weeks before. The bridge was reopened to civilian traffic once it had been secured, shortly after the accident, though no one had found the time to wash the blood from the asphalt. The Harrisburg Marines who guarded the Saddam Canal Bridge had renamed it "Al's Diamond Cabaret Memorial Bridge," in honor of the Pennsylvania strip club where they planned to have their homecoming party.

Abraham frequently went to the bridge to visit with his old platoon, to deliver cigarettes and soda that he had access to from his travels around and outside of Nasiriyah, and to gather intelligence from the locals who congregated—sometimes a little too close into his personal space—around the Marines.

With schools indefinitely closed, children from Nasiriyah flocked to the soldiers, shouting in the English they had cobbled together, "Mister mister, Bush good, Bush good," as a way to hopefully earn the candy the soldiers gave them from their packaged MREs (meals ready to eat).

Under the bridge, Abraham's old platoon mates told him that the little eight-year-old girl they had befriended was up on the bridge. Abraham had been hearing for weeks now, "Al-Thaibani, you gotta meet this girl."

The girl had captured their hearts with the story villagers told about her. Her entire family had been killed a few years earlier by Saddam Hussein in retaliation for a Shiite uprising in Nasiriyah. His soldiers had killed her father and shot up her house before they showered it with grenades. One had exploded so close to her that she had lost most of her hearing. She was the only one to survive and had been raised by the local village leader, who had taken her as his own child. Several of the Marines had talked about adopting her and had asked Abraham, who had more connections and mobility as an intelligence officer, if he could help them.

Curious, Abraham climbed back up to meet the girl who had mesmerized an entire platoon. Several soldiers were gathered at the north entrance to the bridge, a pack of children in tow. Matthew was there, and he shook his head as he always did when he saw Abraham, as if to say, What the fuck are we doing here? When the Iraqi children would start with the "Bush good, Saddam bad" greeting, Matthew would take them to the side and try to explain in equally simplistic English that it just wasn't that simple.

Another soldier called the girl over. A little blond girl walked toward the soldiers, her flowered dress torn.

Abraham knelt down beside her and told her, "*Ana `arabi*," I'm Arab.

She slowly read his lips and smiled up at him. Abraham felt as if her face—in which he saw pain and survival—betrayed her angelic appearance.

Even though he had heard her story, he asked her, "What happened to your parents?"

She started to move her lips and her hands. She pointed to houses in a nearby neighborhood, and then to herself. She made movements for guns and shooting, and wrapped her arms around her head to show how she had hidden. With each movement, she paused, watching Abraham's reaction to see if he had understood her.

He nodded his head, yes, and to prod her to go on.

The little girl continued. She threw imaginary grenades into a house across the street. Then she threw her arms in a wide arc, spreading her fingers to show an explosion, and then quickly drew her hands back to grab her ears. She then pointed to herself and shook her head. She had no one.

Again she looked at him. Had he understood?

He nodded and stood up, offering her MRE candy. He told her in Arabic, "I'm going to be back if you need anything."

Abraham had decided that he agreed; she should be adopted. But it would be better, he thought, were it by someone who spoke Arabic.

He called Esmihan that night. He told her all about the girl, how her parents had been murdered in front of her, how she had lost her hearing, how she was so beautiful, like a little doll, and how she made him feel like a parent in Iraq.

"This girl has been so strong," he told Esmihan, "she deserves to finally get a break, to have a better life."

He heard his wife crying on the other side of the world.

"Everyone wants to adopt her," he continued. "And," he ventured, "I feel like I should do it." He then confessed to himself what he had not brought himself to say out loud: I would love having this girl as a daughter.

"Why don't you adopt her?" Esmihan asked. Both of them knew, after all, that if things had been different, they would have had a baby girl of their own right now.

"Are you serious?" he asked her. He needed Esmihan's blessing. On Halloween in 2001, Esmihan had miscarried the baby they had been expecting; it had been a girl. At five months old, Abraham was amazed to see that she was fully formed. They could not bear to see her buried in potter's field, where the city disposed of many unborn fetuses. Instead, they had bought her a tiny coffin and buried her in the "Baby Land" section at the Pine Lawn Cemetery under a tombstone that said, simply, "Mariam."

Abraham and Esmihan agreed: he would approach CAG—the civilian affairs group—to see what could be done.

Several weeks after Abraham had asked CAG to look into adopting the little girl he wished to make his daughter, he wondered how badly the grenades had damaged her eardrums. He hoped that maybe doctors back home could save some of her hearing. He continued to see her on the bridge, and when she was not wearing the flowered dress, she had on her other outfit, a pair of purple pants and a T-shirt with a cartoon character he did not recognize.

Abraham was hopeful; CAG had helped many military personnel adopt children and had helped Marines who fell in love with Iraqi women get engaged. Abraham had persistently begged a CAG Marine to persuade the village elder, who was the girl's guardian, to let her go. As far as Abraham could tell, the CAG woman had been equally zealous in bringing his dream to fruition, even going to her superiors. But the elder would not agree, and he had similarly turned down other Americans who had tried to obtain his consent with the help of a local Iraqi who had interpreted for them on the bridge.

Abraham finally decided to talk to the elder personally. "*Ana `arabi*," he told the old man, "*wa ana muslim*." I am Arab, and I am Muslim. Abraham didn't think it mattered he was Sunni, and not Shiite like the girl. "I'll make a better home for her," he pleaded. "She'll get everything she needs." Abraham knew the man had to care for several of his own kids and had seen the poverty in which the man—the entire village, in fact—lived.

Just weeks before, Abraham had delivered flour to this same village. The children had surrounded him then, smiling and chanting his name in Arabic, "I-bra-him, I-bra-him," and as they had begun to close in on him, Abraham had had to wave his gun to push them back.

"*Haram*," Abraham continued, poor thing. "She's alone, she has only you." And, Abraham tried to say it as delicately as he could, "You're old."

The man looked Abraham square in the eyes and said, "No my son, she's like my daughter."

Abraham realized the old man—poor as he may have been—loved her too.

CAG had told him in the event her guardian refused to let her go, they would intervene only if abuse could be proven.

Abraham tried to imagine all the trauma the girl had already survived. To take her from the only person she really knew, without his blessing, would have given her only more to bear.

This is out of my hands now, he thought. More and more in Iraq, much as he tried to deny it, he found himself coming to that same conclusion.

One month after President Bush swooped down in a jet onto an aircraft carrier and declared "Mission Accomplished," Abraham had come to the Tallil Air Force base to run a quick errand. But everything moved slower in the June heat, especially the unorganized lines that spilled out of buildings and entrances everywhere. By then people were standing in lines for water, jobs, pensions, food, fuel, answers, justice, and, of course, medical care.

Right outside the entrance to Tallil—guarded by barbed wire—nearly a hundred Iraqis pleaded to be let into the base's hospital. As Abraham passed by in his Humvee, parents held up their children as if trying to show him proof of their afflictions as they shouted out in English, "Please, please."

Abraham hopped out of the Humvee to speak with the Iraqi interpreters. The crowd overheard him speaking in Arabic and rushed him. Several took his hand and kissed it, and others cried, "I beg of you, help us get in."

Abraham felt ashamed and embarrassed. He went up to CAG's office. "Listen," he told them. "There's a bunch of people out there needing treatment."

The hospital at Tallil treated American soldiers first and foremost. Only in cases where the Americans had been responsible for civilian injuries were Iraqis to be treated there now. Abraham tried to argue that from a counterintelligence standpoint, it was important to build good relations with the people whose country they were occupying. But he could not persuade anyone. Even the Americans had begun to run out of supplies.

Abraham realized that many of his fellow Americans resented their own impotence. But only Abraham could comprehend what the words the desperate Iraqis cried meant. Yet he never wished he could turn off his ability to understand Arabic. What good would I be then? he thought. I would just be another person at the checkpoint.

Abraham had tried to help Iraqis with the minor things, like securing stitches, IVs, and Band-Aids. They were people in need, and they reminded him of his mother and his father. The way the women screamed reminded him of when his own mother scolded him.

But looking out at the crowds gathering, Abraham realized all his empathy could not stay the individual tragedies potentially awaiting each and every Iraqi. The best he could do, he decided, was work to avert the coming disaster that he felt would soon engulf Iraq in its entirety.

As Abraham and his partner sat in traffic coming back from As Samawah, a town west of Nasiriyah farther up the Euphrates River, Abraham suggested they go visit the Bedou. His partner took a sharp turn off the road and drove out into the desert, weaving over the mound of rocks that rose out of the sand. The Bedouin encampment—two large tents made of a heavy canvas pitched close to each other surrounded by some chickens and sheep—lay only a mile into the desert, but for those who did not know to look, it would never be found. The modest tents and the people he considered the Amish of Iraq were Abraham's escape from the war.

Unlike most everyone else in Iraq, the Bedou had no interest or stake in politics. As a power broker in the country, Abraham heard mostly complaints from Iraqis, but the Bedou never complained. He reasoned that because the Bedouins were self-sufficient—the only modern thing Abraham could see at the camp was a truck—they didn't need anything from him. There were never any conditions or requests attached to their hospitality; they feared nothing, including the Americans, and thus had the courage to be friendly to them. Abraham marveled at how they seemed to live life simply and for their family. In the middle of the chaos that had begun to make the ground in Iraq constantly tremble, the Bedou remained tranquil. When Abraham could no longer take the corruption, the chaos, or the inequity that characterized his interactions with Iraqis, he went to the Bedou tents for refuge. And even though they were in the middle of the desert, the Bedou sometimes came across useful intelligence to share with the Marines.

Abraham would go with the pretense of just passing by to say hello, but he knew the Bedou would insist he stay for some *shai*, lightly brewed tea heavily sweetened and flavored with fresh sprigs of mint. He was always happy to take a seat inside the tent on the rattan carpet and lean back against the large burgundy pillows.

As the Marines parked their Humvee, the patriarch of the family—an old man in an *abayeh*—walked out to greet them. His wife and daughter—a woman Abraham thought looked like Monica Bellucci with her silver-colored eyes—followed right behind. He kissed Abraham and his partner on both their cheeks, and said, "*Tfaddula, tfaddula*," Come in, come in. He immediately dispatched his wife to begin brewing some tea, and the three men proceeded into the tent.

As the men sat discussing *Amreeka*, Iraq, and Arab history, Abraham knew the sun had begun to set by the change of light on the sand visible just past the partly raised entrance flap of the tent. He loved the sun in Iraq, with its fiery color, which set so low in the sky that Abraham always felt it was right by his face.

But as much as he loved being with the Bedouins, he had to wonder, if he had been born in the same circumstances—who knows where he would be if his parents had stayed in Yemen—would he have had the good sense to get out and see the rest of the world?

Before the soldiers could rise to go, relatives soon arrived, and no one would let the Americans leave without dinner. Abraham, who interpreted for the other Marine, answered the typical barrage of questions during another round of *shai*. What's life like in *Amreeka*? How does it compare to Iraq? How is Times Square? Do women walk around naked?

Soon the food began arriving from the other tent, behind which Abraham had seen an oven built from a mound of bricks. There was bread baked in the camp, lamb, and fish from the nearby Euphrates, which Abraham did not trust—he had seen one too many Iraqi bathe in the filthy river. The meal ended with fruit, and as they picked at some grapes, the father and his visiting cousin each reached for a *dirbakkeh*, the Arabic bongo. The cousin began to sing.

He sang old Iraqi songs, and to Abraham the odes were uplifting despite their melancholic tones. The lyrics told of ancient Iraq, how in its embrace, civilization had begun. They spoke of Iraq's beauty and how much the bard loved his country. The songs were clearly patriotic, but free of any militaristic nationalism. To Abraham, they sounded much more like love songs.

He leaned back against the pillows and relaxed, lost in the moment. In Iraq, he never separated from his caution; even in sleep he found no real comfort. Here, he did not have to be on guard as much as in Baghdad or Nasiriyah. But even though he had placed his weapon to the side, it was still within reach, and he was only a movement away from the pistol holstered to the inside of his right shin.

These nights with the Bedou were straight out of the movies about the Middle East that Abraham had watched as a little boy. But the Middle East he had come to know in Iraq was not in its entirety like these romantic renderings of a place noble in its simplicity and sincerity.

And yet there was something familiar—even though he had been to his parents' native land only once, when he was five—he had grown up in the Yemeni community in Carroll Gardens. At the Yemeni houses back in Brooklyn, on rare occasions he had shared a meal also sitting on the floor, listening to Arabic conversation and folklore. But back outside those houses, all around him, were the wrought-iron stair rails of rows of brownstones, the small grass front yards with manicured shrubs, the tall black lampposts, the orderly parked cars, the pizzeria where he worked as a kid—not the desert, not ancient dwellings, not palm trees.

Abraham and his partner exchanged looks; they should be leaving, the sun had set long ago.

When Abraham heard in July of 2003 that he would return home later that summer, he thought of all the things he could teach Farid. He had been so afraid he would not return that he had long ago stopped counting the days till the end of his service and had told himself he was not going back.

One month later in North Carolina, Abraham waited to see that all his fellow Marines from the 225th had made it back alive. When he was

sworn in as a Marine years before, he had thought that serving his country was about lofty ideals of protecting freedom from its enemies. But
once he knew he would be going to Iraq, serving his country became
about his friends, his brothers, and their commitment to each other that
they would all return back home on their feet. Thinking of it that way
meant he never had to worry about the politics of Washington, D.C., tar-
nishing any of the ideals.

Once he saw his entire platoon safe and sound again at Camp Lejeune,
he felt he could finally stop holding his breath. He realized he was proud
of himself. Serving without seeing combat was one thing, but serving in
wartime in another country and seeing what he saw in Iraq was another.
He felt his service was all the more real and legitimate. When he enlisted,
he always knew that there was a possibility he would one day face soldiers
that were Arab like him. But he had always deferred those thoughts by
telling himself, "I'll cross that bridge when I come to it." But that bridge
had come and gone, and he had crossed it, taking any opportunity to help
civilians who came his way. The war would have happened regardless if
he were there or not; his presence, Abraham realized, guided by trying to
do something right, had served a purpose.

When it came time to board the buses for Long Island, Abraham
would not let Esmihan and Farid come to Garden City to meet him; he
knew that with the swarms of family, he would hold them again in his
arms more quickly if he instead went to them.

When he returned home, he stayed indoors with his family for a week.
He needed to adjust to the loud bangs, jarring honks, and screeching
brakes and realize they meant different things in New York than they did
in Nasiriyah.

After that week, he decided to leave the house to take a walk. He
stopped next door at Sweet Melissa's, bought a cup of coffee, and started
walking with no destination in mind. He walked down Court Street, up
Dean Street, down Atlantic Avenue, then back up Atlantic, stopping to say
hello to all the Arab grocers along that Arab-American thoroughfare.

He walked for three hours straight before he realized he was walking in circles. He was mesmerized by seeing adults go to work and children go to school. Normalcy—non-Iraqi normalcy—was all new again.
In Iraq, when people saw his uniform, they stopped him with their prob-

lems, their needs, their pains. Here in Brooklyn, he slowed down as if by reflex when another person passed him on the sidewalk, ready to hear their woes. In response, people several times gave him the *what the fuck you lookin' at* look, and Abraham had to laugh—he was at home.

In these same streets that he had walked as a child during Gulf War I, he noticed that even though Gulf War II was just beginning to slip into the violent abyss he knew would befall it, there were no yellow ribbons anywhere. And now his little brother would soon be leaving for Iraq. Abraham knew that Ismael's Iraq would be different; the country was changing by the day to one of violent and cynically sectarian rage, one with no end it seemed, as President Bush had vowed that August, "No Retreat."

Abraham finally ended up at the Promenade, the tree-lined walkway along the East River just south of the Brooklyn Bridge, with a view of Manhattan's scarred skyline. From a distance he saw some children skating by on rollerblades; others just played in the grass. Different time, different place, Abraham marveled, thinking of children pushing donkey carts in Iraq.

As he continued along the river, a group of children ran toward him. Abraham raised his hand to wave as he had with all those flocks of children in Iraq who would sprint toward him, yelling, "Mister! Mister!" and when they knew him, "Ibrahim! Ibrahim!"

The children in New York now instead barely glanced at him, the same kind of unimpressed look of indifference on their little faces that the adults had frowned at him. As they dashed past him uninterested, Abraham caught his hand in midwave and lowered it sheepishly back into his pocket.

EPILOGUE

Ed died right before Christmas in 2001. Two of his sons also played baseball and football at the University of Alabama. Ann, who misses him, still lives in Birmingham in the same house they bought in 1963.

Luba regrets she never returned to Ramallah to live but has succumbed to the idea that going back home is no longer possible; she would not want to leave her three daughters and three granddaughters. However, she walks her village's streets in her mind on the many nights when she cannot fall asleep.

Alan was the first Arab American elected to public office in Dearborn, serving a school board that governed both the K–12 and the community college. Today he is the director of community development and outreach in the administration of the Wayne County Executive. He is a single father of three.

John is a successful engineering executive with a nationally recognized architectural and engineering firm in Chicago. He has been involved in numerous award-winning buildings in Chicago and throughout the world. He has established a scholarship fund to help sponsor bright, needy university students from Baqa'a Camp that at one point was managed by his late mother. He is married and has three boys.

Norma has not remarried; every year she travels to Washington, D.C., to receive an in-person update from the FBI as to the status of her late husband's still-open murder case. She has asked the FBI to return Alex's notebook but has yet to receive it. In 1994, a memorial statue honoring Alex was unveiled in front of the library in the civic center of the Orange County seat. The following lines from one of Alex's poems are engraved on the base of the pedestal: "Lies are like still ashes. When the wind of truth blows, they are dispersed like dust and disappear."

After graduating from Yale law school, clerking on the Ninth Circuit Court of Appeals, and working at a law firm, **Omar** moved to the Palestinian Territories in 1999. There he served as a legal adviser to the Palestinian team in peace talks with Israel until 2001 and as a political officer on the peace team of United Nations envoy Terje Roed-Larsen. In 2004, he joined the faculty at the University of the Pacific's McGeorge School of Law, where he teaches and writes about international law, conflict resolution, and contracts.

Farah used the $5,000 she won from the pageant to help pay for college. Today she is a film director. **Issam** still practices medicine in Laketown and hopes to retire to Mexico. **Zayneb** has moved back to the Middle East and while it feels more like home, she is saddened to be away from her children after having spent most of her life in America far from her parents and siblings. **Sawsan** is an attorney living in a major American city. She follows the Palestinian plight closely and may have inherited her father's unhealthy obsession with the nightly news of the Middle East. She is still an outspoken advocate for justice and peace in Palestine.

Rabih lives in Minneapolis. He is a supporter and a contributor to *MIZNA,* the Arab-American literary journal, and his health care practice is on the verge of its third decade. On 8/8/08 at 8:08 P.M., after 8 years of living together, Rabih proposed to his partner. They planned to escape the Minnesota winter and marry in California later that year, though their plans were thwarted by, ironically, Proposition 8.

After years of working in Washington, D.C.—both doing advocacy work for an NGO and legislative work for a member of Congress on the Hill— **Maya** cofounded her own private consulting company to improve U.S. bilateral relations with the Arab and Muslim world on the economic, political, and cultural fronts. She is married, has two young children and, having survived the last eight years of Bush, is delighted to do her part as our nation rebuilds under the leadership of President Barack Hussein Obama.

Randa is president of Fahmy Hudome International (FHI), a strategic consulting firm based in Washington, D.C., that provides advisory services to an elite group of international and domestic clients. She is still a "Baker-Powell-Scowcroft-Hagel" Republican awaiting another Ronald Reagan!

Ignace retired from the Brooklyn church in 2006 and now teaches at the Maronite Seminary in Washington, D.C.

Abraham was honorably discharged from the Marines and is a New York police officer. He is divorced and is devoting his time to raising his son. His brother was awarded the Purple Heart for his service in Iraq.

AFTERWORD

In July 1974, my mother carried me over from Syria in her womb when she came to live in America with my father. That December, I was born an American, the first in my family. Though my father had arrived in America almost exactly five years before on New Year's Eve in 1969, he would not become a citizen until 1980, and my mother not until 1981. By then, my three siblings had all been born American as well.

In the early days, we were Americans in name alone. Inside our house we spoke Arabic, ate Arabic, and lived Arabic. I came to think of the world outside our split-level single-family house in a suburban cul-de-sac as *America* and the children with straight blonde hair and names like Mary Jane as *Americans*. Inside, we understood our hybrid reality of 1969 Damascus—the last Damascus my father had known—and 1980s Baltimore to be different, mostly because our parents made it clear we were not to behave like our American neighbors—no soda, no TV, no Bs in school, no sleepovers, and no dating, for what seemed like forever. We believed then that we could not afford the same relaxed attitude to life we thought our neighbors possessed because our position in America was precarious; we had no one but one another. In our big bay window, we would sit propped up on our elbows and watch our neighbors receive visits from their grandparents; ours were like imaginary friends that we had to yell to across the world through the telephone, if it would connect, and only on holidays.

We didn't feel that America thought we were real Americans either. We understood this in many ways, from the most malignant, like the silencing of our dissent, to the most benign as well. At gift shops I would scan the stands of mugs, key chains, and magnets personalized with every name from A to Z for one that said *Alia*, as if that would be proof America anticipated my presence here. But where it would have been—somewhere between Alexandra and Alice—I never found anything.

Soon I understood that we would experience differently much of what happened in America. Unlike me, my classmates at school were unfettered by the evening news, which told me in advance that what I thought about the Middle East and Arabs was wrong; they did not worry about their fathers losing their jobs to people who did not have accents, accents which I was ashamed to admit embarrassed me sometimes. They did not learn to pray early on that it not be Arabs when a plane crashed or anything exploded; they did not feel implicated by the ugly stereotypes present everywhere in pop culture; and their trips to the mall for new lipstick never ended with men following their families through the parking lot because of a war between Americans and Arabs in a faraway Arab world.

Though I knew my ancestors' history was ancient, I did not know of any larger history in the United States that would make me feel as American as the people I thought of as "real Americans," namely anyone of European origin or African Americans (sadly, Native Americans weren't even on my radar screen). Only vaguely did I realize that my family's lived reality was likely similar to that of Arab Americans across the country. It also didn't occur to me that it was indeed akin to the experiences of other post-1965 immigrants from other developing countries and their children. I definitely did not understand then that collectively those realities were as quintessentially American as any other way of growing up.

I wished for some reflection of our existence, whether it was in the census, on TV, in books, or on the lips of political or cultural leaders. When as an adolescent I saw for the first time hummus and falafel sandwiches being sold at a mall food court in Boston (apparently more diverse than Baltimore in those days), I was nearly delirious from joy. Along with fried rice, pizza, hot dogs, and tacos, our cuisine as well—*we* as well— were somehow part of the American mosaic.

That same yearning for visibility, normalization, and affirmation stayed with me, and is what partly drove me to want to become a civil rights lawyer. Though the civil rights laws are birthed from the African-American experience, they remain an essential mechanism in realizing our national ideal that *all* women and men are created equal. And since the passage of the Civil Rights Act in 1964 and its legislative progeny, the framework has expanded to work on behalf of many of America's peoples, including those brought and born here because of the 1965 Immigration Act.

As I worked in that sphere, especially after 9/11, I realized that litigating for people's rights—including Arab Americans'—would be better served if their lived reality, their voices, their faces, their names were less foreign to their fellow Americans. I also came to believe that making these narratives heard would allow us all to more thoroughly understand our collective American society and history and to more accurately imagine ourselves as Americans. Because we cannot move forward until we better understand the history and the lived experiences of all *our* peoples, until we better understand who *we* are.

Since 1974, America itself has hardly been static; it has continued to evolve, changing in ways that hopefully were made more tangible by the chapters preceding this afterword. Today, one can buy many Arabic foods in a regular grocery store (as well as Mexican, Jamaican, or Pakistani ingredients), and there's been a proliferation of babies being given Arabic names by all kinds of Americans as well. The parameters of the debates about the Middle East have been greatly expanded—though there is much further to go—and many Americans readily dissent about their country's policies in the region. In 2008, the nation elected an African-American president with an Arabic name and his own developing-world immigrant pedigree, just years after the 9/11 attacks threatened to see us become as ugly as we were when we interned Japanese Americans almost a century ago.

But Arab Americans are still struggling to be seen as a part of this country, and as human individuals who are part of a larger community that is as American as any other immigrant or native-born group. As an adult, I continue to seek out books, articles, and films with these narratives. They have begun to appear—I have seen parts of our story in works by and about, to name a few, Indian Americans, Asian Americans, African Americans, Hispanic Americans, and of course other Arab Americans.

My hope for this book, *A Country Called Amreeka*, is that it adds to the growing way of how we Americans and Arab Americans alike see who we are and how we work together to write the next century of chapters in our joint history.

A NOTE ON SOURCES

This book offers the stories of individuals. As such, the primary source for each chapter is the main character (or in the case of Ed Salem, his family as he is deceased). However, they are not the only source. While the chapters tell the moments in time through the eyes of one person, I of course interviewed other people in addition to the main characters. I also relied on news accounts of the major event that each chapter discusses as well as for the events that make up each person's story. I used many a local newspaper, and I encountered some incredibly helpful librarians across the country at universities, historical societies, and local public branches. Where television news footage or other videos were available, I made use of them. Many of those I interviewed also had personal pictures and videos that they shared with me. These inputs helped me re-create events and understand the ethos of times and places, as well as confirm information provided by those portrayed. With the exception of the 1991 chapter, I have not changed any names or locations. In the 1995 chapter, the last name given is Rabih's pen name.

I have tried to render a listing of those sources, though this is by no means an exhaustive list. Many of the sources listed in one chapter were also used in the interstitials or other chapters; I have not double-listed.

SEPTEMBER 15, 1963: PROLOGUE

"Auburn 0 Alabama 55." *Corolla Yearbook*, The University of Alabama, 1949.
Birmingham's Lebanese: The Earth Turned to Gold. Birmingham: Birmingham Find, 1981.
Bolton, Clyde. *The Crimson Tide: A Story of Alabama Football*. Huntsville, AL: Strode, 1972.
Bostany, Bee. Personal interview. Nov. 2008.
Bostany, Joe. Personal interview. June 2006, Nov. 2008.
Bostany, Philip. Personal interview. June 2006, Nov. 2008.

Corley, Robert G. Professor, University of Alabama, Birmingham. Personal interview and e-mail exchanges. June 2006, Nov. 2008.

Davis, Charles. Former Alabama football player. Personal interview. Nov. 2008.

Faires Conklin, Nancy and Nora Faires. " 'Colored' and Catholic: The Lebanese in Birmingham, Alabama." *Crossing the Waters: Arabic-Speaking Immigrants to the United States Before 1940*. Ed. Eric James Hooglund. Washington, DC: Smithsonian Institution Press, 1987, 69–84.

Farley, Bob, ed. *Bloodfeud: The Storied Rivalry of Alabama-Auburn Football*. Birmingham, AL: Epic Sports, 2000.

Feldman, Lynne B. *A Sense of Place: Birmingham's Black Middle Class Community 1890–1930*. Tuscaloosa, AL: University of Alabama Press, 1999.

Files of the FBI's investigation into the church bombing.

Fortunado, Steve. Former Alabama football player. Personal interview. Nov. 2008.

Gryska, Clem. Former Alabama football player and coach. Personal interview. Nov. 2008.

Gualtieri, Sarah. "Strange Fruit? Syrian Immigrants, Extralegal Violence, and Racial Formation in the Jim Crow South." 26 *Arab Studies Quarterly* (Summer 2004): 63.

Haddad, Janisse Boustany. Personal interview. Nov. 2008.

Higham, John. *Strangers in the Land: Patterns of American Nativism 1860–1925*. New Brunswick, NJ: Rutgers University Press, 1955.

Khalaf, Samir. "The Background and Causes of Lebanese/Syrian Immigration to the United States before World War I." *Crossing the Waters*. 17–35.

McWhorter, Diane. *Carry Me Home: The Climactic Battle of the Civil Rights Revolution*. New York: Touchstone, 2001.

———. Personal interview and e-mail exchanges. June 2008 and Nov. 2008.

Melof, Fred. "History of St. George Melkite Church of Birmingham, Alabama."

Mizerany, Mike. Former Alabama football player. Personal interview. Nov. 2008.

Saad, Richard. Priest, St. Elias Maronite Church. Personal interview. Nov. 2008.

Salem, Ann. Personal interview. Nov. 2008.

Salem, George. Personal interview. Nov. 2008.

Salem, Mark. Personal interview. Nov. 2008.

Schoor, Gene. *100 Years of Alabama Football: A Century of Champions, 1892–1992*. Atlanta, GA: Longstreet Press, 1991.

The Phoenician Club of Birmingham: Celebrating 100 Years of Tradition, Centennial Commemorative Issue. Birmingham: The Phoenician Club, 2005.

Tuscaloosa News Staff. *Greatest Moments in Alabama Crimson Tide Football History.* Birmingham, AL: Epic Sports Classics, 2003.

"Your Guide to St. Elias Maronite Church, Birmingham, Alabama."

Zaidan, Judy. Personal interview. June 2006 and Nov. 2008.

Legal Citations:

In re Najour, 174 F. 735 (C.C.N.D.Ga. 1909).

In re Balsara, 171 F. 294 (C.C.S.D.N.Y. 1909).

In re Halladjian, 174 F. 834 (C.C.D.Mass. 1909).

In re Mudarri, 176 F. 465 (C.C.D.Mass. 1910).

In re Ellis, 179 F. 1002 (D. Or. 1910).

Ex parte Shahid, 205 F. 812 (E.D.S.C. 1913).

Ex parte Dow, 211 F. 486 (E.D.S.C. Feb. 18, 1914).

In re Dow, 213 F. 355 (E.D.S.C. April 15, 1914).

Dow v. United States, 226 F. 145 (4th Cir. 1915).

In re Ahmed Hassan, 48 F.Supp. 843 (E.D.Mich. 1942).

Ex parte Mohriez, 54 F.Supp. 94 (D.C. Mass. 1944).

JUNE 5, 1967: HOME

Abraham, Sameer and Nabeel. "The Southend: An Arab-Muslim Working Class Community." *Arabs in the New World: Studies on Arab-American Communities.* Ed. Sameer and Nabeel Abraham. Detroit, MI: Wayne State University, 1983.

Abu-Jaber, Kamel S. "U.S. Policy Toward the June Conflict." *The Arab-Israeli Confrontation of June 1967: An Arab Perspective.* Ed. Ibrahim Abu-Lughod. Evanston, IL: Northwestern University Press, 1970.

Aruri, Naseer. Personal interview. 22 April 2008.

Aruri, Naseer. "Arab Americans and the Vital American Political Center." Banquet address, Arab Students Union.

Aswad, Barbara. *Arabic-Speaking Communities in American Cities.* New York, NY: Center for Migration Studies, 1974.

Baldwin, Hanson. "Why Israel Prevailed: Her Spirit and Modern Organization Are Contrasted with Arab Feudalism." *The New York Times,* 8 June 1967.

CBS News Clips. The following films were viewed at CBS Archives in New York City: "Jerusalem Situationer: Israel Takes Over," *CBS News,* 7 June 1967; "Security Council President on Ceasefire," CBS News, 7 June 1967; "Security Council Passes Ceasefire," *CBS News,* 7 June 1967; "Wallace Hears Reporters on Mid-East War," *CBS News,* 5 June 1967; "Nahal Oz Border

Kabbutz," *CBS News*, 6 June 1967; "Special Report: War in the Middle East," *CBS News*, June 1967.

Colony of Aden. Certificate of Service, 16 July 1958.

Dresch, Paul. *A History of Modern Yemen*. Cambridge, UK: Cambridge University Press, 2000.

Farrell, William. "Israel Settlers Are Holding Out at Illegal Camp." *The New York Times*, 12 Dec. 1976.

Feron, James. "Time Stands Still in an Israeli-Occupied Town." *The New York Times*, 17 May 1970.

————. "Tourists Crowd Jerusalem's Holy Places." *The New York Times*, 8 July 1967.

Finney, John W. "U.S. Providing $5 Million for Mideast War Victims." *The New York Times*, 28 June 1967.

Gavin, R. I. *Aden Under British Rule 1839–1967*. London, UK: C. Hurst & Co. Publishers Ltd., 1975.

Haddad, Yvonne. "Arab Muslims and Islamic Institutions in America." *Arabs in the New World: Studies on Arab-American Communities*. Ed. Sameer and Nabeel Abraham. Detroit, MI: Wayne State University: 1983.

"Israel Rules Out Return to Frontiers." *The New York Times*, 11 June 1967.

Jabara, Abdeen. "The American Left and the June Conflict." *The Arab-Israeli Confrontation of June 1967: An Arab Perspective*. Ed. Ibrahim Abu-Lughod. Evanston, IL: Northwestern University Press: 1970.

Kerr, Malcolm. "Foreword." *The Arab-Israeli Confrontation of June 1967: An Arab Perspective*. Ed. Ibrahim Abu-Lughod, Evanston, IL: Northwestern University Press, 1970.

Langston, Anna. Letter of reference, 13 March 1961.

Mansour, Nadya. Personal interview. 12 Sept. 2008.

Robbins, William. "A New Skyline Climbs Baltimore Horizon." *The New York Times*, 4 June 1967.

Jane Rostek, Halifax Seed, e-mail message to author, Sept. 11, 2008.

Said, Edward. "The Arab Portrayed." *The Arab-Israeli Confrontation of June 1967: An Arab Perspective*. Ed. Ibrahim Abu-Lughod. Evanston, IL: Northwestern University Press, 1970.

Semple Jr., Robert B. "Cities Seek Shift of Slum Burdens." *The New York Times*, 5 June 1967.

Sihwail, Luba. Personal interviews. 6 May 2006; 21 March 2008; 21, 22, 23, 29 April 2008; 3, 11 June 2008; 1, 2, 8, 10 July 2008; 12 Sept. 2008.

Stookey, Robert W. *South Yemen: A Marxist Republic in Arabia*. Boulder, CO: Westview, 1982.

Suhwail, Aziz. Personal interview. 10 July 2008.

Suleiman, Michael. "American Mass Media and the June Conflict." *The Arab-Israeli Confrontation of June 1967: An Arab Perspective.* Ed. Ibrahim Abu-Lughod. Evanston, IL: Northwestern University Press, 1970.

Swados, Harvey. "The Bridge on the River Jordan." *The New York Times,* 26 Nov. 1967.

U.S. Customs Service. Passenger list, *Saturnia.* 12 Sept. 1959.

"U.S. Grants Visas to 5,633 Refugees." *The New York Times,* 8 July 1954.

OCTOBER 17, 1973: DISSENT

Abraham, Nabeel. Personal interview. 4 Sept. 2008.

Ahmed, Ishmael. "Organizing an Arab Workers Caucus: Middle East Research and Information Project. Jan. 1975: 17–22. JSTOR. Online. 16 Jan. 2008."

———. Personal interview. 23 Oct. 2008.

Alhobashi, Moshin. Personal interview. 5 Sept. 2008.

Almaklani, Ali. Personal interview. 5 Sept. 2008.

Amen, Alan. Personal interviews. 24 July 2008; 20 Aug. 2008; 3, 25 Sept. 2008; 9, 21 Oct. 2008.

Amen, Alice. Personal interview. 27 Oct. 2008.

Amen, Karen. Personal interview. 28 Oct. 2008.

Katherine Amen et al., v. *City of Dearborn.* D.C.Mich. Aug. 14, 1973. 363 F.Supp. 1267.

Katherine Amen et al., v. *City of Dearborn.* 6th Cir. March 24, 1976. 532 F.2d 554.

Amen, Ron. Personal interviews and e-mail exchanges. 1 Sept. 2008; 21, 23, 28 Oct. 2008.

"The Arab-Americans Awaken." *AAUG Newsletter,* Dec. 1973:10.

"Arabian Leaders Demand Return to Occupied Land." *Detroit Free Press,* 29 Nov. 1973:8-B.

"Arabs in Academe." *Time,* 19 Nov. 1973. http://www.time.com/time/magazine/article/0,9171,944733,00.html.

"The Arabs' New Oil Squeeze: Dimouts, Slowdowns, Chills." *Time,* 19 Nov. 1973. http://www.time.com/time/magazine/article/0,9171,944743,00.html.

"Auto Industry Layoffs." *World News Digest,* 20 Sept. 1975. *LexisNexis,* 25 Oct. 2008.

"Auto Industry Problems." *World News Digest,* 11 Jan. 1975. *LexisNexis,* 25 Oct. 2008.

"Auto Makers Report Earnings Drop." *World News Digest,* 1 March 1975; *LexisNexis,* 25 Oct. 2008.

Barron, James. "Parks News Racial Issue in Dearborn." *The New York Times,* 19 Jan. 1986, *LexisNexis,* 25 Oct. 2008.

Bartlett, J.A., "One Day in Your Life: October 1973." *PopDose.* 15 Oct. 2008. 2
    Oct. 2008. http://popdose.com/one-month-in-your-life—1973.
Beck, Jason. "Horton Reflects on Detroit's Past." MLB.com 17 Feb. 2005. http://
    mlb.mlb.com/news, 8 Nov. 2008.
Bisharat, Mary. "Yemeni Farmworkers in California." *Middle East Research and
    Information Project,* Jan. 1975: 22–26; http://www.jstor.org, 16 July 2008.
"Black October: Old Enemies at War Again." *Time,* 15 Oct. 1973; http://www.
    time.com/time/magazine/article/0,9171,910794,00.html.
"Bnai B'rith Fetes Woodcock, Arabs Stage a Protest." *Detroit Free Press,* 30 Nov.
    1973.
"Cashbox Top 100 Singles." *Cashbox* magazine, 25 Oct. 2008. http://cashbox
    magazine.com.
Chappel, Lindsay. "Henry Ford—Warts and All." *Automotive News,* 15 June
    2003: 67. *LexisNexis,* 25 Oct. 2008.
"City's Arabs Pledge Support." *Detroit Free Press,* 15 Oct. 1973.
Crellin, Jack, Susan Silk, and Mark Lett. "A Precedent in Chrysler Shutdown?"
    The Detroit News, 25 June 1973: 1.
Cusumano, John. "Southend Renewal Ruled 'Illegal.' " *The Dearborn Press,* 16
    Aug. 1973: front cover.
"Dearborn Rally for Arabs: UAW Chided on Israeli Bonds." *The Detroit News,*
    15 Oct. 1973: 13A.
"Detroit Arabs Fight City Hall." *AAUG Newsletter,* Aug. 1973: 3.
"Detroit Hits a Roadblock." *Time,* 2 Jun. 1980; http://www.time.com/time/
    magazine/article/0,9171,924166,00.html.
"Earnings of Ford Tumbled 76% in Final '73 Quarter." *The New York Times,* 13
    Feb. 1974: 53.
"The Fire This Time." *Time,* 4 Aug. 1967. http://www.time.com/time/
    magazine/article/0,9171,837150-1,00.html.
"Fires and Looters Run Rampant in Detroit." *The Dearborn Press,* 27 July
    1967:2A.
Foley, Eileen. "Detroit's Arab Community." *Detroit Free Press,* 3 Feb. 1973: 1D.
"Fuel Shortage Crisis Tackled." *The Dearborn Press,* 15 Nov. 1973: front cover.
Georgakas, Dan. "Arab Workers in Detroit." *Middle East Research and Informa-
    tion Project,* Jan. 1975: 13–17. http://www.jstor.org, 16 July 2008.
——— and Marvin Surkin. *Detroit I Do Mind Dying.* Updated ed. Cambridge,
    MA: South End Press, 1998.
"Hubbard Says: 'Take Up Arms' Shoot Straight and Deadly." *The Dearborn Press*
    3, Aug. 1967: front cover.
"Israeli, Arab Demonstrators Clash in N.Y." *The Detroit News.* 15 Oct. 1973: 13A.
"It Is Now Up to You." *The Dearborn Press,* 29 Nov. 1973.

Jabara, Abdeen. Personal interview. 25 Sept. 2008.

Jabara, Abdeen. "Workers, Community Mobilized in Detroit." *AAUG Newsletter*, June 1974: 10.

Kennedy, Shawn G. "Orville L. Hubbard of Dearborn; Ex-Mayor a Foe of Integration." *The New York Times*, 17 Dec. 1982. *LexisNexis*, 25 Oct. 2008.

Khoury, George. Personal interviews. 21, 28 Oct. 2008.

Koski, Al. "Terror While the City Burned." *The Dearborn Press*, 27 July 1967.

Kresnak, Jack. "Arabs Here Attack U.S. Mideast Policy." *Detroit Free Press*, 10 Oct. 1973:4A

"Layoffs Affect Arab Laborers." *AAUG Newsletter*, June 1974: 10.

Meredith, Robyn. "5 Days in 1967 Still Shake Detroit." *The New York Times*, 23 July 1997. *LexisNexis*, 8 Nov. 2008.

Nawash, Hassan. Personal interview. 23 Oct. 2008.

Nelson, Gerald L. "Arabs Protest Outside Cobo." *The Detroit News*, 30 Nov. 1973.

"Nixon Cuts Heating Oil, Gas Quotas." *Detroit Free Press*, Nov. 26 1973: 10A.

"Oldsmobile 1890–1900." *Wayne State University Library*, 8 Nov. 2008. www.lib.wayne.edu/resources/special_collections/local/cfai/pages/oldsmobile.html.

"Orders: 'Shoot on Sight.'" *The Dearborn Press*, 27 July 1967: front cover.

"The Painful Change to Thinking Small." *Time*, 31 Dec. 1973. http://www.time.com/time/magazine/article/0,9171,910904,00.html.

Postrel, Virginia. "The Long-term Consequences of the Race Riots in the Late 1960s Come into View." *The New York Times*, 30 Dec. 2004; *LexisNexis*, 8 Nov. 2008.

"Pushing the Arab Cause in America." *Time*, 23 June 1975. http://www.time.com/time/magazine/article/0,9171,913175,00.html.

"Rationing, Tax—or White Market?" *Time*, 3 Dec. 1973. http://www.time.com/time/magazine/article/0,9171,908220,00.html.

"REO: The Man & the Machine." *Michigan State University Archives*, 8 Nov. 2008.

"Risky Road of Retaliation." *Time*, 3 Dec. 1973. http://www.time.com/time/magazine/article/0,9171,908219,00.html.

Rosenfeld, Steven P. "Layoffs Spread as Economic Decline Deepens." *The Associated Press*, 15 Nov. 1981; *LexisNexis*, 25 Oct. 2008.

Salpukas, Agis. "Skilled Trades Reject Pact at Ford." *The New York Times*, 14 Nov. 1973: 1.

"Saudi Arabia Threatens U.S. Oil Cutoff, Paper Says." *Detroit Free Press*, 14 Oct. 1973:3A.

Shehadeh, Mary. Personal interview. 18 Nov. 2008.

Silk, Leonard. "Impact Is Wide When Detroit Goes Flat." *The New York Times*, 8 Dec. 1974: 1.

Stanley, Bob. "Panic in Detroit." *The Guardian*, 4 Jan. 2008; *LexisNexis*, 25 Oct. 2008.

"Stations to Be Shut on Sundays." *Detroit Free Press*, 26 Nov. 1973.

Stevens, William K. "Moslems in Dearborn Fight for Survival of Community." *The New York Times*, 21 Feb. 1973: 45.

Stork, Joe and Rene Theberge. "Any Arab or Others of a Suspicious Nature." *MERIP Reports*, Feb. 1973: 3–6, 13.

"They Buried Civil Rights." *The Dearborn Press*, 27 July 1967:2-A.

"Two Societies (1965–1968)." Narrator, Julian Bond. *Eyes on the Prize*. PBS, 1989.

UPI, "Arabian Leaders Demand Return of Occupied Land." *Detroit Free Press*, 29 Nov. 1973: 8B.

"U.S. Aid to Israel Protested Nationality." *AAUG Newsletter*, Dec. 1973: front cover.

Wolcott, Victoria W. *Remaking Respectability: African-American Women in Interwar Detroit*. Chapel Hill, NC: University of North Carolina Press, 2001.

Yost, Pete. *The Associated Press*, 22 July 1977. *LexisNexis*, 8 Nov. 2008.

Yunis, Don. Personal interview. 24 Oct. 2008.

NOVEMBER 4, 1979: DRIVEN

Bumiller, Elisabeth. "Arabian Knights and Western Ways." *The Washington Post*, 19 Aug. 1980: B1.

Dasoqi, John. Personal interviews. 17, 18 Nov. 2008; 1, 7 Dec. 2008.

"Federal Harassment of Iranian Students Raises Grave Concern." *Association of Arab-American University Graduates, Inc. Newsletter*, Dec. 1979–March 1980: 9.

Feinsilber, Mike. "Washington Dateline." *The Associated Press*, 15 Nov. 1979.

Gedda, George. "Washington Dateline." *The Associated Press*, 5 Dec. 1979.

Jamil, Allan. Personal interview. 2 Dec. 2008.

Levitt, Lisa. "Midwest Islamic Center Under Attack." *The Associated Press*, 3 Dec. 1979.

McAlister, Melani. *Epic Encounters: Culture, Media, & U.S. Interests in the Middle East Since 1945*. Berkeley, CA: University of California Press, 2005.

Pandya, Abha. "Iranian Immigrants in the U.S." *The Christian Science Monitor*, 6 April 1987: 35.

Pitvorec, Kathy. Personal interview. 25 Nov. 2008.

OCTOBER 11, 1985: SILENCED

ABC World News. October 15, 1985.

"Another Victim." Editorial. *The Washington Post*, 15 Oct. 1985: A22. *Lexis Nexis*, March 2007.

"Anti-Semitism, Anti-Murder." Editorial. *The New York Times*, 14 Nov. 1985: A34. *LexisNexis*, March 2007.

Black Jr., Charles L. "Terrorism Killed a 2d American During the Achille Lauro Affair." Letter. *The New York Times*, 1 Nov. 1985: A34; *LexisNexis*, March 2007.

"Bomb Injures Officers." *The Washington Post*, 17 Aug. 1985: A9; *LexisNexis*, March 2007.

"Bomb Kills Leader of U.S. Arab Group." *The New York Times*, 12 Oct. 1985: A5; *LexisNexis*, March 2007.

"F.B.I. Investigates Bombing of a U.S. Arab Group." *The New York Times*, 14 Oct. 1985: A25. *LexisNexis*, March 2007.

Findley, Paul. "The Alex Odeh Case." *Christian Science Monitor*, 25 Oct. 1985: Opinion 13; *LexisNexis*, March 2007.

Geyelin, Philip. "Victims of Terror." *The Washington Post*, 1 Nov. 1985: A25. *LexisNexis*, March 2007.

Harris, Lyle V. "American Arab Office in NW Gutted by Fire." *The Washington Post*, 30 Nov. 1985.

Hiltermann, Joost R. *Behind the Intifada*. Princeton, NJ: Princeton University Press, 1991.

Ingwerson, Marshall. "American Arabs Face Increasing Hostility." *Christian Science Monitor*, 21 Oct. 1985: National 3; *LexisNexis*, March 2007.

"Inquiry on Attacks on U.S. Arabs." *The New York Times*, 6 Dec. 1985: A3; *LexisNexis*, March 2007.

"Links Between Bombs in Boston Area Sought." *The New York Times*, 18 Aug. 1985: A22; *LexisNexis*, March 2007.

Mathews, Jay. "Alex Odeh: Arab-American Victim of Hate." *The Washington Post*, 13 Oct. 1985: A18; *LexisNexis*, March 2007.

———. "JDL Named in Probe; F.B.I. Sees 'Possible Link' to Arab American's Death." *The Washington Post*, 9 Nov. 1985: A2; *LexisNexis*, March 2007.

Mokhibar, Albert. Personal interview. 12 May 2007.

NBC Nightly News. October 11, 1985; December 6, 1985.

"No to Domestic Terrorism." Editorial. *Christian Science Monitor*, 23 Oct. 1985: Opinion 15; *LexisNexis*, March 2007.

Odeh, Norma. Personal interviews. Jan. 2007; 15, 16, 17 Feb. 2007; 13 May 2007.

Odeh, Sami. Personal interview. Jan. 2007.

Richey, Warren. "Former Senator Says Anti-Arab Violence in U.S. Ignored."
    Christian Science Monitor, 6 Dec. 1985: National 3; *LexisNexis*, March
    2007.

Winter, Greg. "Jewish Militant's Road to Jail Was Filled with Arrests." *The New
    York Times*, 15 Dec. 2001. *LexisNexis*, March 2007.

DECEMBER 8, 1987: BOUND

"Attacks No Route to Peace." Letter. *The Daily Northwestern*, 21 Jan. 1988: 4.

Balinksy, Michael. "Mideast Problems Continue." Letter. *The Daily Northwest-
    ern*, 11 Feb. 1988: 4.

Bannister, David. "Israel Must Seek Peace." Letter. *The Daily Northwestern*, 28
    Jan. 1988: 4.

Barrish, Jonathan. "Give and Take Key to Mideast Peace." *The Daily Northwest-
    ern*, 26 Jan. 1988: 4.

————. "Israel Troubled by Situation." Letter. *The Daily Northwestern*, 5 Feb.
    1988: 4.

————. "Violence No Route to Peace." Letter. *The Daily Northwestern*, 12 Jan.
    1988: 4.

Dajani, Omar. "Israel Spurs Arab Violence." Letter. *The Daily Northwestern*, 14
    Jan. 1988: 4.

————. Personal interviews. 11, 12 Aug. 2008; 19 Oct. 2008; 2, 8, 11, 12, 14
    Nov. 2008.

Diesenhof, Michael. "Attacks No Route to Peace." Letter. *The Daily Northwest-
    ern*, 21 Jan. 1988: 4.

Katz, Dan. "Mideast Needs Leaders." Letter. *The Daily Northwestern*, 2 Feb.
    1988: 4.

Meersman, Lynn and Michelle Martin. "Palestinians Protest at Israeli Consul-
    ate." *The Daily Northwestern*, 8 Jan. 1988: 1.

Rand, Allison. Personal interview. 10 Nov. 2006.

Review of Middle East in *The Daily Northwestern*, 2 Jan.–11 Feb. 1988.

JANUARY 16, 1991: UNDER SUSPICION

"Arab Americans Report Rise in Violent Harassing Incidents." *Associated Press*,
    7 Feb. 1991; *LexisNexis*, 31 Jan. 2006.

Bridis, Ted. "Neighbors Aid, Comfort Iraqi Whose House Burned in Suspected
    Hate Crime." *Associated Press*, 23 Feb. 1991. *LexisNexis*, 31 Jan. 2006.

Cohen, Sharon. "Arab Americans Live with Fear and Frustration During Gulf
    War." *Associated Press*, 30 Jan. 1991. *LexisNexis*, 31 Jan. 2006.

Coleman, Joseph. "Arabs in America Brace for Anti-Arab Backlash." *Associated Press*, 18 Jan. 1991; *LexisNexis*, 31 Jan. 2006.

"Do you think there is any reason to suspect that Arab-American citizens are more sympathetic to Iraq than other American citizens are, or not?" Public Opinion Poll. *Roper Center at University of Connecticut*, 19 Jan. 1991. *LexisNexis*, 31 Jan. 2006.

"Excerpts from Recent Editorials in Newspapers in the U.S. and Abroad." *Associated Press*, 20 Feb. 1991. *LexisNexis*, 8 Feb. 2006.

Feinsilber, Mike. "Bush Says Alliance Is Holding, Deplores Anti–Arab-American Bias." *Associated Press*, 25 Jan. 1991; *LexisNexis*, 31 Jan. 2006.

"From the Home Front." *Associated Press*, 21 Jan. 1991. *LexisNexis*, 31 Jan. 2006.

Ganguly, Dilip. "500 Dead from Allied Raid, Called 'Well Planned Crime.' " *Associated Press*, 13 Feb. 1991; *LexisNexis*, 8 Feb. 2006.

Gillerman, Margaret. "On Campus, 'Scared' Is Often-Heard Word." *St. Louis Post Dispatch*, 13 Jan. 1991: 1D. *LexisNexis*, 7 Feb. 2006.

Graham, Victoria. "Bombing in Baghdad Condemned as U.N. Council Prepares to Debate Gulf." *Associated Press*, 13 Feb. 1991. *LexisNexis*, 8 Feb. 2006.

Haller, Vera. "Pan Am Accused in Lawsuit of Discriminating Against Arabs." *Associated Press*, 1 March 1991. *LexisNexis*, 31 Jan. 2006.

Hampson, Rick. "Arab Americans: Dual Loyalties and Nagging Worries." *Associated Press*, 20 Jan. 1991. *LexisNexis*. 31 Jan. 2006.

Horn, John. "Arabs Targeted as Hollywood's New Villains." *Associated Press*, 18 Jan. 1991. *LexisNexis*, 31 Jan. 2006.

O'Rourke, Lawrence M. "Bush Seeks Students' Support; White House Denies Draft Plan." *St. Louis Post Dispatch*, 11 Jan. 1991: 19A. *LexisNexis*, 7 Feb. 2006.

Putnam, Walter. "Deadly Attack in Iraq Widens Split in Arab World." *Associated Press*, 14 Feb. 1991. *LexisNexis*, 8 Feb. 2006.

Pyle, Richard. "U.S. Claims Baghdad Bunker Was Military Command Center." *Associated Press*, 13 Feb. 1991. *LexisNexis*, 8 Feb. 2006.

Pyle, Richard. "U.S. Says Strike in Baghdad Hit Military Site." *Associated Press*, 13 Feb. 1991; *LexisNexis*, 8 Feb. 2006.

Ramirez, Lyng Hou. "U.S.: Anti Terrorist Drive Brings Violence Against Arabs." *IPS-Inter Press Service*, 19 Feb. 1991. *LexisNexis*, 31 Jan. 2006.

"Rodeo Officials Pull Reins on Use of Saddam Effigy." *United Press International*, 22 Feb. 1991; *LexisNexis*, 31 Jan. 2006.

Rosso, Henry David. "ACLU Decries Gulf War Related Harassments." *United Press International*, 28 Jan. 1991; *LexisNexis*, 31 Jan. 2006.

Shepard, Robert. "Edwards Warns of Dangers to Civil Liberties." *United Press International*, 16 Jan. 1991. *LexisNexis*, 31 Jan. 2006.

"Shocked Audience Views Tapes of Bombing in Iraq." *United Press International*, 13 March 1991; *LexisNexis*, 31 Jan. 2006.

"U.S. Marine General Tells Joke About Convenience Stores, Iraq." *Associated Press*, 16 Feb. 1991; *LexisNexis*, 31 Jan. 2006.

Walker, Martin. "The Gulf War: 'Hundreds Killed' in Bunker—U.S. Says Bombed Baghdad Shelter Where 400 Died Was Military Command Post." *The Guardian* (London), 14 Feb. 1991; *LexisNexis*, 8 Feb. 2006.

APRIL 19, 1995: COMING OUT

Abowd, Mary. "Arab-Americans Suffer Hatred After Bombing." *The Chicago Sun Times*, 13 May 1995: 14.

AbuSahan, Rabih. Personal interviews. Jan., Feb., March 2007.

ADC Times: News and Opinions of ADC. Washington, DC: American Arab Anti-Discrimination Committee, Spring 1995.

"American Terror: Special Report on the Oklahoma Explosion." *St. Petersburg Times*, 20 April 1995; *LexisNexis*, 30 Jan. 2007.

Appleby, Timothy. "Muslims Caught in Bombing Backlash; Children Harassed in Schools, Mosques Because of Early Speculation Pointing to a Middle East Connection." *The Globe and Mail*, 22 April 1995.

Tony Brown Productions. http://www.tonybrown.com (accessed Jan. 15, 2007).

CNN Transcripts: All available for April 19 and 29, 1995, in addition to the following: *Survivors Seem Doubtful in Oklahoma City Explosion*, Transcript, CNN, 19 April 1995; *FBI Press Conference on Oklahoma City Bombing*, Transcript, CNN, 20 April 1995; *Janet Reno Press*, Transcript, CNN, 20 April 1995; *FBI Moves to Quickly Apprehend Bombing Suspects*, Transcript, CNN, 20 April 1995.

Culver, Virginia. "Local Muslims Denounce Bombing, But Officials Get Hate Calls." *Denver Post*, 21 April 1995: A7.

Donayre, Marta. Personal interview. 11 Dec. 2008.

Doyle, Leonard. "An Islamic Terrorist Under Every Arab Bed?" *The Independent* (London), 21 April 1995: 15.

Falcone, David. "Muslims in Hub Worry of Backlash Against Them." *The Boston Herald*, 21 April 1995: 6.

"FAQs—Frequently Asked Questions About Stonewall 25." *Queer Resources Directory*, 15 January 2008; http://www.qrd.org/qrd/events/stonewall25/faq.very.general.

Grunwald, Michael. "Muslims Fear Being Made Scapegoats." *The Boston Globe*, 21 April 1995: 1.

Guy, Jeff. "Battling Over Bedroom Out in the Open." *The Sunflower* (Wichita State University), 18 Oct. 1993: 1.

Hanne, Matt. "Before There Were Soldiers." *The Liberty Press*, January 2008: 24–28.

Kelly, L. "Wichita's Gays, Lesbians Salute Their Progress with Parade Today." *The Wichita Eagle*, 17 June 1995.

"Leader of Gay-Rights Group Will Speak in Wichita." *The Wichita Eagle*, 13 Oct. 1993: 4D.

Mansnerus, Laura. "Word for Word/Gay Magazines." *The New York Times*, 26 June 1994: 4:7.

Mayhood, Kevin. "Muslim Leader Says Backlash Was Severe." *Columbus Dispatch*, 6 May 1995: 3C.

McKinley Jr., James C. "From the Gay World's Every Reach, A Sea of Marchers, All with Stories." *The New York Times*, 27 June 1994: B2.

———. "The Mayor's in the Middle." *The New York Times*, 26 June 1994: 25.

McKinney, B.A. "From Silence to Celebration: Wichita Pride 1995." *The Liberty Press*, July 1995: 12–13.

Moghrabi, Hamzi. "A Rush to Judgement—Again." *The Plain Dealer*, 23 April 1995: 3C.

Nakagawa, Scott. E-mail message to author, Sept. 9, 2008.

Nasrulla, Amber. "Attacks on Islam Anger Community 'Why Do They Always Blame Us?' " *The Globe and Mail*, 22 April 1995.

1995 Report on Anti-Arab Racism. Washington, D.C.: American Arab Anti-Discrimination Committee, 1995.

Norman, Bud. "Oppression of Gays Will Threaten Everyone's Freedom, Activist Says." *The Wichita Eagle*, 18 Oct. 1993: 3C.

Parker, Kristi. Editor, Liberty Press. Personal interview. 18 Mar. 2008.

Qasem, Bassam. Personal interview. April 2008.

Rojas, Aurelio. "Arabs Scapegoated, Even though FBI Is Seeking Whites." *The San Francisco Chronicle*, 21 April 1995: A12.

Shideler, Karen. "Groups Turn Focus to AIDS Funding." *The Wichita Eagle*, 17 June 1995.

Talbot, David. "Islamic Community Concerned for Safety." *The Boston Herald*, 21 April 1995: 6.

"Tiny Terror Victims Mourned." *Courier-Mail* (Australia), 26 April 1995.

"Video Almanac 1995." CNN. http://www.cnn.com/resources/video.almanac/1995/index2.html#okc.bombing (accessed 15 Feb. 2008.)

Wilson, Mike and Katherine Shaver. "Muslims Fear a Backlash." *St. Petersburg Times*, 21 April 1995: 1A.

"WSU Speaker to Discuss Attacks on Gays, Lesbians." *The Wichita Eagle*, 17 Oct. 1993: 4B.

NOVEMBER 7, 2000: COURTED

AAPAC newsletter. Dearborn, MI: Arab American Political Action Committee, 7 Nov. 2000.

AAPAC newsletter. Dearborn, MI: Arab American Political Action Committee, 5 Nov. 2002.

"About MPAC." *Muslim Public Affairs Council*, 13 Oct. 2008. http://mpac.org/about.

Abunab, Neal. "Arab American Political Action Group Endorses Bush." *The Arab American News*, 14–20 Oct. 2000.

———. "The Lieberman Factor." *The Arab American News*, 26 Aug.–8 Sept. 2000.

———. "Gore Loses Even Diehard Arab Democrats." *The Arab American News*, 21 Oct.–3 Nov. 2000.

American Demographics. Jan. 1994.

American Muslim Council, 13 Oct. 2008. http://amcnational.org.

Arab Americans: A Century of Political and Cultural Achievement. Washington, DC: The Arab American Institute, 2000.

Arab-American Roundtable, 5 Oct. 2000.

"Arab Americans for Bush 2000 by State." Arab Americans for Bush/Cheney 2000.

"Arab Americans for Gore 2000 by State." Arab Americans for Gore 2000.

Archibold, Randal C. "G.O.P. Ends Calls Linking Some Clinton Donors to Terrorism." *The New York Times*, 30 Oct. 2000; http://query.nytimes.com, 5 Oct. 2008.

Arellano, Amber. "Arab-American Group for Bush." *Detroit Free Press*, 16 Oct. 2000: 1B.

———. "Texan Scores Points During Recent Debates." *Detroit Free Press*, 16 Oct. 2000.

Benson, Miles. "American Muslims Seek Reassurance on Lieberman's Mideast Approach." *Religion News Service*, 17 Aug. 2000.

Berry, Mary Francis. Letter to Representative David E. Bonior, United States Commision on Civil Rights, Washington DC, July 2001.

Berry, Maya. Personal interviews. May 2006; 23 July 2008; 5, 6, 26, 29 Aug. 2008; 23 Sept. 2008; 3, 5, 13 Oct. 2008.

"Biography." *U.S. Senator Joe Lieberman, Connecticut*. http://lieberman.senate.gov/about, 13 Oct. 2008.

"The Birth of an Arab-American Lobby." *The Economist*, 14 Oct. 2000

Bray, Thomas J. "Gore's Arab-American Problem." *The Wall Street Journal*, 17 Oct. 2000. http://www.opinionjournal.com.

Bruni, Frank and Michael Cooper. "The 2000 Campaign: The Texas Governor;

Bush Camp Sees Unrest as Validation of Its Views." *The New York Times,* 14 Oct. 2000. http://query.nytimes.com, 5 Oct. 2008.

Burns, John F. and Steven Lee Myers. "The Warship Explosion: The Overview; Blast Kills Sailors on U.S. Ship in Yemen." *The New York Times,* 13 Oct. 2000; http://query.nytimes.com, 5 Oct. 2008.

"Camp David Summit 2000." Anti-Defamation League, 13 Oct. 2008. http://www.adl.org/israel/advocacy/glossary/camp_david_summit.asp.

Campaign 2000: Empowering Arab Americans. A summary report of the Arab-American Institute National Leadership Conference. Dearborn, MI. 5–7 Nov. 1999.

"Campaign 2008." *The Sun-Times News Group,* 6 Oct. 2008. http://elections.suntimes.com.

"Demographic Watch: Major Arab American Meeting." *National Journal,* 4 Nov. 1999.

"The Department of Justice and the Civil Rights of Arab Americans." Arab American Institute. March 1998.

Edwards, Catherine. "Arab-Americans Rise in Influence." *In-Sight,* 19 Feb. 2001. Allied-Media Corp., 6 Oct. 2008. http://www.allied-media.com.

Ehrenberg, Betty. "International Briefs." Institute for Public Affairs, June 1998. http://www.ou.org/public/news/intlbriefs/intl698.htm.

Engler, John. Former governor of Michigan. Personal interview. 9 Oct. 2008.

Foster, Julie. "Arab-Americans Side with Democrats, Discuss Position on Lieberman as Jewish V.P. Nominee." *World Net Daily,* 17 Aug. 2000.

Ghalwash, Mae. "Arab Americans Face Voting Quandary; In Michigan, Gulf War Hurts Bush, but Israel Policy Hounds Clinton." *The Washington Post,* 1 Nov. 1992; *LexisNexis,* 16 Oct. 2008.

Gordon, Craig. "Ticket Worries Arab-Americans." *Newsday,* 17 Aug. 2000.

Gordon, Michael R. "The Warship Explosion: Military Analysis; Superpower Suddenly Finds Itself Threatened by Sophisticated Terrorists." *The New York Times,* 14 Oct. 2000.

"Gore Announces Support for Secret Evidence Repeal." Arab American Institute. Press release.

Gore, Al. Memo to Arab-American constituent, National Headquarters, Nashville, TN. 19 Oct. 2000.

———. Speech. Arab American Institute National Convention. Arab American Institute, Dearborn, MI. 6 Nov. 1999.

"Governor Bush on Racial Profiling." *George W. Bush for President.* Austin, TX.

Hammoud, Abed. Personal interview. 4 Sept. 2008.

Horowitz, Nitzan. "Tough Times for American Jews." *The Arab American News,* Oct. 2000, 14–20.

Hudome, Randa Fahmy. Memo to Tom Bray. 16 Oct. 2000.

————. Personal interviews. 13 Aug. 2008; 19, 23 Sept. 2008; 9, 15, 21 Oct. 2008.

Isgro, Francesco. "Immigration Litigation Update." *Migration World Magazine*, 1996; *ProQuest*, 8 Oct. 2008.

Isikoff, Michael. "Their Support Could Make the Difference in Close States." *Newsweek*, 23 Oct. 2000.

Khan, Suhail. Personal interview. 31 Oct. 2008.

Kifner, John. "All Sides Resist Plan by Clinton for the Mideast." *The New York Times*, 31 Dec. 2000. http://query.nytimes.com, 5 Oct. 2008.

Koszczuk, Jackie. "Arabs Back Lieberman for Siding with Them." *Detroit Free Press*, 16 Aug. 2000:10A.

"Lebanon; Flicker in the Darkness." *The Economist*, 17 Jan. 1976; *LexisNexis*, 16 Oct. 2008.

"Lieberman Reaches out to Arab Americans." *The Arab American News*, 26 Aug.–8 Sept. 2000.

Lieberman, Joe and Karenna Gore Schiff. Speech, Democratic National Convention. Los Angeles, CA. 16 Aug. 2000.

McConnell, Darci. "Lieberman Romances the Area's Undecided." *Detroit Free Press*, 28 Aug. 2000: 1A

McConnell, Darci and Amber Arellano. "Visit Is Vital for Nominee." *Detroit Free Press*, 26 Aug. 2000:1A.

Michigan Advisory Committee to the U.S. Commission on Civil Rights. *Civil Rights Issues Facing Arab Americans in Michigan*. May 2001.

"Michigan Democrat Activist Endorses Governor Bush." Bush/Cheney 2000, Inc. press release, 6 Oct. 2000.

"Mondale Camp Returns Funds to U.S. Arabs." *The New York Times*, 25 Aug. 1984. http://query.nytimes.com, 5 Oct. 2008.

Montemurri, Patricia. "Gore Goes Full Bore to Sweep Michigan." *Detroit Free Press*, 30 Oct. 2000: 1A.

————, Time Jones, and May Nne. "Chief Exec Welcomes New Citizens." *Detroit Free Press*, 2 Oct. 1984.

Muasher, Marwan. "New Relationships That Are Reshaping the Middle East." Speech, AIPAC Policy Conference, Washington, DC. May 1998. http://www.jordanembassyus.org, 8 Oct. 2008.

Myers, Stephen Lee. "Inquiry Faults the *Cole*'s Captain and Crew." *The New York Times*, 9 Dec. 2000. http://query.nytimes.com, 5 Oct. 2008.

Nassar, David. "Re: October 19 Endorsement Meeting." Memo to Arab American and Chaldean Leadership Council of Michigan, 2 Oct. 2000.

————. Personal interview. 18 Sept. 2008.

Netanyahu, Benjamin. "Address by Prime Minister Netanyahu to AIPAC's 39th

Conference." Speech, Washington, DC. 17 May 1998. http://www.mfa. gov.il, 8 Oct. 2008.

"Notes on discussion with Joe Lieberman." 27 Aug. 2000.

Okwu, Michael. "Arab-Americans Call for Boycott of 'Rules of Engagement.'" *CNN*, 25 April 2000. http://archives.cnn.com, 5 Oct. 2008.

"Our Vision, Mission and Core Principles." Council on American-Islamic Relations. http://www.cair.com, 13 Oct. 2009.

"Poll Shows Major Change in Choice of Presidential Candidates." *The Arab American News*, 14–20 Oct. 2000.

"Presidential Candidate Profile: Governor George W. Bush." Arab American Institute, Washington, DC.

"Presidential Candidate Profile: Vice President Al Gore." Arab American Institute, Washington, DC.

"Presidential Results Summary for All States." *CNN*. http://www.cnn.com/ ELECTIONS/2000/results/president/index.html, 6 Oct. 2008.

"Proceedings of the Arab American National Leadership Conference." *Arab American Institute*, May 1998.

Rees, Matthew. "Arabs, Poles, and Other Key Voters." *The Weekly Standard*, 30 Oct. 2000.

"Remarks at Naturalization Ceremonies for New United States Citizens in Detroit." 1 Oct. 1984.

"Remarks by the President: Arab American Institute Conference." The White House, press release, 7 May 1998.

Rove, Karl C. and Tim Goeglein. "Re: Muslim Outreach." E-mail exchange. 14–15 June 2001.

Saffuri, Khaled. Personal interview. 4, 15, 17 Oct. 2008.

Salan, Jennifer. Personal interview. 1, 5 Oct. 2008.

Salem, George. Personal interview. 1 Oct. 2008.

"Secretary of Energy Spencer Abraham." The White House, http://whitehouse. gov/government/abraham-bio.html, 6 Oct. 2008.

Shoha, Jennifer. Fairland Club, Dearborn, MI. 3 Oct. 2000.

———. Personal interview. 3 Oct. 2008.

Sweet, Matthew. "Movie targets Arabs are the latest people to suffer the racial stereotyping of Hollywood—and nowhere more so than in William Friedkin's new film." *The Independent*, 30 July 2000, *ProQuest*, 5 Oct. 2008.

"2000 Debates." Commission on Presidential Debates. http://www.debates.org/ pages/his_2000.html, 25 Oct. 2008.

"2000 DLC National Conversation Agenda." Democratic Leadership Council. http://www.ndol.org, 13 Oct. 2008.

20th Anniversary Tribute 1985–2005. CD-ROM. Arab American Institute.

"Voter Guide." Fax to Arab-American Institute, Gore Lieberman 2000. 11 Sept. 2000.

Wald, Matthew L. "Panel on Air Security May End Without Reaching a Consensus." *The New York Times,* 26 Jan. 1997. http://query.nytimes.com, 8 Oct. 2008.

———. "Panel to Recommend Steps for Cutting Air Crash Rate." *The New York Times,* 12 Feb. 1997. http://query.nytimes.com, 8 Oct. 2008.

Warikoo, Niraj. "Arab Americans Flex Their Voting Muscle But Experts Say They Need to Build Mass." *Detroit Free Press,* 15 Nov. 2000: 3B Zone.

———. "Bush Chats with Arab Americans on Issues." *Detroit Free Press,* 6 Oct. 2000: 8A.

———. "Michigan News Briefs." *Detroit Free Press,* 1 Nov. 2000: 2B.

———. "Voters Flexing New Political Muscle." *Detroit Free Press,* 8 Nov. 2000: 12A.

Warikoo, Niraj and Amber Arellano. "Arab-American Groups Back Bush Outreach to Community Cited." *Detroit Free Press,* 20 Oct. 2000: 3B Zone.

———. "His Outreach Is Cited; Late Gore Pitch Fails." *Detroit Free Press,* 20 Oct. 2000.

Zacharia, Janine. "Arab Americans Send Record Number of Delegates to Convention." *The Jerusalem Post,* 17 Aug. 2000, http://jpost.com.

Zogby, James J. "RE: Post-convention update and preparing for November." Letter, 7 Sept. 2000.

———. "Update on Transition 2001 and Party News." Memo to Arab American Democratic Leaders, 15 Feb. 2001.

———. Testimony, DNC platform hearing, 2000.

SEPTEMBER 11, 2001: BEGINNINGS

Chang, Jeff. "9/11: The Fallout." *Bad Subjects,* Feb. 2002. http://bad.eserver.org, 13 Dec. 2006.

"Dedicate Maronite Church." *The New York Times,* 18 Dec. 1916.

Dreher, Rod. "City's Lebanese Know All About Horrors of War." *New York Post,* 19 Sept. 2001: 10.

———. "Trouble in My 'Hood: The Muslim Question in Brooklyn." *National Review,* 2003. 31 Oct. 2006.

Goldberg, Michelle. "My Arab Street." Salon.com, 7, March 2003. 31 Oct. 2006.

Habib, Claire. Personal interview. 10 Nov. 2008.

Hassan, Salah D. "Arabs, Race and the Post-September 11 National Security

State." *Middle East Report*, Fall 2002: 16–21. http://www.jstor.org, 11 Dec. 2008.

Howell, Sally and Andrew Shryock. "Cracking Down on Diaspora: Arab Detroit and America's 'War on Terror.' " *Anthropological Quarterly* 76.3 (Summer 2003): 443–462.

Karpf, Ruth. "Street of the Arabs." *The New York Times*, 11 Aug. 1946.

Lichtblau, Eric and William Glaberson. "Cleric Boasted of Supporting al-Qaida." *The New York Times*, 5 March 2003. http://query.nytimes.com, 31 Oct. 2006.

Marini, Francis J., J.D., J.C.O.D. "A Brief History of the Maronites of New York City: Saint Joseph's Church in Manhattan and Our Lady of Lebanon Church in Brooklyn; Two Parishes and One Maronite Community."

Newman, Andy. "Brooklyn Mosque Becomes Terror Icon, but Federal Case Is Unclear." *The New York Times*, 9 March 2003. http://query.nytimes.com, 13 Oct. 2008.

"New York's Syrian Quarter." *The New York Times*, 20 Aug. 1899.

Sadek, Ignace. Personal interviews. Dec. 2006; 30 Oct. 2008; 1, 14 Nov. 2008.

Shifrel, Scott. "Arab-Americans, Mosques Targeted in Bias Attacks." *Daily News*, 15 Sept. 2001. *LexisNexis*, 10 Oct. 2008.

"Sights and Characteristics of New York's 'Little Syria.'" *The New York Times*, 29 March 1903.

"Syrian Colony of New York and Its Characteristics." *The New York Times*, 25 May 1902.

"Syrian Young Men Oppose Cobble Hill Rehabilitation." *The New York Times*, 2 Oct. 1962.

"The Syrian Colony." *Harper's Weekly*, 10 Aug. 1895.

Zain, Thomas. Dean of St. Nicholas Antiochian Orthodox Church. Personal interview. 12 Nov. 2008.

MARCH 20, 2003: NATIVE FOREIGNER, FOREIGN NATIVE

Al-Thaibani, Abraham. Personal interviews. April, May 2006.

"Arab American U.S. Marine—Wounded in Fallujah Fighting." Association of Patriotic Arab Americans in Military, http://apaam.org/injuredfalluja.htm, 9 March 2006.

Baadani, Jamal S. "We Have to Choose Who and What We Want to Be!" *Association of Patriotic Arab Americans in Military*, 28 Jan. 2005. http://www.apaam.org/ChooseWhowhat.htm, 9 March 2006.

Becker, Maki. "Daddy Has to Go Fight the Bad Guys." *Daily News*, 13 March 2003; *LexisNexis*, 16 April 2006.

Brooks, Jennifer. "Arab Americans in military juggle patriotism, suspicion." *The Detroit News*, 15 Dec. 2004. Association of Patriotic Arab Americans in Military, http://www.apaam.org/DetroitNews1204.htm, 9 March 2006.

"Commander in Chief Lands on USS Lincoln." CNN.com. 2 May 2003. 12 April 2006.

Gonzalez, John W. "Arab American in military battle against stereotyping." *Houston Chronicle 7*, March 2003. Association of Patriotic Arab Americans in Military, http://patrioticapaam.org/3.07.03Gonzalez.htm, 7 March 2006.

Habib, Claire. Personal interview. 12 Nov. 2008.

Lieberman, Brett. "Echo Company Moves into Iraq." *Penn Live.com*, 4 April 2003. http://pennlive.com, 16 April 2006.

———. "Marines Settle into Baath Complex." *Penn Live.com*, 10 April 2003. http://pennlive.com, 16 April 2006.

———. "Shooting Deaths of 2 Infants Shake Harrisburg-based Marines." *Penn Live.com*, 12 April 2003. http://pennlive.com, 16 April 2006.

———. "Bridge Renamed after Reading Cabaret." *Penn Live.com*, 20 April 2003. http://pennlive.com, 16 April 2006.

———. "Troops spread joy to orphans with toys, food, friendship." *Penn Live. com*, 20 April 2003. http://pennlive.com, 16 April 2006.

———. "Schools Open, but Kids, Teachers Play Hooky." *Penn Live.com*, 21 April 2003. http://pennlive.com, 16 April 2006.

Winik, Lyric Wallwork. "Don't Ask Me to Take Off the Uniform." 17 April 2005. Association of Patriotic Arab Americans in Military, http://apaam.org/PARADEarticle4.17.htm, 9 March 2005.

GENERAL REFERENCES

Abraham, Nabeel and Andrew Shryock, eds. *Arab Detroit: From Margin to Mainstream*. Detroit, MI: Wayne State University Press, 2000.

Abraham, Sameer Y. and Nabeel, eds. *The Arab World and Arab-Americans: Understanding a Neglected Minority*. Detroit, MI: Wayne State University, 1981.

Abu-Laban, Baha and Faith T. Zeadley, eds. *Arabs in America: Myths and Realities*. Medina University Press, 1975.

Akram, Susan M. "The Aftermath of September 11, 2001: The Targeting of Arabs and Muslims in America." *Arab Studies Quarterly* (Spring-Summer 2002).

Ameri, Anan and Yvonne Lockwood. *Images of America: Arab Americans in Metro Detroit, A Pictorial History*. Chicago, IL: Arcadia, 2001.

Aruri, Naseer H. "The Middle East on the U.S. Campus." *The Link* 18.2 (May–June 1985).

Aryain, Ed. *From Syria to Seminole: Memoir of a High Plains Merchant.* Lubbock, TX: Texas Tech University Press, 2006.

Benson, Kathleen and Philip M. Kayal, eds. *A Community of Many Worlds: Arab Americans in New York City.* New York: Museum of City of New York/ Syracuse University Press, 2002.

Cainkar, Louise. "No Longer Invisible: Arab and Muslim Exclusion After September 11." *Middle East Report* 224 (Autumn 2002): 22–29.

"Chronology of Arab-Israeli Wars." *The Associated Press*, 18 Oct. 1991.

Fischbach, Michael R. "Government Pressures Against Arabs in the United States." *Journal of Palestine Studies* 14.3 (Spring 1985): 87–100.

Gabriel, Judith. "Palestinians Arrested in Los Angeles Witch Hunt." *Middle East Report* (March–April 1987).

Hassan, Salah D. "Arabs, Race, and the Post September 11 National Security State." *Middle East Report* 224 (Autumn 2002): 16–21.

"History of Mideast Conflict." *BBC News*, http://news.bbc.co.uk/2/hi/in_depth/ middle_east/2000/mideast_peace_process/340237.stm, 1 Dec. 2008.

Hitti, Philip K. *The Syrians in America.* New York: George H. Doran Company, 1924.

Howell, Sally and Andrew Shryock. "Cracking Down on Diaspora: Arab Detroit and America's 'War on Terror.'" *Anthropological Quarterly* 76.3 (Summer 2003): 443–462.

"Israel and the Palestinians: A History of Conflict." *BBC News.* http://news. bbc.co.uk/2/shared/spl/hi/middle_east/03/v3_ip_timeline/html/2002. stm, 1 Dec. 2008.

Meleis, Afaf I. "Arab Students in Western Universities: Social Properties and Dilemmas." *The Journal of Higher Education* 53.4 (1982): 439–447.

Mitchell, Alison. "After Blast, New Interest in Holy-War Recruits in Brooklyn." *The New York Times*, 11 April 1993: 23.

Nigem, Elias T. "Arab Americans: Migration, Socioeconomic and Demographic Characteristics." *International Migration Review* 20.3 (Autumn 1986): 629–649.

"Obstacles to Peace: Borders and Settlements." *BBC News*, http://news.bbc. co.uk/2/hi/middle_east/6669545.stm, 1 Dec. 2008.

Orfalea, Gregory. *The Arab Americans: A History.* Northampton, MA: Olive Branch Press, 2006.

Reaven, Marci and Steve Zeitlin. *Hidden New York: A Guide to Places That Matter.* New Brunswick, NJ: Rivergate Books.

Rizek, Martin, Barbara Rizek, and Joanne Medvecky. *Images of America: The*

Financial District's Lost Neighborhood 1900–1970. Portsmouth, NH: Arcadia 2004.

Sadd, David J. and G. Neal Lendenmann. "Arab American Grievances." *Foreign Policy* 60 (Autumn 1985): 17–30.

Scott, Joan W. "Middle East Studies Under Siege." *The Link* 39.1 (Jan.–March 2006).

Suleiman, Michael, ed. *Arabs in America: Building a New Future.* Philadelphia: Temple University Press, 1999.

Swedenburg, Ted. "The Post September 11 Arab Wave in World Music." *Middle East Report* 224 (Autumn 2002): 44–48.

"Ties to Sheik Omar Abdel Rahman." *The Washington Post,* 11 July 1993: A16.

"Timeline: Algeria." *BBC News,* http://news.bbc.co.uk/2/hi/middle_east/country_profiles/811140.stm, 1 Dec. 2008.

"Timeline: Egypt." *BBC News,* http://news.bbc.co.uk/2/hi/middle_east/790978.stm, 1 Dec. 2008.

"Timeline: Iraq." *BBC News,* http://news.bbc.co.uk/2/hi/middle_east/737483.stm, 1 Dec. 2008.

"Timeline: Jordan." *BBC News,* http://news.bbc.co.uk/2/hi/middle_east/country_profiles/828993.stm, 1 Dec. 2008.

"Timeline: Lebanon." *BBC News,* http://news.bbc.co.uk/2/hi/middle_east/country_profiles/819200.stm, 1 Dec. 2008.

"Timeline: Morocco." *BBC News,* http://news.bbc.co.uk/2/hi/middle_east/country_profiles/2431365.stm, 1 Dec. 2008.

"Timeline: Syria." *BBC News,* http://news.bbc.co.uk/2/hi/middle_east/country_profiles/827580.stm, 1 Dec. 2008.

"Timeline: Yemen." *BBC News,* http://news.bbc.co.uk/2/hi/middle_east/country_profiles/1706450.stm, 1 Dec. 2008.

Wright, Claudia. "The Prohibition Against the Training or Support of Terrorist Organizations Act of 1984." *Journal of Palestine Studies* 13.4 (Summer 1984): 134–144.

ACKNOWLEDGMENTS
(*Shukran!*)

Many folks deserve a round of applause for bringing this book to fruition. First and foremost, I want to express my deepest gratitude to all my main characters for sharing their lives with me and now with those who read *A Country Called Amreeka*. Thank you to the Salem family and to Luba, Alan, John, Norma, Omar, the Nabulsi family, Rabih, Maya, Randa, Monsignor Sadek, and Abraham for your courage, wit, self-reflection, memories, and hours upon hours—on the phone and in person.

In Birmingham, thank you particularly to Judy Zaidan for being a fantastic fixer. Also thanks to her daughter Zana Zaidan Lord and all the members of the Bostany family for opening me to a whole world I never knew—there is nothing more sweet than Arabic with an Alabaman accent! In addition, thank you Father Richard for your deadpan humor and help.

To coach Clem Gryska and to Director Ken Gaddy and especially Assistant Curator Brad Green at the Paul W. Bryant Museum in Tuscaloosa, a hearty thanks for opening your archives to me. Roll Tide!

Thank you also Diane McWhorter, not only for your bible on Birmingham but also for guiding me through the history of your city. And thank you for introducing me to Professor Bob Corley, who deserves thanks for his generously shared insights on the Magic City.

For lending me their precious copies of *Hathihe Ramallah*, thank you Maher and Judy Ajluni. In Dearborn, particular thanks are owed to Ron Amen; I could not have done the 1973 chapter without him. So by extension, thank you Mona! Thank you Professor Nabeel Abraham for invaluable insights into the time and place. Thank you to all the former UAW members and community activists who shared their memories. Also in Dearborn, thank you Abed Hammoud for your help in securing printed materials for the 2000 chapter.

In Brooklyn, thank you Claire Habib, Joseph Shaia, Father James Root, and Father Thomas Zain for helping unravel the history of Lebanese and Syrian churches in New York City.

In Kansas, thank you to Joe Kleinsasser at Wichita State University, Kristi Parker at *Liberty Press*, Stacy Goble at the *Sunflower*, and Michelle Enke at the Wichita Public Library. In addition, thank you to the following librarians and researchers: Miranda Schwartz at The New York Historical Society; Sara Wakefield and Daniel Necas at the Immigration History Research Center, University of Minnesota; William LeFevre at the Walter P. Reuther Labor Library, Wayne State University; Allen Streicker at Northwestern University; and the folks at the TV News Archive at Vanderbilt University.

For help in Lebanon, *merci kteer* Dominique Tohme.

For her invaluable research assistance, *shukran* Laura Kasinof! And thanks as well to Joseph Nakhleh and Fatimah Baeshen for supplemental research. Thanks to Daniel Martin, statistician at the Department of Homeland Security, for his help in pulling all the necessary data.

Alf shukr to Sinan Antoon for the transliterations. On a similar note, thank you Mickey Lee Bukowski and Kareem Roustom for making sure my music writing was right. And thank you Tia Letras for all her design input.

To Abdeen Jabara and Albert Mokiber; to ADC's Nabil Mohammed, Kareem Shora, and Nawar Shora; and especially to AAI's Helen Samhan, *shukran* for keeping the records and memories of Arab American activism.

Thank you to my friends and family for the moral support, thoughts, and even occasional research and Excel spreadsheet assistance!

Of course, many thanks to Sam Freedman, who started as a professor, became a mentor, and is now a friend. Thank you Lynton family for the fellowship for book writing while I was at Columbia. Thank you agent-extraordinaire Anna Ghosh for understanding this project and getting it into the right hands, and thank you Amber Qureshi, in whose grasp it landed. Also at Simon & Schuster, thank you Jennifer Weidman for due diligence, and to the copyeditors Susan Norton and Edith Lewis, a very humble, properly punctuated thank you!

And to all the Arab Americans who participated in one way or another by sharing their lives, experiences, thoughts, analysis, and insights with me, *shukran jazeelan!*

INDEX